S0-BNB-091

# THE ROUGH GUIDE TO

# Beijing

This fifth edition updated by

Martin Zatko

ROUGH GUIDES

roughguides.com

# Contents

# Introduction to
# **Beijing**

Crisscrossed by freeways, spiked with high-rises and soaked in neon, Beijing (北京, běijīng) represents China at its most dynamic. This vivid metropolis leaves an indelible impression on every traveller who passes through – by turns brash, gaudy, elegant, charming, filthy and historic, Beijing is never, *ever* dull. Yet despite its relentless modernity, the city remains rooted in the past: much of the drama of China's imperial history was played out here, the emperors of the Ming and Qing dynasties enthroned at the centre of the Chinese universe in the Forbidden City, now one of Asia's most famous draws. Though Beijing is a very different city today, it remains spiritually and geographically the buzzing heart of the nation, an irresistible lure to the many Chinese who come to fulfil their dreams.

According to some accounts, this was the first city in the world to hit a population of one million, and it should come as little surprise to see the remote control of urban development stuck on permanent fast-forward here. The Chinese character for "demolish" (拆, chāi), painted in white on old buildings – and the cranes that skewer the skyline – attest to the speed of **change**, though this affects more than just the city's architecture: as China embraces capitalism, social structures are also being revolutionized. The government is as determined as ever to repress dissent, but outside the political arena just about anything goes these days. Students in the latest fashions while away their time in internet cafés, dropouts mosh in punk clubs, bohemians dream up boutiques over frappuccinos. New **prosperity** is evident everywhere – witness all the Mercedes-driving businessmen – but not everyone has benefited: migrant day-labourers wait for work outside the stations, and homeless beggars, not long ago a rare sight, are now as common as in Western cities.

The first impression of Beijing, for both foreigners and visiting Chinese, is often of a bewildering vastness, not least in the sprawl of uniform apartment buildings in which most of the city's 22 million-strong population are housed, and the eight-lane

**ABOVE** THE FORBIDDEN CITY **RIGHT** THE CBD

freeways that slice it up. It's a perception reinforced on closer acquaintance by the concrete desert of **Tian'anmen Square**, and the gargantuan buildings of the modern executive around it. The main **tourist sights** – the Forbidden City, the Summer Palace and the Great Wall – also impress with their scale, though more manageable grandeur is offered by the city's attractive **temples**, including the Tibetan-style Yonghe Gong, the Taoist Baiyun Guan, and the astonishing Temple of Heaven, once a centre for imperial rites.

With its sights, history and, by no means least, delicious **food** (all of China's diverse cuisines can be enjoyed cheaply at the city's numerous restaurants and street stalls), Beijing is a place almost everyone enjoys. But it's essentially a private city, one whose surface, though attractive, is difficult to penetrate. The city's history and unique character are in the details: to find and experience these, check out the little antiques **markets**; the local shopping districts; the smaller, quirkier sights; the **hutongs**, the city's twisted, grey stone alleyways that are – as one Chinese guidebook puts it – "fine and numerous as the hairs of a cow"; and the **parks**, where you'll see old men sitting with their caged songbirds. Take advantage, too, of the city's burgeoning **nightlife** and see just how far the Chinese have gone down the road of what used to be deemed "spiritual pollution". Keep your eyes open, and you'll soon notice that **Westernization** and the rise of a brash consumer society is not the only trend here; just as marked is the revival of **older Chinese culture**, much of it outlawed during the more austere years of communist rule. Witness, for example, the sudden re-emergence of the **teahouse** as a genteel meeting place, and the renewed interest in traditional music and opera and imperial cuisine – dishes once enjoyed by the emperors.

# What to see

The absolute centre of China since the Ming dynasty, the wonderful **Forbidden City** remains Beijing's most popular sight – and rightly so. Immediately to its south is **Tian'anmen Square**, a bald expanse with a hairy history; sights on and around the square include the colossal National Museum and three grand city gates, as well as the corpse of Chairman Mao, lying pickled in his sombre mausoleum.

The wide area spreading north of the Forbidden City is one of the city's most pleasant quarters. First comes **Beihai Park**, the old imperial pleasure grounds, centred on a large lake. North again are two further lakes, **Qianhai** and **Houhai**, surrounded by one of the city's most appealing *hutong* areas – though, as elsewhere in the city, one that's living on borrowed time. The *hutongs* are tricky to navigate, but getting lost is part of the fun – nowhere else in Beijing is aimless rambling so amply rewarded. Many sights west of the lakes are remnants of the imperial past, when the area was home to princes, dukes and eunuchs. For a more contemporary side of Beijing head east instead to the charming street of **Nanluogu Xiang**, one of Beijing's most fashionable areas – youngsters from all over the city come here to stroll and sup coffee, tourists (both foreign and domestic) go trinket mad, while expats tend to make a beeline for the craft breweries.

Further to the east is the **Yonghe Gong**, a spectacular Lamaist temple, which lies across the road from the wonderful **Confucius Temple** – less showy but just as worthy of your time. The areas to the east and south are some of the most important pieces of Beijing's modern jigsaw – **Sanlitun**, still the city's prime nightlife spot after all these years; the **CBD**, boasting high-rises aplenty and with plenty more to come; and **Wangfujing**, with

**ABOVE** DONG'ANMEN NIGHT MARKET **RIGHT** THE WATER CUBE

## BEIJING ARCHITECTURE

Since the days of dynasty, Beijing has always been image-conscious – anxious to portray a particular face, both to its citizenry and to the world at large. It was during the Ming dynasty that the city took on much of its present shape, including the grid pattern still followed by many of the major streets. Some splendid buildings and complexes from this time remain, including the Forbidden City, Yonghe Gong, the Temple of Heaven and the Drum Tower. One of the world's most vaunted pieces of engineering also took shape at this time – the glorious Great Wall. Rather more humble, though forming an essential part of the city's fabric, were the traditional *hutong* houses that most Beijingers lived in. Though declining in number with each passing year, many of those you'll see today went up in **Qing** times.

Beijing took on an entirely different form during early **Communist rule**. When Mao took over, he wanted the feudal city of the emperors transformed into a "forest of chimneys"; he got his wish, and the capital became an ugly industrial powerhouse of socialism. The best (or worst, depending upon your point of view) buildings from the Mao years are the Military Museum, the National Exhibition Hall, or any of the buildings on or around Tian'anmen Square. In the 1980s, when the Party embraced capitalism "with Chinese characteristics", bland international-style office blocks were erected with a pagoda-shaped "silly hat" on the roof as a concession to local taste.

**Modern Beijing**, eager to express China's new global dominance, has undergone the kind of urban transformation usually only seen after a war. Esteemed architects from across the globe have been roped in for a series of *carte blanche* projects; the results have been hit and miss, but some have been astounding. The best include the fantastic venues built for the 2008 Olympics (the "Bird's Nest" and "Water Cube"), Paul Andreu's National Center for the Performing Arts (the "Egg"); and Zaha Hadid's curvy, sci-fi-like Galaxy Soho, completed in 2013. Perhaps most striking of all, however, is the new CCTV state television headquarters (the "Twisted Doughnut") by Dutch architect Rem Koolhaas, which appears to defy gravity with its intersecting Z-shaped towers.

## CHINESE SCRIPT

**Chinese characters** are simplified images of what they represent, and their origins as pictograms can often still be seen, even though they have become highly abstract today. The earliest known examples of Chinese writing are predictions, which were cut into "oracle bones"; these were used for divination during the Shang dynasty, more than three thousand years ago, though the characters must have been in use long before, for these inscriptions already amount to a highly complex writing system. As the characters represent concepts, not sounds, written Chinese cuts through the problem of communication in a country with many different dialects. However, learning the writing system is ponderous, taking children an estimated two years longer than with an alphabet. Foreigners learning Mandarin use the modern **pinyin** transliteration system of accented Roman letters – used in this book – to help memorize the sounds (see p.188).

its array of places to shop and Beijing's most prominent night markets. The best sight hereabouts is the little oasis of calm that is the **Ancient Observatory**, where Jesuit priests used to teach the charting of the heavens.

South of the Forbidden City you'll find **Qianmen Dajie**, a shopping street reconstructed along dynastic lines. This eventually leads to the magnificent **Temple of Heaven**, a superb specimen of Ming-dynasty design surrounded by pretty parkland. There's less to see west of the Forbidden City, but there are still a few sights worth visiting. These include a couple of charming temples; the **Military Museum**, monument to a fast-disappearing communist ethos; the modern **Capital Museum**; and the city **zoo** and **aquarium**.

In the far north of Beijing proper, you'll find three contrasting groups of sights. Farthest west, providing one of the most pleasant areas to escape from the city bustle, is the **Summer Palace**, centred around peaceful Kunming Lake; Yuanmingyuan, the "old"

**ABOVE** GALAXY SOHO

# Author picks

Our indefatigable author has explored every highway, byway and *hutong* of Beijing to bring you some unique travel experiences. Here are some of his personal favourites.

**Hidden treasures** Everyone knows about the Wall, the Forbidden City and the Temple of Heaven but to avoid the crowds head a little off the beaten track to the Confucius Temple (p.69), Ancient Observatory (p.74) and Baiyun Guan (p.88).

**Get on your bike** For all its high-octane development, Beijing remains a great cycling city (p.26). Wend your way through the *hutong* alleys around the Shicha lakes (p.59), cycle south to the Imperial Palace, past Mao's portrait, and pedal back up along the Forbidden City canal.

**Contemporary art** Beijing's prolific art scene is centred around the famed 798 Art District (p.102) but there are some good galleries closer to the city centre, such as the wonderful Red Gate Gallery (p.75).

**Shopping** Beijing's mix of earthy markets, boutique districts and super-modern mall complexes make it a fine place to shop (p.155): green tea, fans, name chops and antiques are all popular souvenirs, and the city remains a highly affordable place for tailored clothing.

**Courtyard living** Though many *hutong* dwellings have fallen foul of the wrecking ball (p.60), a fair few remain, and it's quite possible to stay in one of many artfully redecorated courtyard houses (p.129).

**Park life** To de-stress from the city bustle, make for one of Beijing's principal parks – Ditan (p.70), Tiantan (p.80) and Ritan (p.73). They're at their most attractive around sunrise and sunset, when you may see locals practising *tai ji*, dancing in formation, or doing the odd-looking "backwards walk".

> Our author recommendations don't end here. We've flagged up our favourite places – a perfectly sited hotel, an atmospheric café, a special restaurant – throughout the Guide, highlighted with the ★ symbol.

**FROM TOP** ANCIENT OBSERVATORY; COTE COUR HOTEL; RITAN PARK

summer palace, lies nearby. East of here, past the university district, is the **Olympic Green**, home to some of the remaining venues from the spectacular 2008 Summer Games. East again, en route to the airport, is the fascinating **798 Art District**, centre of Beijing's burgeoning art scene.

Beijing's sprawling outskirts are a messy jumble of farmland, housing and industry, but here you'll find the giant parks of **Badachu** and **Xiangshan**, and the impressive **Tanzhe**, **Fahai** and **Jietai temples**. Well outside the city – but an essential stop for many visitors well within the scope of a day-trip – is the **Great Wall**, which winds over lonely ridges only a few hours' drive north of the capital, while for those with time to spare, the imperial pleasure complex of **Chengde** is easily accessible capital by train and bus.

# When to go

Beijing's year starts off mean. The long **winter** (November to March) sees temperatures plummet below freezing – sometimes as low as -20°C (-4°F) – and the mean winds that whip off the Mongolian plains feel like they're freezing your ears off. However, pack the right clothing and this can actually be an enjoyable time to visit, not least since crowds are thin even at the most popular sights. The run-up to **Chinese New Year** (falling in late January or early to mid-February) is a great time to be in the country: everyone is in festive mood and the city is bedecked with decorations. This isn't a good time to travel around, however, as much of the population is on the move, and transport systems become hopelessly overstretched. It's best to avoid Beijing during the first three days of the festival itself, as everyone is at home with family, and a lot of businesses and sights are closed.

The city's short **spring** (April and May) is a lovely season to visit Beijing – it's dry and comfortably warm at this time, though can be windy. Fortunately, the spring dust storms that once plagued the city have lessened of late, though they still occur. **Summer** itself (June to August) is muggy and hot, with temperatures up to 30°C (86°F) and often beyond; in high summer the city is ripe for dining alfresco, and beer consumption goes through the roof. July and August see also plenty of rainfall, though most of it deluges all at once and even then there's still a fair amount of sun.

Ultimately, when all's said and done, the best time to visit Beijing is in the **autumn** (September and October), when the weather is dry and clement. This is also the most likely time for Beijing's semi-mythical "blue-sky days", when air pollution is said to be at its lowest, to occur – the perfect time to climb up Jingshan and see the Forbidden City at its most beautiful.

## AVERAGE TEMPERATURES AND RAINFALL IN BEIJING

| | Jan | Feb | Mar | Apr | May | Jun | Jul | Aug | Sep | Oct | Nov | Dec |
|---|---|---|---|---|---|---|---|---|---|---|---|---|
| Max/min (°C) | 1/-10 | 4/-8 | 11/-1 | 21/7 | 27/13 | 31/18 | 31/21 | 30/20 | 26/14 | 20/6 | 9/-2 | 3/-8 |
| Max/min (°F) | 34/14 | 39/18 | 52/30 | 70/45 | 81/55 | 88/64 | 88/70 | 86/68 | 79/57 | 68/43 | 48/28 | 37/18 |
| Rainfall (mm) | 4 | 5 | 8 | 17 | 35 | 78 | 243 | 141 | 58 | 16 | 11 | 3 |

**FROM TOP** NATIONAL CENTER FOR THE PERFORMING ARTS (AKA THE "EGG"); TEAHOUSE; OLD MEN PLAYING CHINESE CHESS

# 19

# things not to miss

It's not possible to see everything Beijing has to offer in one short trip – and we don't suggest you try. What follows is a selective taste of the city's highlights: stunning temples, delicious food, artsy districts and fascinating excursions beyond the city. All entries have a page reference to take you straight into the Guide, where you can find out more.

1

### 1 FORBIDDEN CITY
Page 40

For five centuries centre of the Chinese universe and private pleasure ground of the emperor, this sumptuous palace complex ranks as the city's main attraction.

### 2 BEIJING OPERA
Page 151

Largely incomprehensible to foreigners, and many Chinese, but still a great spectacle.

### 3 PEKING DUCK
Page 134

You won't be eating the city's most famous dish every day (doing so would probably guarantee heart failure), but try it out at least once, as it's supremely tasty.

### 4 MAO'S MAUSOLEUM
Page 51

Join the queue of awed peasants shuffling past the pickled corpse of the founder of modern China in his giant tomb, fronted by suitably bombastic Socialist Realist statuary.

### 5 BAIYUN GUAN
Page 88

See China at prayer in this attractive and popular Taoist temple, where devotees play games such as throwing coins at the temple bell.

### 6 AN EVENING BY THE TOWERS
Page 62

The famed Drum (pictured) and Bell towers are justly popular sights by day, though it's also worth popping by around sunset time, when the area takes on a notably more relaxed atmosphere.

### 7 A BEIJING BREAKFAST
Page 134

Start your day the local way: hunt down some *jian bing* (a kind of savoury pancake), and wash it down with a pot of delicious Beijing yoghurt.

### 8 798 ART DISTRICT
Page 102

This huge complex of art galleries has become Ground Zero for the city's bohemians and fashionistas.

### 9 YONGHE GONG
Page 68

A lively, flamboyantly decorated Tibetan temple, where the air is often heady with incense smoke.

### 10 SUMMER PALACE
Page 95

Once the exclusive retreat of the emperors, this beautiful landscaped park, dotted with imperial buildings, is now open to all.

### 11 THE CBD
Page 73

The heart of new Beijing, the Central Business District is essentially a playground for some of the world's foremost architects – most dramatically in the seemingly gravity-defying CCTV Headquarters.

### 12 NANLUOGU XIANG
Page 63

In vogue with local hipsters, this trendy *hutong* of restaurants and boutiques is the perfect spot for a quick cappuccino and a read of the paper.

6

7

8

### 13 GREAT WALL AT SIMATAI
Page 108

A dramatic stretch of crumbly, vertiginous fortifications three hours from Beijing.

### 14 TEMPLE OF HEAVEN
Page 80

Set in the centre of an elegant park, this temple is often regarded as the zenith of Ming architecture.

### 15 SANLITUN
Page 70

Famed as Beijing's main nightlife area, Sanlitun now also boasts a superb range of cosmopolitan places to eat, as well as impressively designed new shopping zones such as the Tai Koo Li complex.

### 16 HUTONGS
Pages 60 & 77

The maze of alleys and traditional courtyard buildings around Dazhalan or Houhai reveal the city's real, private face.

### 17 ACROBATICS
Page 152

The style may be vaudeville, but the stunts, performed by some of the world's greatest acrobats, are breathtaking.

### 18 NIGHTLIFE
Page 144

Experience Beijing's cultural explosion by catching one of the new bands in a smoky bar, or just bop with the beautiful people in a club – like erstwhile favourite *World of Suzie Wong* (p.148).

### 19 HOUHAI
Page 61

Beautiful and serene in the early morning, Houhai lake is the perfect setting for a boat ride or rooftop meal, and has a lively bar scene after dark.

BEIJING CYCLISTS

# Basics

# Getting there

**Beijing is China's main international transport hub, with plenty of direct flights from European capitals and from American, Australian and other Asian cities. You can also get here by train from cities all over China, or even from far-away Moscow on the vaunted Trans-Siberian Express.**

**Airfares** vary by season, with the highest fares from Easter to October and around Christmas, New Year and just before the Chinese New Year (which falls between late January and mid-February). Note also that flying at weekends is slightly more expensive; prices quoted below assume midweek travel.

## Flights from the UK and Ireland

The only **nonstop flights** to Beijing **from the UK** are with Air China and British Airways, both flying from London Heathrow (10hr); figure on a minimum of £500 return. It's not a problem to book from other UK airports or **from the Republic of Ireland**, though you'll end up either catching a connecting flight to London or flying via your airline's hub city.

There are plenty of **indirect flights** to Beijing from London with airlines such as Emirates, Qatar Airways, Lufthansa and Aeroflot, stopping off in the airline's hub city. These are a little cheaper than direct flights, with prices starting from around £400 in low season, rising to £700 in high season. Prices can be substantially higher from the Republic of Ireland; you may want to consider taking a cheap flight to London first.

## Flights from the US and Canada

There's no shortage of **direct flights** to Beijing **from North America**; carriers include Air China, Air Canada and United. It takes around 13hr to reach Beijing **from the west coast**; add 7hr or more to this if you start **from the east coast** (including a stopover on the west coast en route). Some flights cross the North Pole, shaving a couple of hours off the flight time.

In low season, expect to pay US$850–1200 from the west coast (Los Angeles, San Francisco, Vancouver), or US$1100–1400 from the east coast (New York, Montreal, Toronto). To get a good fare during high season it's important to buy your ticket as early as possible, in which case you probably won't pay more than US$200 above low-season tariffs.

## Flights from Australia, New Zealand and South Africa

You can fly **direct** to Beijing **from Melbourne and Sydney** with, among others, Singapore Airlines, JAL, Malaysia Airlines and China Eastern. Otherwise, you will need to **stop over**, probably in Hong Kong. Alternatively, once in Hong Kong you have the option of continuing your journey by train; direct services run from Kowloon, and in 2015 a new high-speed link should be completed. Alternatively, consider taking a short hop on the train to Guangzhou or Shenzhen, from which flights to other Chinese cities are cheaper than direct ones from Hong Kong. Direct Air China flights to Beijing from Sydney (12hr) start at around Aus$1200. Some of the cheapest transit fares are with Royal Brunei Airlines, though they only serve **Brisbane and Darwin**. Their return fares to Hong Kong, via a stopover in Brunei, are around Aus$1100.

There are now no direct flights **from New Zealand** to Beijing, though Air New Zealand fly from Auckland to Shanghai (11hr 30min) and Hong Kong (11hr), both costing around NZ$2000 return. Malaysia Airlines and other carriers also fly via other Southeast Asian cities to Hong Kong and Beijing.

**From South Africa**, South African Airways have direct flights to Beijing (14hr), costing ZAR10,000–18,000.

## Organized tours

**Tour operators** generally include Beijing as one of a number of destinations in a tour of China. There are very cheap, off-season **flight-and-hotel**

---

### A BETTER KIND OF TRAVEL

At Rough Guides we are passionately committed to travel. We believe it helps us understand the world we live in and the people we share it with – and of course tourism is vital to many developing economies. But the scale of modern tourism has also damaged some places irreparably, and climate change is accelerated by most forms of transport, especially flying. All Rough Guides' flights are **carbon-offset**, and every year we donate money to a variety of environmental charities.

**packages** to Beijing, at prices that sometimes go as low as £600/€700/US$1000. Since six or seven nights in a four-star hotel are included, you're effectively getting accommodation for free, considering the cost of the flight alone. Don't forget, though, that quoted prices in brochures usually refer to the low-season minimum, based on two people sharing – the cost for a single traveller in high season will always work out more expensive.

# By train

The classic **overland route to Beijing** is through Russia on the **Trans-Siberian Express**, a very memorable way to begin or end your stay in China. There are two rail lines from Moscow to Beijing: the first, the **Trans-Manchurian line**, runs almost as far as the Sea of Japan before turning south through Dongbei to Beijing, and takes six days. The second **Trans-Mongolian** line is more popular with tourists as it rumbles past Lake Baikal in Siberia, the grasslands of Mongolia, and the desert of northwest China. It takes around five days.

You'll need tourist **visas** for Russia, and possibly Mongolia too if you use the Trans-Mongolian train (US citizens don't need these). For detailed, up-to-date **information** on all ways to get tickets, check w seat61.com.

Sorting out your travel arrangements on your own from abroad is a complex business and usually more trouble than it's worth; simply turning up in Russia and buying a ticket from a train station is unlikely to succeed as tickets sell out quickly. British travellers can cut the complications by using the **online booking system** offered by **Real Russia** (w realrussia.co.uk); they mark up prices by about 20 percent but do save you a lot of hassle. A second-class Moscow to Beijing ticket booked with them costs around £550 – and of course they will then help you sort out your visas for a small fee (as will all other agencies). They also offer **tours**, as do a number of Russia-based agencies.

It's also possible to reach Beijing by train from other neighbouring countries. There are direct trains from Hanoi in **Vietnam** (2 weekly; 40hr), and daily services via Nanning. From **Kazakhstan** there are weekly services from both Astana and Almaty; you'll have to change in Urumqi. There's also a weekly service from Pyongyang in **North Korea**, though you'll only be able to take this as part of a tour, and even then it's usually prohibitively expensive.

# Airlines, agents and operators

## AIRLINES

**Aeroflot** w aeroflot.ru.
**Air Canada** w aircanada.com.
**Air China** w airchina.com.
**Air New Zealand** w airnewzealand.com.
**British Airways** w ba.com.
**China Eastern Airlines** w flychinaeastern.com
**JAL (Japan Airlines)** w jal.com.
**Lufthansa** w lufthansa.com.
**Malaysia Airlines** w malaysiaairlines.
**Qatar Airways** w qatarairways.com.
**Royal Brunei** w bruneiair.com.
**Singapore Airlines** w singaporeair.com.
**South African Airways** w flysaa.com.
**United Airlines** w united.com.

## AGENTS

**w flychina.com.** US Good for discount fares from the States.
**North South Travel** UK ☎ 01245 608291, w northsouthtravel .co.uk. Discounted fares worldwide. Profits are used to support projects in the developing world, especially the promotion of sustainable tourism.
**STA Travel** UK ☎ 0870 160 0599, US & Canada ☎ 1 800 781 4040, Australia ☎ 1300 733 035, New Zealand ☎ 0508 782 872; w sta-travel.com. Worldwide specialists in low-cost flights and tours for students and under-26s, though other customers are welcome too.
**Trailfinders** UK ☎ 020 7628 7628, Republic of Ireland ☎ 01 677 7888, Australia ☎ 02 9247 7666; w trailfinders.com. One of the best-informed and most efficient agents for independent travellers.

## SPECIALIST TOUR OPERATORS

**Abercrombie & Kent** US ☎ 1 800 554 7016, w abercrombiekent .com. Luxury tours, including a 12-day "Highlights of China" trip covering Shanghai, Guilin, Xi'an and Beijing.
**Adventures Abroad** US ☎ 1 800 665 3998, w adventures-abroad.com. Small-group specialists with two-week tours from Beijing and Shanghai to Hong Kong, plus interesting Silk Road trips from Uzbekistan to Beijing, and Yunnan/Tibet adventures.
**Backroads** US ☎ 1 800 462 2848, w backroads.com. Cycling and hiking between Beijing and Hong Kong.
**China Highlights** China ☎ 773 283 1999, w chinahighlights.com. China-based company that offers a set of tours of Beijing and the surrounding area.
**China Odyssey** China ☎ 773 585 4000, w chinaodysseytours.com. Short city tours and longer trips that take in other destinations in China.
**CTS Horizons** ☎ 020 7868 5590, w ctshorizons.com. The China Travel Service's UK branch, offering an extensive range of tours including some cheap off-season hotel-and-flight packages to Beijing, and tailor-made private tours.
**Destinations Worldwide Holidays** Republic of Ireland ☎ 01 855 6641, w destinations.ie. Two-week tours that include Hong Kong and Beijing.

**Hayes and Jarvis** UK ☎ 0843 636 2863, ⓦ hayesandjarvis.co.uk. Among the most inexpensive Beijing flight-and-hotel-only packages available to British travellers.

**Intrepid Adventure Travel** UK ☎ 0800 781 1660, Australia ☎ 03 9473 2673, New Zealand ☎ 0800 174 043; ⓦ intrepidtravel .com. Small-group tours, with the emphasis on cross-cultural contact and low-impact tourism. Covers the staples, including hikes along the Great Wall near Beijing.

**Koryo Tours** China ⓦ koryogroup.com. Beijing's most unusual tour agency, arranging visits (heavily controlled, of course) to the paranoid hermit kingdom of North Korea.

**The Russia Experience** UK ☎ 0845 521 2910, ⓦ trans-siberian .co.uk. Besides detailing their Trans-Siberian packages, the website is a veritable mine of information about the railway. More expensive than similar tours offered by Russian agencies, but probably the most hassle-free option.

**Travel China Guide** US & Canada ☎ 1 800 892 6988, ⓦ travelchinaguide.com. A Chinese company with a wide range of three- and four-day group tours of Beijing and around.

**Wild China** ⓦ wildchina.com. Reliable agency for adventure travel around China, including a tour linking Beijing with Ulan Bator in Mongolia.

**World Expeditions** UK ☎ 0800 074 4135, Australia ☎ 1300 720 000, US ☎ 1 888 464 8735, Canada ☎ 1 800 567 2212; ⓦ worldexpeditions.com. Offers a 21-day Great Wall trek, starting in Beijing and heading well off the beaten track, and cycling tours too.

# Arrival and departure

**Those who arrive by train are lucky to find themselves already at the heart of the city; all others will find themselves outside the Second Ring Road with a long onward journey. It's best not to tussle with the buses, especially if you're bearing luggage, so head for the metro or a cab rank. There aren't many shady cabbies in Beijing, but the few there are hang around arrival points – ignore offers from freelance operators and head straight to the officially monitored taxi ranks.**

Booking **onward transport** is a simple matter, but for peak seasons – the two-week-long holidays and just before Chinese New Year (see box, p.28) – it's best to organize it long in advance.

## By plane

**Beijing Capital Airport** (北京首都机场, běijīng shǒudū jīchǎng; ⓦ bcia.com.cn) is 29km northeast of the centre. It serves both international and domestic flights, and has three terminals (T1, T2 and T3) – if you're departing Beijing, be sure to figure out which one you'll be using before heading to the airport. There are banks and ATMs here, and commission rates are the same as everywhere else.

### Taxis to the centre

You'll be pestered in the arrivals hall itself by charlatan taxi drivers; ignore them and use the official **taxi ranks**. A trip to the city centre will cost ¥80–150, including the ¥10 toll, depending upon where you're headed. It's a good idea to get the name of the hotel you're staying at printed out in Chinese; alternatively, staff at the airport information desks can scribble it down for you.

### Airport Express to the centre

The **Airport Express** light rail runs from T3 and stops at T2 (connected by walkway and free shuttle bus to T1); it then hits Sanyuanqiao (line 10), before terminating at Dongzhimen (lines 2 & 13). The ride from the airport to Dongzhimen takes about 30min from terminal 3, and 20min from terminal 2; tickets cost ¥25. The trains run every 15min from 6.30am to 10.30pm. If you want to continue your journey from Dongzhimen by cab, note that cabbies at the Dongzhimen exit commonly gouge new arrivals, so walk a little way and hail a cab from the street.

## ORIENTATION

Beijing's **ring roads** – freeways arranged in nested rectangles centring on Tian'anmen Square – are rapid-access corridors around the city. The Second and Third ring roads, **Erhuan** and **Sanhuan Lu**, are the two most useful, as they cut down on journey times but extend the distance travelled; they are much favoured by taxi drivers. Within the Second Ring Road lie most of the **historical sights**, while many of the most modern buildings – including the smartest hotels, restaurants, shopping centres and office blocks – are along or close to the Third. You'll soon become familiar with the experience of barrelling along a freeway in a bus or taxi, not knowing which direction you're travelling in, let alone where you are, as identical blocks flicker past.

### Buses to the centre

Airport **buses** (¥16) to the city depart from T3, stopping at T2 and T1 on the way; buy tickets from desks inside the terminals. They run regularly along eleven routes; the most useful are line 1 for Guomao, a station near the Central Business District to the east of the centre; and line 3 for Dongzhimen and the main train station. The same routes return to the airport from the city. Journeys take at least 1hr each way.

### Tickets

You can buy onward **airline tickets** from hotels and all travel agencies, which sometimes charge a small commission (¥30 or so). The latter include CITS offices (see p.26), and the Aviation Office at 15 Xichang'an Jie in Xidan (☎010 66013336 for domestic flights, ☎010 66016667 international; 24hr). These days, however, it's easy to buy domestic tickets **online** at ⓦelong.com.cn or ⓦctrip.com.cn; some international credit cards are accepted, and you'll need a phone number (your hotel's will do) to confirm your purchase.

## By train

Beijing has three giant train terminals: main, West and South. The latter two host most **high-speed services**, for which new lines are being added all the time; finding the right service can save you hours, though of course tickets will cost more.

**Beijing station** (北京站, běijīng zhàn) is the most central station, though it has few high-speed services. Most arrivals will depart by taxi (follow signs to the rank), or subway (it's on line 2). **Beijing West** (北京西站, běijīng xī zhàn) is Asia's largest rail terminal, and serves destinations south and west of the capital, including Hong Kong on the high-speed line. Getting away is easy by taxi, since there's an official rank; the station is also on subway lines 7 & 9.

By far the most modern and attractive of Beijing's stations, **Beijing South** (北京南站, běijīng nán zhàn) is where most high-speed trains arrive. It's easy to leave by taxi from the official rank, while it's also on subway line 4 (and, by the end of 2014, line 14 too).

Lastly, **Beijing North** (北京北站, běijīng běi zhàn) is a shabby affair to the north of town, near Xizhimen station on subway lines 2 and 13. It has little to offer travellers, though can be used to access Chengde, and parts of the Great Wall.

All stations have **left-luggage** offices.

### Tickets

There are a number of ways in which to buy **tickets**. However you obtain them, it will be necessary to bring your passport, which you'll also need to board the trains. The first, and most obvious, is to head to the **stations** themselves; this is often troublesome, however, since queues can be maddening and incredibly long, and signage is poor – there's little more dispiriting than spending half an hour waiting in line, only to discover that you're actually in the ticket cancellation queue.

It's far, far easier to have tickets **purchased for you** – almost all hotels provide this service for a fee of around ¥30 per ticket. If you're feeling adventurous, and can speak a few words of Chinese, it's cheaper (¥5 fee) to book at the **official ticket booking offices** strewn across town – ask staff at your accommodation to point you to the nearest one.

Tickets for busy routes should be booked at least a day in advance, and can be booked up to ten days ahead.

## By bus

You're unlikely to encounter Beijing's fearsomely busy bus stations unless you're going to or from **Chengde**, or as part of an independent trip to the **Great Wall**.

**Dongzhimen** (东直门公共汽车站, dōngzhímén gōnggòng qìchēzhàn; subway lines 1, 2 & 13), on the northeast corner of the Second Ring Road, is the largest bus station; it handles services to China's northeast, though Beijing travellers are more likely to use it as a means of accessing the 798 Art District (p.102). Those heading to Chengde (see p.117) are advised to use **Sihui** bus station (四惠公共汽车站, sìhuì gōnggòng qìchēzhàn; subway line 1) to the southeast of town; another option is **Liuliqiao** (六里桥公共汽车站, liùlǐqiáo gōnggòng qìchēzhàn; subway lines 9 & 10), way to the southwest. Some sights around Beijing are served by buses from stops, rather than stations; details are given in the individual accounts.

## By ferry

There are plenty of international ferries linking China with **South Korea**. On the Korean side, all depart from Incheon, a port city 1hr west of Seoul by subway. On the Chinese side, the closest port to Beijing is **Tanggu**, near Tianjin city (see map, p.106); high-speed trains link Tanggu with Beijing South station (55min; ¥78), with Tanggu station itself a ¥20–30 taxi-ride to or from the port. The ride takes

24hr on a highly comfortable vessel.

Services leave Korea every Tuesday and Friday (the latter service arrives later in the day, making it harder to get to Beijing), and Tanggu every Thursday and Sunday. **Tickets** are available at both ports, though leaving China it's best to buy from travel agents in Beijing; CITS is highly recommended (see p.26). The cheapest tickets (around W110,000 from Korea, and ¥888 from China) will get you a comfy bed, with curtains to seal yourself off from the communal corridors. Pay a little more, and you'll get a bed in an en-suite private room.

# City transport

**Getting around Beijing isn't quite the challenge it once was, thanks to the excellent new subway lines. Still, the public transport system often feels overstretched. Buses can be a hassle and taxis get stuck in gridlock, so sometimes the best way to get around is to hire a bike.**

## Subway

Clean, efficient and very fast, the **subway** (daily 5.30am–11pm; Ⓦ bjsubway.com) is preferable to the bus, though be prepared for enforced intimacies during rush hour. Station entrances are marked by a logo of a rectangle inside a "G" shape. You're obliged to pass bags through an airport-style scanner on entry, though this is not necessary for handbags and man-bags if you give staff a quick flash of what's inside. **Tickets** cost ¥2 per journey from station ticket offices or when using a transport card. All stops are signed in *pinyin* (the anglicized spelling out of Chinese characters) and announced in English and Chinese over the intercom when the train pulls in.

---

### TRANSPORT CARDS

Anyone staying more than a couple of weeks and intending to use public transport regularly should consider buying a swipe-style **transport card** (一卡通, yīkǎtōng). Available from subway stations, these are valid for bus and subway journeys, getting you a 60 percent discount on the former; they can also be used in taxis, and for payment in some convenience stores. The deposit is ¥20, which you receive back when you return it, and you can put as much money on the card as you like.

---

## Buses

Getting around Beijing by bus can be a bit of a challenge – destinations are not marked in English at stops or on the buses themselves, and services can be packed to the gills at rush hour. The city's two hundred-plus **bus and trolleybus services** cost ¥1, or an incredible ¥0.4 when using a transport card. **Double-deckers** (¥2), operated on some services, are comfortable – you're more likely to get a seat on these – and run along main roads. **Luxury buses** (¥3–10), which run to certain tourist sights, are modern, air-conditioned, and quite pleasant. **Tourist buses** (¥10–60) – which look like ordinary buses but have route numbers written in green – make regular trips (mid-April to mid-Oct) between the city centre and certain out-of-town attractions, including sections of the Great Wall; we've listed useful routes in the Guide.

## Taxis

Taxis cost ¥2.3 per kilometre, with a minimum **fare** of ¥13, and tips are never expected. Using a taxi

---

### STREET NAMES

**Beijing street names** appear bewildering at first, as a road can have several names along its length, but they are easy to figure out once you know the system. Some names vary by the addition of the word for "inside" or "outside" – **nèi** (内) or **wài** (外) respectively – which indicates the street's position in relation to the former city walls. More common are directional terms – north (**běi**, 北), south (**nán**, 南), west (**xī**, 西), east (**dōng**, 东) and central (**zhōng**, 中). Central streets often also contain the word **men** (门, gate), which indicates that they once passed through a walled gate along their route. **Jiē** (街) and **lù** (路) mean "street" and "road" respectively; the word **dà** (大), which sometimes precedes them, simply means "big". Thus Jianguomenwai Dajie literally refers to the outer section of Jianguomen Big Street. Some of these compound street names are just too much of a mouthful and are usually shortened; Gongrentiyuchang Beilu, for example, is usually referred to as Gongti Beilu.

after 11pm will incur a surcharge of 20 percent. You can pay either by cash or using a transport card (see box, p.25). Drivers are generally honest (except the ones who hang around transport links), but if they don't put the meter on, you can insist by saying "**dǎ biǎo**". If you're concerned about being taken on an expensive detour, have a map open on your lap, or on your phone.

Don't let yourself get hustled into a taxi, as unscrupulous drivers look out for newly arrived foreigners with luggage; walk a short distance and hail one, or find a rank (there's one outside each train station). If you feel aggrieved at a driver's behaviour, take his or her number (displayed on the dashboard) and report it to the taxi **complaint office** (☎010 68351150). Indeed, just the action of writing their number down can produce a remarkable change in demeanour.

These days, it can be a little hard to get a taxi in certain places at certain times of the day. Wangfujing can be a nightmare to escape during the day's shopping hours, while it can be just as hard to move on from the Forbidden City; buses and subways are on hand to solve these problems, though this cannot be said for the Sanlitun bar area around kicking-out time – unless you're willing to pay an extortionate motor-rickshaw fare (and risk being ripped off), you could be in for a fair wait.

## Bicycles

Renting or buying a bike gives you much more independence and flexibility – and they're often faster than taxis. There are **bike lanes** on all main roads and you'll be in the company of plenty of other cyclists. If you feel nervous at busy junctions, just dismount and walk the bike across – plenty of Chinese do.

### Renting a bike

Almost all hotels – certainly all the hostels – **rent** out bikes for ¥10–30 a day, plus a ¥200–400 deposit. Upmarket hotels charge ¥50 a day for the same bikes. You can also rent from many places in the *hutongs* around Houhai (see p.59). Always test the brakes on a rented bike before riding off, and get the tyres pumped up. Should you have a problem, you can turn to one of the bike repair stalls – there are plenty of these on the pavements next to main roads.

The city has recently been laying out ranks of decent (for now, at least) **rental bikes**. The scheme was still in its infancy at the time of writing, and only local residents were able to make use of it, but

it's planned to roll this out to foreign tourists in due course. Assuming that prices are the same as for locals, bikes will be free for the first hour, then ¥1 per hour thereon to a maximum of ¥10 per day, using a transport card (see box, p.25), after first throwing down a ¥400 deposit at a subway station.

### Buying a bike

You can **buy** cheap city bikes from shops around town. Used models cost from around ¥200, though you'll likely pay at least ¥350 for a bottom-of-the-range new one; for something reliable, try Carrefour (see p.162) or the strip of bike shops on the south side of Jiaodaokou, just west of the Ghost Street (Gui Jie) restaurants (see p.142). You'll need a good lock, as **theft** is very common.

## City tours

**Organized tours** of the city and its outskirts offer a painless, if expensive, way of seeing the main sights quickly. All big hotels offer them, and **CITS** has a variety of one- and two-day tour packages bookable from their offices (see box below), or from the information desk in the Friendship Store. These tours aren't cheap, though the price includes lunch and pays for a tour guide: a trip to the Summer Palace, Yonghe Gong and a pedicab jaunt around the *hutongs* is ¥360.

The one-day tours offered by the **cheaper hotels** offer better value than similar jaunts run by classier places, and you don't have to be staying with them to go along; figure on around ¥120 for a typical tour. All the **youth hostels** offer good-value evening trips to the acrobatics shows and the opera a few times a week (essentially the same price as the event ticket, with transport thrown in), and trips (occasionally overnighters) to the Great Wall (see p.105). You must book these at least a day in advance.

### CITY TOUR COMPANIES

**Beijing Sideways** ⓦ beijingsideways.com. Dash around Beijing in a sidecar, its adjoining motorbike driven by a local expat. Plenty of options available, including *hutong* tours, night tours, and trips to the Great Wall.

★ **Bike Beijing** ☎ 133 81400738, ⓦ bikebeijing.com. Small company with a big reputation, thanks to their excellent programme of rides to areas in and around Beijing. They've everything from half-day *hutong* jaunts to 15-day grassland excursions; see their wwebsite for full details.

**CITS** ⓦ cits.net; branches include; Parkson Building, 103 Fuxingmen Dajie ☎ 010 66011122 (daily 9am–5pm); the Beijing Hotel, 33 Dongchang'an Jie ☎ 010 65120507; and the New Century Hotel, opposite the zoo ☎ 010 68491426. This state-run behemoth is the biggest operator, though certainly not the best. They offer tours of the city and surroundings, and advance ticket booking within China for trains, planes and ferries, with a commission of around ¥30 added to ticket prices.

**City Bus Tour ☎ 400 6500760, Ⓦ www.citybustour.com.** Runs similar standard city tours to those run by CITS (see opposite) but scores for convenience, since you can book online. Their coaches are modern and you'll have an English-speaking guide.

★ **The Hutong Ⓦ thehutong.com.** This excellent outfit runs some interesting tours, including informative culinary and tea-market trips.

# The media

Hopes that a newly wealthy, post-Olympics China would relax its hard line on dissent have been dashed; if anything, the heavy hand of the state censor has tightened since the Games. All Chinese media is so heavily controlled that it shouldn't be relied on, though the country's increasingly net-savvy populace is finding new ways to source information.

### Newspapers and magazines

Despite the censorship, the official English-language **newspaper**, the *China Daily* (Ⓦ chinadaily .com.cn), is a decent enough read; surprisingly, the same can be said of the *Global Times* (Ⓦ globaltimes .com.cn), an offshoot of the nationalistic *People's Daily*. Imported news publications (sometimes censored) such as *Time* and *The Economist*, and Hong Kong's *South China Morning Post* (Ⓦ scmp .com), can be bought at shops in four- and five-star hotels.

There are a number of **free magazines** aimed at the expat community, which contain up-to-date entertainment and restaurant listings and are available at expat bars and restaurants. Look for *The Beijinger* (Ⓦ thebeijinger.com), *City Weekend* (Ⓦ cityweekend.com.cn/beijing) and *Time Out* (Ⓦ timeoutbeijing.com), all of which have listing and event sections, with addresses written in *pinyin* and Chinese.

### Television

There is the occasional item of interest on Chinese **TV**, though you'd have to be quite bored to resort to it for entertainment. Domestic travel and wildlife programmes are common, as are song-and-dance extravaganzas, the most enjoyable of which feature dancers in weird fetishistic costumes. Soap operas and historical dramas are popular, and often feature a few foreigners; in keeping with the global norm, talent and dating shows are currently all the rage.

**CCTV**, the state broadcaster, has an English-language rolling news channel, CCTV News; their dedicated sports channel, CCTV5, often shows European football games. Satellite TV in English is available in the more expensive hotels.

# Festivals and events

The rhythm of festivals and religious observances that used to mark the Chinese year was interrupted by the Cultural Revolution, and only now, more than forty years on, are old traditions beginning to re-emerge. The majority of festivals celebrate the turning of the seasons or propitious dates, such as the Double Ninth festival held on the ninth day of the ninth lunar month, and are times for gift-giving, family reunions and feasting.

## A festival calendar

Traditional festivals take place according to dates in the **Chinese lunar calendar**, in which the first day of the month is when the moon is a new crescent, with the middle of the month marked by the full moon. By the Gregorian calendar, these festivals fall on a different date every year.

### JANUARY/FEBRUARY

**New Year's Day** Jan 1.

**Spring Festival Starts between late Jan and mid-Feb.** The Chinese New Year celebrations extend over the first two weeks of the new lunar year (see box, p.28).

**Tiancang (Granary) Festival** Chinese peasants celebrate with a feast on the twentieth day of the first lunar month, in the hope of ensuring a good harvest later in the year.

### MARCH

**Guanyin's Birthday** Guanyin, the goddess of mercy and China's most popular Buddhist deity, is celebrated on the nineteenth day of the second lunar month, most colourfully in Taoist temples.

**China Open** Late March/early April. Snooker is becoming increasingly popular in China as the country finds itself ever more integral to the sport's future. This edition of the world tour takes place at Beijing University.

## SPRING FESTIVAL

The **Spring Festival**, usually falling in late January or the first half of February, is marked by two weeks of festivities celebrating the beginning of a new year in the lunar calendar (and thus also called **Chinese New Year**). In Chinese astrology, each year is associated with a particular animal from a cycle of twelve, and the passing into a new astrological phase is a momentous occasion. There's a tangible sense of excitement in the run-up to the festival, when China is perhaps at its most colourful, with shops and houses decorated with good luck messages, and stalls and shops selling paper money, drums and costumes. However, the festival is not an ideal time to travel – everything shuts down, and most of the population is on the move, making public transport impossible or extremely uncomfortable.

The first day of the festival is marked by a family feast at which *jiaozi* (dumplings) are eaten, sometimes with coins hidden inside. To bring luck, people dress in red clothes (red being regarded as a lucky colour) – a particularly important custom if the animal of their birth year is coming round again – and each family tries to eat a whole fish, since the word for fish (*yu*) sounds like the word for surplus. Firecrackers are let off to scare ghosts away and, on the fifth day, to honour Cai Shen, god of wealth. Another ghost-scaring tradition you may notice is the pasting up of images of door gods at the threshold. If you're in town at this time, make sure you catch a temple fair (see box, p.177).

## APRIL

**Qingming Festival** April 4 & 5. This festival, Tomb Sweeping Day, is the time to visit the graves of ancestors, leave offerings of food, and burn ghost money – fake paper currency – in honour of the departed.

**Beijing International Film Festival** Mid- to late April ⓦ bjiff.com /en. BJIFF, the city's main cinematic event, is increasingly giving Asia's larger festivals – Hong Kong, Singapore and Busan – a run for their money.

**Midi and Strawberry** Late April/early May. Quite why the city's two biggest rock festivals have to take place on the same weekend is a mystery, but on the plus side, at least you have a choice. Midi (ⓦ www.midifestival.com) is larger and more commercial, while Strawberry tends to branch out into wider musical genres.

## MAY

**Labour Day** May 1. Labour Day is a national holiday, during which all tourist sites are extremely busy.

**Youth Day** May 4. Commemorates the student demonstrators in Tian'anmen Square in 1919, which gave rise to the nationalist "May Fourth" Movement. It's marked in Beijing with flower displays in Tian'anmen Square.

## JUNE

**Children's Day** June 1. Most school pupils are taken on excursions at this time, so if you're visiting a popular tourist site be prepared for mobs of kids in yellow baseball caps.

**Dragon Festival** The fifth day of the fifth lunar month is a one-day public holiday. Traditionally, this is a time to watch dragon-boat racing and eat treats wrapped in leaves.

## JULY

**Genghis Khan Extreme Grassland Marathon and Mountain Bike Adventure** ⓦ genghiskhanmtbadventure.com. The Genghis Khan team organizes two major events in July: first comes a marathon that, while standard length, runs through the Mongolian grasslands; later

in the month comes a 206km bike ride.

**Beijing Dance Festival** ⓦ beijingdancefestival.com. A delightful mix of dance – mostly contemporary, with a few traditional and Chinese ethnic minority strands thrown in. Events held at various venues across a couple of weeks.

## AUGUST

**Beijing International Beer Festival** A great time to sample the wares of Beijing's ever-increasing number of microbreweries, plus a few from elsewhere in China. Venue varies.

**Beijing International Music Festival** ⓦ bimfa.org. China's premier classical music event; with as many local as international performers, it's a great opportunity to see how well the scene is developing here.

## SEPTEMBER

**Moon Festival** Also known as the Mid-Autumn Festival, this is marked on the fifteenth day of the eighth lunar month. It's a time of family reunion, celebrated with fireworks and lanterns. Moon cakes, containing a rich filling of sweet bean paste, are eaten, and plenty of *maotai* – a strong white spirit distilled from rice – is consumed.

**Double Ninth Festival** Nine is a number associated with *yang*, or male energy, and on the ninth day of the ninth lunar month qualities such as assertiveness and strength are celebrated. It's believed to be a profitable time for the distillation (and consumption) of spirits.

**Beijing International Art Bienniale** Late Sept in even-numbered years. See p.181.

**Confucius Festival** Sept 28. The birthday of Confucius is marked by celebrations at all Confucian temples.

## OCTOBER

**National Day** Oct 1. Everyone has three days off to celebrate the founding of the People's Republic.

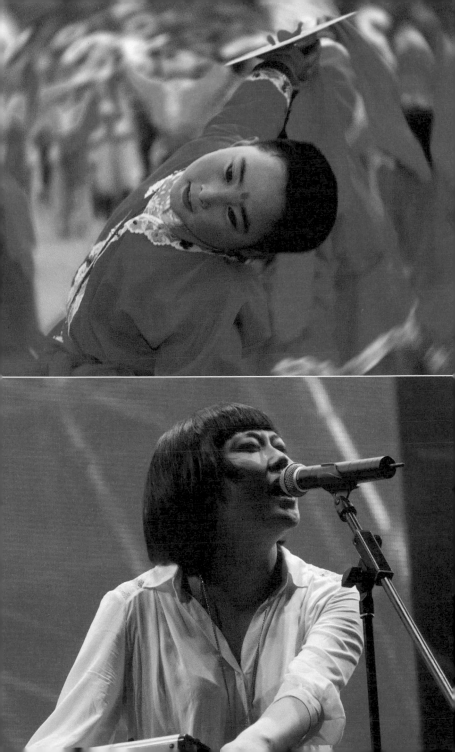

**DECEMBER**

**Ice and Snow Festival** Dec–Feb. Enjoy the Beijing chill at this small festival, held throughout the city's long winter at Yuyuantan Park. There's lots of sledding, and the opportunity to ride a horse-drawn carriage.

# Culture and etiquette

**When Confucius arrives in a country, he invariably gets to know about its society. Does he seek this information, or is it given him? Confucius gets it through being cordial, good, respectful, temperate and deferential.**

**Confucius, *The Analects***

**Privacy** is a luxury largely unheard of in China – indeed, Chinese doesn't have an exact translation of the word. Public toilets are built with low partitions, no one eats alone in restaurants, all leisure activities are performed in noisy groups, and a curiosity – such as a visiting Caucasian, or "big nose" as the Chinese like to say – can find him- or herself the subject of frank stares and attention.

The best thing to do in such situations is smile and say "nǐ hǎo" – a simple hello. A desire to be left alone can baffle the Chinese, and is occasionally interpreted as arrogance. Conversely, behaviour seen as antisocial in the West, notably queue-jumping, spitting and smoking, is quite normal in China, though government campaigns to cut down on these are having some effect.

Skimpy **clothing** is fine (indeed fashionably), but looking scruffy will only induce disrespect: all foreigners are assumed to be comparatively rich, so why they would want to dress like peasants is quite beyond the Chinese. **Shaking hands** is not a Chinese tradition, though it is now fairly common between men. Businessmen meeting for the first time exchange business cards, with the offered card held in two hands as a gesture of respect – you'll see polite shop assistants doing the same with your change.

In a **restaurant**, the Chinese don't usually share the bill; instead, diners contest for the honour of paying it, with the most respected usually winning. You should make some effort to stake your claim but, as a visiting guest, you can pretty much guarantee that you won't get to pay a jiao. **Tipping** is never expected, and though you might sometimes feel it's warranted, resist the temptation – you'll set an unwelcome precedent. A few upmarket places add a service charge, though it's highly unlikely that the serving staff ever see any of it.

If you visit a Chinese house, you'll be expected to present your hosts with a **gift**, which won't be opened in front of you (that would be impolite). Imported whisky and ornamental trinkets are suitable as presents, though avoid giving anything too practical, as it might be construed as charity.

## Sex, sexuality and gender issues

**Women travellers** in Beijing usually find the incidence of sexual harassment much less of a problem than in other Asian countries. Chinese men are, on the whole, deferential and respectful. Being ignored is a much more likely complaint, as the Chinese will generally assume that any man accompanying a woman will be doing all the talking.

**Prostitution**, though illegal, has made a big comeback – witness all the new "hairdressers", saunas and massage parlours, almost every one a brothel. Single foreign men may find themselves approached inside certain hotels (not fancy ones, or Western chains), and it's common practice for prostitutes to phone around hotel rooms at all hours of the night – unplug the phone if you don't want to be woken up. Bear in mind that consequences may be unpleasant if you are caught with a prostitute.

Beijing, and China as a whole, has become more tolerant of **homosexuality** in recent years; it's been removed from the list of psychiatric diseases and is no longer illegal. Still, the scene is fairly tame and low-key (see p.149).

# Travelling with children

**Foreigners with kids can be expected to receive lots of attention from curious locals – and the occasional admonition that the little one should be wrapped up warmer.**

Local kids generally don't use **nappies**, just pants with a slit at the back – and when baby wants to go, mummy points him at the gutter. Nappies and baby milk are available from modern supermarkets such as Carrefour (see p.162), though there are few public changing facilities. High-end hotels have **baby-minding** services for around ¥150 an hour. **Breast-feeding** in public is acceptable, though more so outside the train station than in celebrity restaurants.

Sights and activities that youngsters might enjoy are the zoo and aquarium (see p.92), pedal boating on Houhai (see p.61), the acrobat shows (see p.152), the Puppet Theatre (see p.152) and the Natural History Museum (see p.82). If you're tired of worrying about them in the traffic, try taking them to pedestrianized Liulichang Jie (see p.77), the Olympic Green (see p.101), the 798 Art District (see p.102), or the parks – Ritan Park (see p.73) has a good playground and Chaoyang Park has boating. Note that most Beijing attractions are free for children under 1.2m high.

Check ⓦbeijing-kids.com for more suggestions and advice.

# Travel essentials

## Costs

In terms of **costs**, Beijing is a city of extremes. You can, if you wish to live it up, spend as much here as you would visiting any Western capital; on the other hand, it's also quite possible to live extremely cheaply – most locals survive on less than ¥2000 a month.

Generally, your biggest expense is likely to be **accommodation**. **Food** and **transport**, on the other hand, are relatively cheap. The minimum you can live on comfortably is about £15/€18/US$25/¥150 a day if you stay in a dormitory, get around by bus and eat in simple restaurants. On a budget of £40/€50/US$65/¥400 a day, you'll be able to stay in a modest hotel, travel in taxis and eat in good restaurants. To stay in an upmarket hotel, you'll need to have a budget of around £100/€120/US$160/¥1000 a day.

**Discounts** on admission prices are available to students or elderly travellers with relevant ID; note that rules governing student discounts are far from uniform, and that some places will only give them to those studying in China, or those who are Chinese themselves. An international youth hostel card gets small discounts at affiliated hostels (and can be bought at the front desk).

## Crime and personal safety

With all the careful showcasing of modernity and rampant consumerism, it's easy to forget that Beijing is the heart of an authoritarian state that has terrorized its subjects for much of its short, inglorious history. Not that this should physically

affect visitors too much; the state is as anxious to keep tourists happy as it is to incarcerate democracy activists, bloggers and the like. Indeed, Chinese who commit crimes against foreigners are treated much more harshly than if their victims had been compatriots. **Crime** is, however, a growth industry in China, partly thanks to appalling disparities in income, and the prevailing get-rich-quick ideology. Official corruption is rampant, and the state sometimes shoots scapegoats in an effort to cut it down (it's called "killing the chicken to frighten the monkeys").

### Con artists

Getting **scammed** is by far the biggest threat to foreign visitors, and there are now so many professional con artists targeting tourists that you can expect to be approached many times a day at places such as Wangfujing and on Tian'anmen Square. A sweet-looking young couple, a pair of girls, or perhaps a kindly old man will ask to practise their English or offer to show you round. After befriending you – which may take hours – they will suggest some refreshment, and lead you to a teahouse. After a traditional-looking tea ceremony you will be presented with a bill for thousands of yuan, your new "friends" will disappear or pretend to be shocked, and some large gentlemen will appear. In another variation, you will be coaxed into buying a painting (really a print) for a ridiculous sum. Never drink with a stranger if you haven't seen a price list, and try to select the venue yourself if at all possible.

### Theft

While there is no need for obsessive paranoia – Beijing is still safer than most Western cities – you do need to take care. Tourists are an obvious target for petty **thieves**. Passports and money should be kept in a concealed money belt; a bum bag offers much less protection and is easy for skilled pickpockets to get into. It's a good idea to keep a few large-value notes separate from the rest of your cash, together with copies of all your important documents. Be wary on buses, the favoured haunt of pickpockets, and trains, particularly in hard-seat class and on overnight journeys. Take a chain and padlock to secure your luggage in the rack.

**Hotel rooms** are on the whole secure, dormitories much less so – in the latter case it's often fellow travellers who are the problem. Most hotels should have a safe, but it's not unusual for things to go missing from these.

On the **street**, flashy jewellery and watches will attract the wrong kind of attention, and try to be discreet when taking out your cash. Not looking obviously wealthy also helps if you want to avoid being ripped off by street traders and taxi drivers, as does telling them you are a student – the Chinese have a great respect for education, and more sympathy for foreign students than for tourists.

### The police

If you do have anything stolen, you'll need to get the police, known as the **Public Security Bureau** or PSB, to write up a loss report in order to claim on your insurance. Their main office is at 2 Andingmen Dong Dajie, 300m east of Yonghegong Lama Temple subway stop (Mon–Fri 8am–4.30pm; ☎010 84015292, ⓦwww.bjgaj.gov.cn/eng), though police boxes across town are open around the clock.

The **police** are recognizable by their dark blue uniforms and caps, though there are a lot more around than you might at first think, as plenty are undercover. They have much wider powers than most Western police forces, including establishing the guilt of criminals – trials are often used only for deciding the sentence of the accused, though China is beginning to have the makings of an independent judiciary. Laws are harsh, with execution – a bullet in the back of the head – the penalty for a wide range of serious crimes, from corruption to rape, though if the culprit is deemed to show proper remorse, the result can be a more lenient sentence.

While individual police often go out of their way to help foreigners, the institution of the PSB is, on the whole, tiresomely officious.

## Electricity

The electrical supply is 220V. **Plugs** come in four types: three-pronged with angled pins, three-pronged with round pins, two flat pins and two narrow round pins. Adaptor plugs are available from hardware and electronic stores; try the Buy Now Mall (see p.161).

## Entry requirements

To enter China, almost all foreign nationals (except those from Japan, the Seychelles, Mauritius or San Marino) require a **visa**; your one exception may be the 72-hour visa-free window allowed to transit passengers with confirmed onward flights (and visas for where you're going, if you need one). Unfortunately, Chinese visa rules are a real can of worms – despite the country's increasing wealth, it is getting harder and more expensive to acquire a visa. Indeed, some embassies have outsourced operations to **travel agencies** (who will require an extra fee); details are given on the websites of China's worldwide embassies.

By far the best advice is to apply for a visa in your own country. The first point of contact should be your embassy; if they no longer issue visas, they'll be able to give details of the agencies you'll need to apply through. The second best place to apply is Hong Kong, where agencies such as Forever Bright (ⓦfbt-chinavisa.com.hk) can issue visas cheaply and quickly (sometimes even the same day), with very little fuss or documentation required; this is also the best option if you want anything longer than a regular tourist visa.

**Single-entry tourist visas** (called "L" visas) must be used within three months of issue, and are valid for a month; some embassies also issue three-month visas. Prices vary depending on your nationality, and where you apply; by way of example, it's US$140 for US citizens (same price for anything up to a one-year multiple-entry visa); Can$81.50 for Canadians (including outsourcing fee); £66 for those from the UK (including outsourcing fee); €40 for Irish citizens; Aus$98.50 for Aussies (including outsourcing fee); NZ$140 for Kiwis; and ZAR250 for South Africans.

To **apply** for a visa you have to submit an application form (available online from the embassy or agency sites), one or two passport-size photographs, your passport (which must be valid for at least another six months from your planned date of entry into China, and have at least one blank page for visas) and the fee (sometimes payable by card or bank transfer only). If you apply in person, processing should take between three and five working days. Postal applications take up to three weeks.

You'll be asked your occupation – don't admit to being a journalist or writer, as you might be called in for an interview and made to get the annoying **journalist visa** (J), which means you'll have to report to police stations in China. At times of political sensitivity you may be asked for a copy of any air tickets and hotel bookings in your name.

A **business visa** (F) is valid for six months and multiple journeys; you'll need an official invitation from a government-recognized Chinese organization to apply for one (it was possible to simply buy one in Hong Kong until recently, and it might be possible again in the future). Twelve-month **work visas** (Z) again require an invitation, plus a health certificate from your doctor. Students intending to study in Beijing for less than six months need an invitation or letter of acceptance from a college there in order to apply for **student visas**. If you're intending to go on a longer course, you have to fill in an additional form, available from Chinese embassies, and will also need a health certificate; then you'll be issued with an X visa, valid for a year, and renewable.

### CHINESE EMBASSIES ABROAD

**Australia** W au.china-embassy.org
**Canada** W ca.china-embassy.org
**Ireland** W ie.china-embassy.org/eng
**New Zealand** W www.chinaembassy.org.nz
**South Africa** W za.china-embassy.org
**UK** W www.chinese-embassy.org.uk/eng
**US** W www.china-embassy.org

### Visa extensions

Once in China, a **first extension** to a tourist visa, valid for a month, is easy to obtain; most Europeans pay ¥160 for this, Americans a little more. To apply for an extension, go to the "Aliens Entry Exit Department" of the PSB offices (see opposite). The staff will **keep your passport** for three working days; note that you can't change money, or even book into a new hotel, while they've got it. Subsequent applications for extensions will be refused unless you have a good reason to stay, such as illness. They'll reluctantly give you a couple of extra days if you have a flight out of the country booked, otherwise, you'll be brusquely ordered to leave the country.

Don't **overstay** your visa even for a few hours – the fine is ¥500 per day, and if you're caught at the airport with an out-of-date visa the hassle that will follow may mean you'll miss your flight.

### Customs allowances

You're allowed to **import** into China up to 400 cigarettes, 2 litres of alcohol, 590ml of perfume and up to 50g of gold or silver. You can't take in more than ¥6000, and foreign currency in excess of US$5000 or the equivalent must be declared. It's illegal to import printed or filmed matter critical of the country, but confiscation is rare in practice.

**Export restrictions** apply on any items over 100 years old that you might buy in China. Taking these items out of the country requires an export form, available from the Friendship Store (see map pp. 66–67); ask at the information counter for a form, take along the item and your receipt, and approval is given on the spot. You needn't be unduly concerned about the process – the "antiques" you commonly see for sale are all fakes anyway.

### Embassies

Most **embassies** are either around Sanlitun, in the northeast, or in the Jianguomenwai compound, north of and parallel to Jianguomenwai Dajie. You can get passport-size photos in booths and photography studios all over the city. Visa departments usually open for a few hours every weekday morning (phone for exact times and to see what you'll need to take). During the application process they might take your passport for as long as a week; remember that you can't change money or your accommodation without it.

### BEIJING EMBASSIES

**Australia** 21 Dongzhimenwai Dajie ☎ 010 51404111, W china.embassy.gov.au.
**Canada** 19 Dongzhimenwai Dajie ☎ 010 51394000, W canadainternational.gc.ca.
**Ireland** 3 Ritan Donglu ☎ 010 65322691, W embassyofireland.cn.
**New Zealand** 1 Ritan Dong'er Jie ☎ 010 65327000, W nzembassy.com/china.
**South Africa** 5 Dongzhimenwai Dajie ☎ 010 65320171, W saembassy.org.cn.
**UK** 11 Guanghua Lu, Jianguomenwai ☎ 010 51924000, W www .gov.uk/government/world/organisations/british-embassy-beijing.
**US** 55 Anjialou (entrance on Tianze Lu) ☎ 010 85313333, W beijing.usembassy-china.org.cn.

## Health

The most common health hazard in Beijing is the host of **cold and flu infections** that strike down a large proportion of the population, mostly in the winter months. The problem is compounded by the overcrowded conditions, chain-smoking, pollution and the widespread habit of spitting, which rapidly spreads infection. More serious epidemics such as **SARS and bird flu** have hit since the turn of the century; outbreaks are largely confined to rural areas, but should another major one occur, it's best to refer to the advice of your home government.

**Diarrhoea** is another common illness to affect travellers, usually in a mild form, while your stomach gets used to unfamiliar food. The sudden onset of diarrhoea with stomach cramps and vomiting indicates food poisoning. In both instances, get plenty of rest, drink lots of water, and in serious cases replace lost salts with oral rehydration solution (ORS); this is especially important with young children. Take a few sachets with you, or make your own by adding half a teaspoon of salt and three of sugar to a litre of cool, previously boiled water. While down with diarrhoea, avoid milk, greasy or spicy foods, coffee and most fruit, in favour of bland food such as rice, plain noodles and soup. If symptoms persist, or if you notice blood or mucus in your stools, consult a doctor.

To avoid stomach complaints, eat at places that look busy and clean and stick to fresh, thoroughly cooked food. Beware of food that has been pre-cooked and kept warm for several hours. Shellfish is a potential hepatitis A risk, and best avoided. Fresh fruit you've peeled yourself is safe; other uncooked foods – salads and the like – may have been washed in unclean water. It's not a good idea to drink local **tap water**, and as such it's usually best to avoid locally made ice drinks.

## Hospitals, clinics and pharmacies

**Medical facilities** in Beijing are adequate: there are some high-standard international clinics, most big hotels have a resident doctor, and for minor complaints there are plenty of pharmacies that can suggest remedies. Most doctors will treat you with Western techniques first, but will also know a little traditional Chinese medicine (TCM; see box below). If you don't speak Chinese, you'll generally need to have a good phrasebook or be accompanied by a Chinese-speaker.

**Pharmacies** are marked by a green cross. There are large ones at 136 Wangfujing and 42 Dongdan Bei Dajie (daily 9am–8pm) or you could try the well-known Tongrentang Pharmacy on Dazhalan for traditional remedies (see box below). For imported non-prescription medicines, try the various branches of Watsons strewn across town.

## HOSPITALS AND CLINICS

**Beijing International SOS Clinic** 国际SOS, guójì SOS Suite 105, Kunsha Building, 16 Xinyuanli ☎ 010 64629199, ⓦ internationalsos.com. Foreign-staffed clinic that's correspondingly a little dear; it'll be at least ¥1000 for a simple consultation. **Daily 24hr.**

**China–Japan Friendship Hospital** 中日友好医院, zhōngrì yǒuhǎo yīyuàn 1 Off Beisanhuan Donglu ☎ 010 64221122, ⓦ english.zryhyy.com.cn. In the northeast of the city, this hospital has a dedicated foreigners' clinic. **Daily 8–11.30am & 1–4.30pm; 24hr emergency unit.**

## TRADITIONAL CHINESE MEDICINE

Chinese traditional medicine has been used for 2200 years – ever since the semi-mythical Xia king Shennong compiled his classic work on medicinal herbs. Around eight thousand "herbs" derived from roots, leaves, twigs, fruit and animal parts are used – usually dried or roasted, but sometimes stir-fried. They are generally taken as a bitter and earthy tasting tea. **Diagnosis** involves feeling the pulse, examining the tongue and face, and listening to the tone of voice. Infections are believed to be caused by internal imbalances, so the whole body is treated rather than just the symptom. In the treatment of flu, for example, a "cold action" herb would be used to reduce fever, another to induce sweating and so flush out the system, and another as a replenishing tonic.

Just as aspirin is derived from willow bark, many Western drugs come from traditional herbal remedies: artemisin, for example, which is an effective anti-malarial treatment. With their presentation boxes of ginseng roots and deer antlers, traditional **Chinese pharmacies** are colourful places; unfortunately, few practitioners or pharmacy staff will be able to speak English, but there are a few good places for international visitors to head to.

**Beijing Hospital of Traditional Chinese Medicine** 北京中医医院 běijīng zhōngyī yīyuàn 23 Meishuguan Houjie ☎ 010 52176852, ⓦ bjzhongyi.com; Nanluoguxiang subway (line 6). Renowned hospital with a range of services and English-speaking staff; call ahead to book an appointment. **Daily 8am–4.30pm.**

**Meridian Massage Center** 明经堂中医诊疗机构 míngjīngtáng zhōngyī zhěnliáo jīgòu 9–10A Fangyuan Xilu ☎ 010 84567010; Sanyuanqiao subway (line 10). More than a mere massage centre, this clinic offers various treatments including cupping, moxibustion and acupuncture; courses of the latter sometimes see electrical charges applied to the needles. **Daily 8am–4.30pm.**

**Tongrentang** 同仁堂 tóngréntáng 24 Dashilan Jie ☎ 010 63030221, ⓦ tongrentang.com; Qianmen subway (line 2). Famed pharmacy with branches all around the country. Their Dashilan branch is the most beautiful of the lot, and particularly useful since it has English-speaking staff; they're able to advise on appropriate herbal purchases, and offer on-the-spot diagnoses for a range of ailments. **Daily 8am–8pm.**

## EMERGENCY MEDICAL CARE

For emergencies, the **Friendship Hospital Foreigners' Service** has English-speaking staff and offers a comprehensive (and expensive) service at 95 Yongan Lu (☎010 63014411). **Ambulances** can be called on ☎120, but taking a taxi will be cheaper and probably quicker.

**International Medical and Dental Centre** 国际医疗中心, guójì yīliáo zhōngxīn S111 Lufthansa Centre, 50 Liangmaqiao Lu ☎ 010 64651384, ⓦ imcclinics.com. Efficiently run clinic with foreign staff and a well-stocked pharmacy. **Mon–Fri 9am–5pm.**

**Peking Union Medical College Hospital** 北京协和医院, běijīng xiéhé yīyuàn 1 Shuaifuyuan, Wangfujing ☎ 010 65295284, ⓦ www.pumch.cn. Hospital with English-speaking clinic; the foreigner unit is south of the inpatient building. **Mon–Fri 8am–4.30pm.**

**United Family Hospital** 和睦家医院, hémùjiā yīyuàn 2 Jingtai Lu, appointment ☎ 010 59277000; emergency ☎ 010 59277120, ⓦ ufh.com.cn. The only completely foreign-operated clinic in town; consultations will cost at least ¥1000. **Mon–Fri 9am–5pm.**

## Insurance

You'd do well to take out an **insurance policy** before travelling, to cover against theft, loss and illness or injury. Before paying for a new policy, however, it's worth checking whether you are already covered: some all-risks home insurance policies may cover your possessions when overseas, and many private medical schemes include cover when abroad.

There's little opportunity for dangerous sports in Beijing (unless crossing the road counts) so a standard policy should be sufficient.

## Internet

**Free wi-fi** is widespread, and it's safe to assume that cafés will have it – they even have it at *McDonald's*. Some hotels charge for wi-fi, typically the more expensive ones; daily fees of over ¥100 are not unheard of. At hostels it's almost always free; the same goes for some of the budget hotels.

Smoky **internet cafés** full of kids playing Counterstrike and MMUDs are legion, and looked on with some disquiet – Beijing's vice mayor has called them the new opium dens, and internet addiction clinics have opened to deal with young adults whose online use has become excessive. At these "vice dens", you'll be asked to show your passport before being allowed near a computer. They're on every backstreet, but are particularly prevalent close to colleges. There's never an English sign; look out for the characters "网吧" (wǎngbā). They're generally ¥5 or so per hour.

All but the smallest hotels have business centres where you can get online, generally for about ¥30 an hour. Better value are the hostels, where getting online is usually free.

## Laundry

You might have a tough time finding a **self-service** laundry; it's said that Chinese housewives wouldn't trust a stranger with the family's clothes. **Hotels** all offer a laundry service.

## Left luggage

There are left-luggage offices at all three of Beijing's main train stations, and there are also several at the airport; all are well signed. Those at the train stations are open daily 5am to midnight, and cost from ¥15/day; the office at the airport is open 24hr, and costs from ¥20/day.

## ROUGH GUIDES TRAVEL INSURANCE

Rough Guides has teamed up with **WorldNomads.com** to offer great travel insurance deals. Policies are available to residents of over 150 countries, with cover for a wide range of adventure sports, 24hr emergency assistance, high levels of medical and evacuation cover and a stream of travel safety information. Roughguides.com users can take advantage of their policies online 24/7, from anywhere in the world – even if you're already travelling. And since plans often change when you're on the road, you can extend your policy and even claim online. Roughguides.com users who buy travel insurance with WorldNomads.com can also leave a positive footprint and donate to a community development project. For more information, go to ⓦ roughguides.com/travel-insurance.

## THE GREAT FIREWALL OF CHINA

Tireless as ever in controlling what its citizens learn and know about, the Chinese government has built a sophisticated **firewall** – nicknamed the new Great Wall of China – that blocks access to undesirable websites. The way this is administered shifts according to the mood of the powers that be – restrictions were loosened, for example, while Beijing was campaigning for the 2008 Olympics (the government was anxious to be seen not to be oppressing its subjects). They've long slammed the gate firmly back down again.

In general, you can be pretty sure you won't be able to access stories deemed controversial from sites such as BBC or CNN, anything about Tibetan freedom or democracy, and **Facebook**, **YouTube** and **Twitter** are all blocked. The firewall isn't impenetrable, it's simply meant to make getting information deemed controversial enough of a hassle that most Chinese people won't bother. You can get around it simply by subscribing to a **virtual private network**, or VPN, such as WiTopia, Hotspot Shield or UltraSurf (just about every foreign business in China does this), all of which cost a few pounds a month and offer a free limited-period trial.

## Living in Beijing

Foreigners are allowed to reside anywhere in the city, though most live in **expat housing**, often in **Chaoyang** in the east of the city. Rent in these districts is expensive, usually at least £1000/€1200/US$1600/¥10,000 a month, which gets you a rough imitation of a Western apartment. Living in ordinary neighbourhoods is much cheaper: a furnished two-bedroom apartment can cost around £450/€550/US$700/¥4500 a month.

The easiest way to find an apartment is through a **real estate agent**, who will usually take a month's rent as a fee. There are lots of agents, and many advertise in the expat magazines – an example is *Wo Ai Wo Jia* (44 Chengfu Lu; ☎010 62557602, ⓦ5i5j.com). **Homestays** can be cheap, but you won't get much privacy; check ⓦchinahomestay.org. As you move in, you and the landlord are supposed to register with the local PSB office – in reality, it's quite possible to let it slide, at least for a while.

## Working in Beijing

There are plenty of jobs available for foreigners in mainland China, with a whole section of expat society surviving as actors, cocktail barmen, models and so on. Many foreign workers are employed as **English-language teachers** – most universities and many private colleges now have a few foreign teachers. There are schemes to place foreign teachers in **Chinese educational institutions** – contact your Chinese embassy (see p.33) for details. Teaching at a university, you'll earn ¥6000–11,000 a month: far more than your Chinese counterparts do, and usually bolstered by free on-campus accommodation. Contracts are generally for one year.

You'll earn up to ¥250 per hour in a **private school**, though be aware of the risk of being ripped off: the most common complaints are being given more classes to teach than you'd signed up for, and being placed in substandard housing.

### Studying in Beijing

There are plenty of opportunities to **study** in Beijing but note that most courses are in Chinese. **Beijing Daxue** (usually referred to as Beida, see p.100; ⓦenglish.pku.edu.cn) and **Tsinghua Daxue** (ⓦwww.tsinghua.edu.cn), both in Haidian in the northwest of the city, are the most famous universities in China.

You can do **short courses** (from two weeks to two months) in Mandarin Chinese at **Beijing Foreign Studies University**, 2 Xierhuan Lu (☎010 68468167, ⓦwww.bfsu.edu.cn); at **Berlitz**, 6 Ritan Lu (☎010 65930478, ⓦberlitz.com); at the **Bridge School**'s various branches (☎010 84517605, ⓦbridgeschoolchina.com), which offer evening classes; or at the **BLCC** at 7 Beixiao Jie, Sanlitun (☎010 65323005, ⓦchinesestudy-lcc.com), where most students are diplomats. For **longer courses** in Chinese, lasting six months to a year, apply to the **Beijing International School** at Anzhenxili, Chaoyang (☎010 64433151, ⓦbiss.com.cn), Beida in Haidian (see p.100), or **Beijing Normal University** (ⓦenglish.bnu.edu.cn).

### USEFUL RESOURCES

**Chinatefl** ⓦ www.chinatefl.com. A good overview of English-teaching opportunities in the Chinese public sector.

**CIEE** ⓦ ciee.org. The Council on International Educational Exchange runs programmes for US students of Mandarin or Chinese studies, with placements in Beijing.

**Teach Abroad** ⓦ goabroad.com. International teaching website with plenty of Beijing positions.

**Zhaopin** ⓦ zhaopin.com. A huge jobs site, in Chinese and English.

# Mail

Main **post offices** are open Monday to Saturday between 9am and 5pm; smaller offices may close for lunch or at weekends. Offices in the *New Otani Hotel* (daily 8am–6pm) and at L115, China World Trade Centre (daily 8am–8pm), keep longer hours.

The **International Post Office** is on Chaoyangmen Dajie, just north of the intersection with Jianguomen Dajie (Mon–Sat 8am–7pm; ☎010 65128114). Here you can rent a PO box, use their packing service for parcels and buy a wide variety of collectable stamps, though staff are not very helpful.

The Chinese **postal service** is, on the whole, fast and reliable. A postcard costs ¥5, while a standard letter is ¥7 or more, depending on the weight; stamps are available from post offices and street kiosks. An **Express Mail Service** (**EMS**) operates to most countries and to most destinations within China and is available from all post offices. Besides cutting delivery times, the service ensures the letter or parcel is sent by registered delivery – though note that the courier service of **DHL** (24hr office 2 Jiuxian Qiao, Chaoyang; ☎010 64662211, ⓦcn.dhl .com) is rather faster, and costs about the same; there are also **FedEx** (ⓦfedex.com) and **UPS** (ⓦups.com) branches around town.

To send **parcels**, turn up at a post office with the goods you want to send – staff sell boxes to pack them in. Once packed, but before the parcel is sealed, it must be checked at the customs window in the post office. A 1kg parcel will cost ¥70–140 to send by surface mail, ¥150 by airmail to Europe or North America; the largest box available holds 30kg and costs over ¥1000 to send. If you are sending valuable goods bought in China, put the receipt or a photocopy of it in with the parcel, as it may be opened for customs inspection farther down the line.

# Maps

A large foldout **map** of the city can come in handy. In general, the free tourist maps – available in large hotels and printed inside tourist magazines – don't show enough detail. A wide variety of city maps are available at all transport hubs and from street vendors, hotels and bookshops; many are labelled in English and Chinese, and have bus routes, sights and hotels marked.

# Money

Chinese **currency** is formally called the **yuan** (¥), more colloquially known as renminbi (RMB) or kuai; a yuan breaks down into units of ten **jiao** (also called mao). One jiao is equivalent to ten **fen**, though these are effectively worthless – you'll only ever be given them in official currency transactions, or see the tiny notes folded up and used to build model dragons or boats. Paper money was invented in China and is still the main form of exchange, available in ¥100, ¥50, ¥20, ¥10, ¥5 and ¥1 notes; though you'll rarely need to use them, there are also notes for jiao and fen, while everything up to and including ¥1 also comes in coin form. At the time of writing the exchange rate was approximately ¥9.5 to £1, ¥6 to US$1 and ¥8.2 to €1.

## Banks and ATMs

Most **ATMs** accept foreign bankcards, connected to the Cirrus, AmEx, Visa, Plus and MasterCard networks. They'll likely charge transaction fees, and your home bank will probably take a slice too. There's usually a maximum of ¥2000 in a single withdrawal, and a maximum 24hr limit of ¥3000–5000, depending on your card.

**Banks** are usually open from Monday to Friday (9am–5pm), though some branches open on weekends too. All are closed on New Year's Day, National Day, and for the first three days of the Chinese New Year, with reduced hours for the following eleven days. All branches of the Bank of China will give cash advances on Visa cards.

## Credit cards and wiring money

**Major credit cards**, such as Visa, American Express and MasterCard, are accepted only at big tourist hotels and restaurants, and by a few tourist-oriented shops. It's possible to **wire money** to Beijing through **Western Union** (ⓦwesternunion .com); funds can be collected from one of their agents in the city, in post offices and the Agricultural Bank of China.

# Opening hours and public holidays

**Offices** and **government agencies** are open from Monday to Friday, usually from 8am to noon and then from 1pm to 5pm; some open on Saturday and Sunday mornings, too. **Shops** are generally open from 9am to 6pm or 7pm Monday to Saturday, with shorter hours on Sunday; large shopping centres are open daily and don't close till around 9pm. **Museums** are either open all week or are shut on one day, usually Monday. We have listed opening hours throughout the Guide.

**Public holidays** have little effect on business, with only government departments and certain banks closing. However, on New Year's Day, during the first three days of the Chinese New Year, and on National Day, most businesses, shops and sights will be shut, though some restaurants stay open.

The best time to sightsee is during the week, as all attractions are swamped with local tourists at weekends. Some attractions have separate low- and high-season opening times and prices; in high season (usually March to November), places often open half an hour earlier, and close half an hour later, and prices sometimes rise by ¥5–10.

## PUBLIC HOLIDAYS

**Jan 1** New Year's Day
**Feb/March** Chinese New Year (first day of first lunar month)
**Early April** Qingming Festival
**May 1** Labour Day
**June** Dragon Boat Festival (fifth day of fifth lunar month)
**September** Mid-Autumn Festival (fifteenth day of eighth lunar month)
**Oct 1** National Day

# Phones

Local calls are free from landlines, and long-distance China-wide calls are fairly cheap. Note that everywhere in China has an **area code** that must be used when phoning from outside that locality; Beijing's is 010.

The most prevalent **public phones** are located on the outside of small stores – you won't have to look long to find one. Simply pick up, dial and pay the amount on the meter afterwards. Most of these however, will not handle international calls. The cheapest way to make long-distance and international calls is with **card phones** (¥0.3/min for domestic, ¥1.8–3.2/min international, with a 50 percent discount after 6pm and at weekends). They take **IC Cards** (*IC kǎ* in Mandarin), which are sold at every little store and in hotels, in units of ¥20, ¥50 and ¥100. You will be cut off when the credit left on the card drops below the amount needed for the next minute. You'll find a card phone in every hotel lobby, and there are many booths on the street. Another option is the **IP card**, which can be used with any phone, and comes in ¥100 units. You dial a local number, then a PIN, then the number you're calling. Rates are as low as ¥2.4 per minute to the US and Canada, ¥3.2 to Europe.

Note that calling from **tourist hotels**, whether from your room or from their business centres, will attract a surcharge that may well be extortionate.

---

## USEFUL DIALLING CODES

To **call mainland China from abroad**, dial the international access code, then 86, then the number (omitting the initial zero). To **call abroad from mainland China**, dial ❶ 00, then the country code (see below), then the number (omitting the initial zero, if any):
**Australia** 61
**New Zealand** 64
**Republic of Ireland** 353
**South Africa** 27
**UK** 44
**US and Canada** 1

---

### Mobile phones

Your **home mobile phone** may already be compatible with the Chinese network, though you will pay a premium to use it abroad, and callers within China have to make an international call to reach you. For more information, check with the manufacturer and/or your telephone service provider. It's also worth contacting your phone company to ask whether they do calling cards that can be charged to your home bill.

Alternatively, once in Beijing you can buy a **SIM card** from any China Mobile shop or street kiosk, which allows you to use your phone as though it's a local mobile, with a new number, as long your phone is unlocked. The SIM card costs ¥60–100, with some variation according to how lucky the digits are – favoured sixes and eights bump up the price, while unlucky fours make it cheaper. Additionally, you'll need to buy **prepaid cards** to pay for the calls. Making and receiving domestic calls this way costs ¥0.7/min for land lines and ¥1.5/min for mobiles; international calls will cost considerably more.

The cheapest phones **to buy** will cost around ¥400; make sure the staff change the operating language into English for you. You can also **rent mobile phones** from China Mobile, which is most conveniently arranged online at ⓦ china-mobile-phones.com. The phone can be picked up from your hotel and left there when you leave. Phones cost ¥80, with an ¥8 per day charge, and all calls are at the local rate.

## Time

Beijing, like the rest of China, is 8hr ahead of GMT, 13hr ahead of US Eastern Standard Time, 16hr ahead of US Pacific Time and 2hr behind Australian Eastern Standard Time. It does not observe daylight saving time.

# Toilets

Chinese toilets can be pretty disgusting, and though Beijing is one of the best places in the country in such regards, it's still common to find loos that are absolutely filthy or provide no privacy whatsoever. Things are certainly improving, though, even in the city's famed *hutong* alleys – many of the communal toilets (which all locals have to use, since they've none of their own) have been spruced up of late, with some now even allowing wheelchair access. Although public toilets are quite common and almost always free, the best advice when around town is to head for the nearest shopping mall or five-star hotel; many of Beijing's sights now also feature decent toilets. Lastly, some facilities only have Chinese markings to designate male and female sections: it's helpful to remember that the ladies' one (女) looks a bit like a (crouching) woman, and the chaps' one (男) somewhat like a fella with a window for a head.

# Tourist information

For details of the government-run CITS offices, see p.26, though as a general rule avoid websites run by them (or any other official agency) as they're dry as dust. For the locations of **Chinese tourist offices abroad**, which can book tours and tickets, see Ⓦcnto.org/offices.htm, and for details of English-language listings magazines, see p.135.

## ONLINE RESOURCES

**The Beijing Page** Ⓦ beijingpage.com. A comprehensive and well-organized page of links, with sections on tourism, entertainment and industry.

**CCTV 9** Ⓦ cctv-9.com. Featuring a live video stream plus other programmes available to watch on demand, this is the website of the Chinese state television's English-language channel.

**China Business World** Ⓦ cbw.com. A corporate directory site with a useful travel section, detailing tours and allowing you to book flights and hotels.

**China Vista** Ⓦ chinavista.com. China-based website with snippets about Chinese culture, history, attractions and food.

**Danwei** Ⓦ danwei.org. English commentary and reporting on what's hot in the Chinese media; very informative, but usually blocked in China.

**Friends of the Great Wall** Ⓦ friendsofgreatwall.org. Covers efforts to maintain and clean up the Great Wall, with useful links.

**Sinomania** Ⓦ sinomania.com. A California-based site with links to current Chinese news stories and a good popular music section, with MP3 downloads available.

**Yesasia** Ⓦ yesasia.com. Online shopping for Chinese movies, CDs, books, collectables, etc.

**Youku** Ⓦ youku.com. With YouTube blocked, this popular site fills the gap, with millions of clips and home videos. In Chinese, but easy enough to navigate.

**Zhongwen.com** Ⓦ zhongwen.com. Especially interesting if you're a student of Chinese, this site includes background on the Chinese script, several classic texts (with links to some English translations) and even a bunch of suggested renderings into Chinese of common first names.

# Travellers with disabilities

Beijing makes few provisions for disabled people. Undergoing an economic boom, the city resembles a building site, with uneven, obstacle-strewn paving, intense crowds and vehicle traffic, and few access ramps. **Public transport** is generally inaccessible to wheelchair users, though a few of the upmarket **hotels** are equipped to assist disabled visitors; in particular, Beijing's several *Holiday Inns* (Ⓦihg.com/holidayinn) and *Hiltons* (Ⓦhilton.com) have rooms designed for wheelchair users.

The disabled in Chinese are usually kept hidden away; attitudes are not, on the whole, very enlightened, and disabled visitors should be prepared for a great deal of staring. Given the situation, it may be worth considering an **organized tour**. Make sure you take spares of any specialist clothing or equipment, extra supplies of drugs (carried with you if you fly), and a prescription including the generic name – in English and Chinese characters – in case of emergency. If there's an association representing people with your disability, contact them early on in the planning process.

MAO PORTRAIT, TIANAN'MEN

# The Forbidden City and Tian'anmen Square

A sealed-off stomping ground for century upon century of emperors, Beijing's lauded Imperial Palace – better known in the West by its unofficial title, the Forbidden City – is the most famous tourist draw in all China. For its five centuries in action, clean through the reigns of 24 emperors of the Ming and Qing dynasties, civilian Chinese were forbidden from even approaching its walls. With its maze of eight hundred buildings and nine thousand chambers, the Forbidden City was the core of the capital, the empire, and (so the Chinese believed) the universe. It remains an extraordinary place today, unsurpassed in China for monumental scale, harmonious design and elegant grandeur.

This jaw-dropping specimen of dynastic splendour sits just off **Tian'anmen Square**, at over 400,000 square metres the greatest public space on earth. Symbolically the heart of the country, the square is an infamous place which in its austerity provides a complete contrast to the luxury and ornament of the palace. Laid out in 1949, it's a modern creation in a city that, traditionally, had no places where crowds could gather. As one of the square's architects put it: "Beijing was a reflection of a feudal society... We had to transform it; we had to make Beijing into the capital of socialist China." They created a vast concrete plain bounded by stern, monumental buildings, not least the **Great Hall of the People** to the west and the **National Museum of China** to the east.

# The Forbidden City

故宫, gùgōng • Daily: April–Oct Mon 8.30am–noon, Tues–Sun 8.30am–5pm; Nov–March Mon 8.30am–noon, Tues–Sun 8.30am–4.30pm • April–Oct ¥60, Nov–March ¥40; audio guide ¥40 • ☎ 010 85007421, ⓦ www.dpm.org.cn • Tian'anmen East or Tian'anmen West subway (both line 1)

Lying at the heart of the city, the **Imperial Palace** – or, most evocatively, the **Forbidden City** – is Beijing's finest monument. To do it justice, you should plan to spend at least a whole day here; you could wander the complex for a week and keep discovering new aspects, especially now that many of the halls are doubling as museums of dynastic artefacts. The central halls, with their wealth of imperial pomp, may be the most magnificent buildings, but for many visitors it's the side rooms, with their displays of the more intimate accoutrements of court life, that bring home the realities of life for the inhabitants in this, the most gilded of cages. It is somewhat ironic that the "Forbidden" City now admits up to 80,000 visitors each day. However, this is the largest palace complex in the world – even at capacity the countless faces, tour guides and sun-umbrellas melt away as you walk under Mao's infamous portrait (see opposite) and into the complex.

The Forbidden City is encased by a moat and, within the turreted walls, employs a wonderful symmetry and geomantic structure to achieve a balance between yin and yang, positive and negative energy (see box below). The City's spine is composed of eleven south-facing halls or gates, all colossal, exquisite and ornate. Branching off from this central vertebrae are more than eight hundred buildings that share the exclusive

---

**FENG SHUI IN THE FORBIDDEN CITY**

Literally "wind and water", **feng shui** (风水, fēng shuǐ) is a form of geomancy, which assesses how objects must be positioned so as not to disturb the spiritual attributes of the surrounding landscape. This reflects Taoist cosmology, which states that the inner harmonies of the landscape must be preserved to secure all other harmonies. Buildings should be favourably oriented according to the compass – tombs, for example, should face south – and protected from unlucky directions by other buildings or hills. Even the minutiae of interior **decor** are covered by feng shui. Some of its handy rules for the modern home include: don't have a mirror at the foot of the bed; don't have sharp edges pointing into the room; cover the television when it's not in use; and don't leave the lavatory seat up.

All the halls of the Forbidden City were laid out according to geomantic theories – the balance between yin and yang, or negative and positive energy. The buildings, signposted in English, face south in order to benefit from the invigorating advantages of yang energy, and as a protection against harmful yin elements from the north, both real and imagined – cold winds, evil spirits and steppe barbarians. Ramparts of compacted earth and a 50m-wide moat isolated the complex from the commoners outside, with the only access being through four monumental gateways in the four cardinal directions. The layout is the same as that of any grand Chinese house of the period: pavilions are arranged around courtyards, with reception rooms and official buildings at the front (south) set out with rigorous symmetry and a labyrinthine set of private chambers to the north.

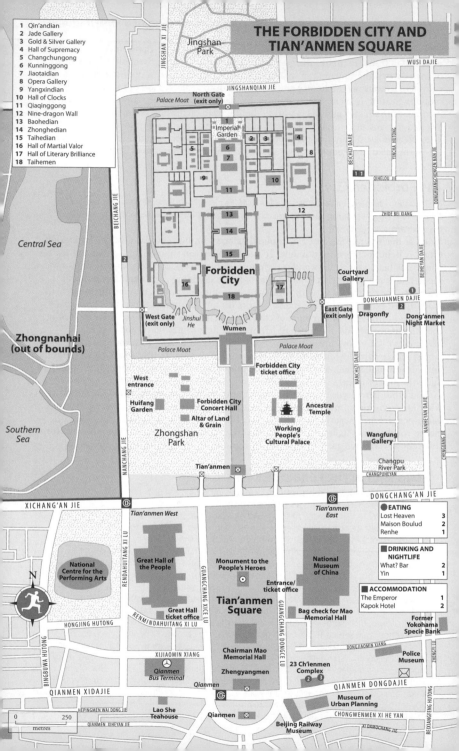

# THE FORBIDDEN CITY AND TIAN'ANMEN SQUARE

1 Qin'andian
2 Jade Gallery
3 Gold & Silver Gallery
4 Hall of Supremacy
5 Changchungong
6 Kunninggong
7 Jiaotaidian
8 Opera Gallery
9 Yangxindian
10 Hall of Clocks
11 Qiaqinggong
12 Nine-dragon Wall
13 Baohedian
14 Zhonghedian
15 Taihedian
16 Hall of Martial Valor
17 Hall of Literary Brilliance
18 Taihemen

Jingshan Park

Central Sea

Zhongnanhai
(out of bounds)

Southern Sea

North Gate
(exit only)

Imperial Garden

Palace Moat

Forbidden City

Courtyard Gallery

West Gate
(exit only)

Jinshui He

Wumen

East Gate
(exit only)

Dragonfly

Dong'anmen Night Market

Palace Moat

Palace Moat

Forbidden City ticket office

West entrance

Huifang Garden

Forbidden City Concert Hall

Altar of Land & Grain

Zhongshan Park

Ancestral Temple

Working People's Cultural Palace

Wangfung Gallery

Changpu River Park

Tian'anmen

National Centre for the Performing Arts

Tian'anmen West

Great Hall of the People

Great Hall ticket office

Tian'anmen Square

Monument to the People's Heroes

Entrance/ ticket office

Tian'anmen East

National Museum of China

Bag check for Mao Memorial Hall

Chairman Mao Memorial Hall

Zhengyangmen

23 Ch'ienmen Complex

Qianmen Bus Terminal

Qianmen

Former Yokohama Specie Bank

Police Museum

Museum of Urban Planning

Lao She Teahouse

Qianmen

Beijing Railway Museum

## EATING
Lost Heaven        3
Maison Boulud      2
Renhe              1

## DRINKING AND NIGHTLIFE
What? Bar          2
Yin                1

## ACCOMMODATION
The Emperor        1
Kapok Hotel        2

0    250
metres

combination of imperial colours (see box, p.44): red walls and yellow roof tiles. Elsewhere, jade green, gold and azure blue decorate the woodwork, archways and balconies. The doors to the central halls are heavy, red, thick and studded with gold. All in all, the intricacy of the City's design is quite astonishing.

There are a number of interesting and consistent **themes** to follow as you progress deeper into the belly of the Imperial Palace: sundials feature in many squares as symbols of the emperor's authority over time-keeping; huge bronze cauldrons – once used to store water in case of fire – punctuate the open spaces; while statues and carvings of dragons (the symbol of the emperor), cranes (symbolic of longevity) and lions (associated with mystical protective properties) are abundant.

Brief history

Construction of the Forbidden City began in 1407 during the reign of Emperor Yongle, the monarch responsible for switching the capital from Nanjing back to Beijing in 1403 (see p.170). His programme to construct a complex worthy enough to house the Son of Heaven involved up to ten thousand artisans, and perhaps a million labourers, and was completed in 1420. From then until 1644, the Forbidden City served as the seat of successive emperors of the Ming dynasty, as well as the political and ceremonial heart of government. In 1912, upon the abdication of Puyi – the last emperor of China – parts of the City were opened to the public, though Puyi actually lived in its inner sanctums until 1924 with the blessings of the Republican government. The City suffered some damage during the Cultural Revolution, though this was limited by an army battalion that was sent to guard the palace during the uprisings.

**ARRIVAL AND INFORMATION**                                **THE FORBIDDEN CITY**

**Access** The Forbidden City can only be entered from the south, via the Wumen gate. This is most easily accessed via the Tian'anmen gate, just north of Tian'anmen Square; the ticket offices lie approximately 250m onwards. You can enter from the south too, or from alternate gates to the north, east and west. If you're in a taxi, you can be dropped right outside the ticket offices. The throngs can be massive so if you're walking you may wish to consider heading to or from Wumen via Zhongshan Park (see p.49), or the Working People's Cultural Palace (see p.50), rather than going straight from Tian'anmen Square. Visitors have freedom to wander most of the site, though not to access all of the buildings.

**Tours** If you want detailed explanations of everything you see, you can tag along with one of the numerous tour groups, pick up a specialist book (on sale at Wumen), or take the audio tour, also available at the Wumen; though it no longer has Roger Moore's voice, it is GPS-enabled, so automatically provides a short, digestible and informative narrative commentary as you progress through the complex. If you take this option, it's worth retracing your steps afterwards for an untutored view and exploring the side halls that aren't included on the tour.

**Services** There are plenty of clean toilets inside the complex, a few places to get a coffee (though *Starbucks* were kicked out of here after a public campaign), and even an ATM, though it is advisable to bring a packed lunch – a full day is required to sample the delights of the Forbidden City and the cafés are not particularly well stocked or varied.

## Wumen

A huge building whose central archway was reserved for the emperor's sole use, **Wumen** (Meridian Gate) is the largest and grandest of the Forbidden City gates. From a vantage point at the top, each new lunar year the Sons of Heaven would announce to their court the details of the forthcoming calendar, including the dates of festivals and rites, and, in times of war, inspect the army. It was customary for victorious generals returning from battle to present their prisoners here for the emperor to decide their fate. He would be flanked, as on all such imperial occasions, by a guard of elephants, the gift of Burmese subjects. In the Ming dynasty, this was also where disgraced officials were flogged or executed.

In the wings on either side of the Wumen are two drums and two bells; the drums were beaten whenever the emperor went to the Temple of the Imperial Ancestors, the bells rung when he visited the temples of Heaven (see p.80) and Earth (see p.70).

**1**

## IMPERIAL SYMBOLISM

Almost every colour and image in the Imperial Palace is richly symbolic. Yellow was the imperial **colour**; only in the palace were yellow roof tiles allowed. Purple was just as important, though used more sparingly; it symbolized joy and represented the pole star, centre of the universe according to Chinese cosmology (the implication of its use – usually on wall panels – was that the emperor resided in the earthly equivalent of the celestial zenith).

The **sign** for the emperor was the dragon and for the empress, the phoenix; you'll see these two creatures represented on almost every building and stairway. The crane and turtle, depicted in paintings, carved into furniture or represented as freestanding sculptures, represent longevity of reign. The **numbers** nine and five crop up all over the complex, manifested in how often design elements are repeated; nine is lucky and associated with *yang*, or male energy, while five, the middle single-digit number, is associated with harmony and balance. Nine and five together – power and balance – symbolize "the heavenly son", the emperor.

### Jinshui He and Taihemen

On the far side of Wumen you find yourself in a vast paved court, cut east–west by the **Jinshui He**, or Golden Water Stream, with its five marble bridges, one for each Confucian virtue (see box, p.69), each decorated with carved torches (a symbol of masculinity). Beyond is another ceremonial gate, **Taihemen**, the Gate of Supreme Harmony, its entrance guarded by a magisterial row of lions, and further on a larger courtyard where the principal imperial audiences were held. Within this space the entire court – up to 100,000 people – could be accommodated. They made their way in through the lesser side-gates – military men from the west, civilian officials from the east – and waited in total silence as the emperor ascended his throne. Then, with only the Imperial Guard remaining standing, they prostrated themselves nine times.

The galleries running round the courtyard housed the imperial storerooms. The buildings either side are the **Hall of Martial Valor** to the west and **Hall of Literary Brilliance** to the east; the latter under the Ming emperors housed the 11,099 volumes of the encyclopedia Yongle commissioned, though is now the Ceramics Gallery (see box, p.48).

### The ceremonial halls

The three main **ceremonial halls** stand directly north of Taihemen, dominating the court. The main halls, made of wood, are built in traditional style all on the same level, on a raised stone platform. Their elegant roofs, curved like the wings of a bird, are supported entirely by pillars and beams; the weight is cleverly distributed by ceiling consoles, while the walls beneath are just lightweight partitions. Doors, steps and access ramps are always odd in number, with the middle passageway reserved for the emperor's palanquin.

#### Taihedian

Raised on a three-tiered marble terrace is the first and most spectacular of the ceremonial halls, the **Taihedian**, Hall of Supreme Harmony. The vast hall, nearly 38m high, was the tallest in China during the Ming and Qing dynasties – no civilian building was permitted to be taller. Taihedian was used for the most important state occasions: the emperor's coronation, birthday or marriage; ceremonies marking the new lunar year and winter solstice; proclamations of the results of the imperial examinations; and the nomination of generals at the outset of a military campaign. During the Republic, it was proposed that parliament should sit here, though the idea wasn't put into practice.

Decorated entirely in red and gold, Taihedian is the most sumptuous building in the entire complex. In the central coffer, a sunken panel in the ceiling, two gold-plated dragons play with a huge pearl. The gilded rosewood chair beneath, the dragon throne, was the exact centre of the Chinese universe. A marble pavement ramp, intricately carved with dragons and flanked by bronze incense burners, marks the path along which the emperor's sedan chair was carried whenever he wanted to be taken somewhere, while the grain measure and sundial just outside are symbols of imperial justice.

Zhonghedian

Beyond the Taihedian, you enter the **Zhonghedian**, Hall of Central Harmony, another throne room, where the emperor performed ceremonies of greeting to foreign dignitaries and addressed the imperial offspring (the progeny of his several wives and numerous concubines). It owes its name to a quote from the *I-Ching*, a Chinese tome dating back to 200 BC: "avoiding extremes and self control brings harmony", the idea being that the middle course would be a harmonious one. The emperor also examined the seed for each year's crop in the hall, and it was used, too, as a dressing room for major events held in the Taihedian.

Baohedian

The third of the great ceremonial halls, the **Baohedian**, or Preserving Harmony Hall, was the venue for state banquets and imperial examinations; graduates from the latter were appointed to positions of power in what was the world's first recognizably bureaucratic civil service. Huge ceremonies took place here to celebrate Chinese New Year; in 1903, this involved the sacrifice of 10,000 sheep. The hall's galleries, originally treasure houses, display various finds from the site, though the most spectacular, a vast marble block carved with dragons and clouds, stands at the rear of the hall. A Ming creation, reworked in the eighteenth century, it's among the finest carvings in the palace and certainly the largest – the 250-tonne chunk of marble was slid here from well outside the city by flooding the roads in winter to form sheets of ice.

**The imperial living quarters**

To the north of the ceremonial halls, and repeating their hierarchy, are the three principal palaces of the **imperial living quarters**: the Qianqinggong, the Jiaotaidian and the Kunninggong. Emperors also made use of a clutch of surrounding halls.

Qianqinggong

Its terrace surmounted by incense burners in the form of cranes and tortoises (see box opposite) the extravagant **Qianqinggong**, or Palace of Heavenly Purity, was originally the imperial bedroom. It was here in 1785 that Qianlong presided over the famous "banquet of old men" that brought together three thousand men of over sixty years of age from all corners of the empire. Used for the lying-in-state of the emperor, the hall also played a role in the tradition that finally solved the problem of **succession** (hitherto fraught with intrigue and uncertainty, as the principle of primogeniture was

---

**DINING, IMPERIAL STYLE**

The **emperor** ate twice a day, at 6.30am and around noon. Often **meals** consisted of hundreds of dishes, with the emperor eating no more than a mouthful of each – to eat more would be to express a preference, and that information might reach a potential poisoner. According to tradition, no one else was allowed to eat at his table, and when banquets were held he sat at a platform well above his guests. Such occasions were extremely formal and not to everyone's liking; a Jesuit priest invited to such a feast in 1727 complained, "A European dies of hunger here; the way in which he is forced to sit on the ground on a mat with crossed legs is most awkward; neither the wine nor the dishes are to his taste… Every time the emperor says a word which lets it be known he wishes to please, one must kneel down and hit one's head on the ground. This has to be done every time someone serves him something to drink."

**1**

## EUNUCHS AND CONCUBINES

For much of the imperial period, the Forbidden City was home to members of the royal household. Around half of these were **eunuchs**, introduced into the imperial court as a means of ensuring the authenticity of the emperor's offspring and, as the eunuchs would never have any family, an extreme solution to the problem of nepotism. As virtually the only men allowed into the palace, they came into close contact with the emperor and often rose to positions of considerable power. Their numbers varied greatly from one dynasty to the next – the Ming court is supposed to have employed 20,000, but this is probably an overestimate; the relatively frugal Qing Emperor Kangxi reduced the number to nine thousand.

Most of the eunuchs (or "bob-tailed dogs" as they were nicknamed) came from poor families, and volunteered for their emasculation as a way of acquiring wealth and influence. The operation cost six silver pieces and was performed in a hut just outside the palace walls. Hot pepper-water was used to numb the parts, then after the blade had flashed the wound was sealed with a solder plug. The plug was removed three days later – if urine gushed out, the operation was a success. If it didn't, the man would die soon, in agony. Confucianism held that disfiguration of the body impaired the soul, so in the hope that he would still be buried "whole", the eunuch carried his severed genitalia in a bag hung on his belt. One problem eunuchs were often plagued with was bed-wetting, hence the old Chinese expression, "as stinky as a eunuch". Eunuchry was finally banned in 1924, and the remaining 1500 eunuchs were expelled from the palace. An observer described them "carrying their belongings in sacks and crying piteously in high-pitched voices". The last imperial eunuch, Sun Yaoting, died in 1996 at the age of 93, and inspired a fascinating book chronicling the mysteries and horrors of his life at the Imperial Court, Jia Yinghua's *The Last Eunuch of China: The Life of Sun Yaoting*.

Scarcely less numerous than the eunuchs were the **concubines**, whose role varied from consorts to whores. At night, the emperor chose a girl from his harem by picking out a tablet bearing her name from a pile on a silver tray – though the court astrologer had to OK the decision. She would be delivered to the emperor's bedchamber naked but for a yellow cloth wrapped around her, and carried on the back of one of the eunuchs, since she could barely walk with her bound feet. Eunuchs would be on hand for the event, standing behind a screen and shouting out cautions for the emperor not to get too carried away and risking harming the imperial body. Favoured wives and concubines were the only women in dynastic China with power and influence; Dowager Empress Cixi (see box, p.96) was a telling example of just how successful a wily concubine could be.

not used), a practice begun by Qing Emperor Yongzheng. Keeping an identical document on his person, Yongzheng and his successors deposited the name of his chosen successor in a sealed box hidden in the hall. When the emperor died, it was sufficient to compare the two documents to proclaim the new Son of Heaven.

### Jiaotaidian

Beyond the Qianqinggong is the **Jiaotaidian** (Hall of Union), the empress's throne-room where the 25 imperial document seals were kept. The ceiling here is possibly the finest in the complex, a gilt confection with a dragon surrounded by phoenixes at the centre; also here is a fine, and very hefty, water clock. The two characters *wu wei* at the back of the hall mean "no action" – a reference to the Taoist political ideal of not disturbing the course of nature or society.

### Kunninggong

The **Kunninggong**, or Palace of Earthly Tranquillity, was where the emperor and empress traditionally spent their wedding night. By law the emperor had to spend the first three nights of his marriage, and the first day of the Chinese New Year, with his new wife. On the left as you enter is a large sacrificial room, its vats ready to receive

## EXHIBITIONS IN THE FORBIDDEN CITY

The Imperial Palace is increasingly being devoted to museum space – so much so that it arguably constitutes the best museum in China. The numerous buildings spreading out from the Forbidden City's central axis house a variety of fascinating permanent and temporary exhibitions of Chinese and international historical artefacts and treasures; you'll find a map showing their location on the back of your entrance ticket. Check what's on at ⓦ www.dpm.org.cn.

**The Treasure Gallery** In the buildings surrounding the Hall of Supremacy. Gold, silver, pearl and jade items demonstrating the wealth, majesty and luxury of imperial life. ¥10

**Hall of Clocks** This exhibition, always a favourite, displays the result of one Qing emperor's passion for liberally ornamented Baroque timepieces, most of which are English and French, though the rhino-sized water clock by the entrance is Chinese. There's even one with a mechanical scribe who can write eight characters. Some clocks are wound to demonstrate their workings at 11am and 2pm. ¥10

**Ceramics Gallery** Hall of Literary Brilliance. A wonderful, air-cooled selection of fine pots, statutes and porcelain treasures; keep an eye out for the Ming and Qing vases. Free

**Painting and Calligraphy Gallery** Hall of Martial Valor. Pieces demonstrating the art, skill and beauty of artists and literary aesthetics. Free

**Jade Gallery** Palace of Accumulated Purity. A selection of intricate jade objects from the Imperial Court. Free

**Gold and Silver Gallery** Palace of Great Brilliance. Precious religious, decorative, dress and sacrificial items. Free

**Opera Gallery** Hall for Viewing Opera. Fascinating display of all the finery of the Chinese opera. Free

offerings (1300 pigs a year during the Ming dynasty). The wedding chamber is a small room off to one side, painted entirely in red and covered with decorative emblems symbolizing fertility and joy. It was last pressed into operation in 1922 for the wedding of 12-year-old Pu Yi, the last emperor, who, finding it "like a melted red wax candle", decided that he preferred the Mind Nurture Palace (see below) and went back there.

### Yangxindian and Changchungong

One of a group of palaces to the west of the Kunninggong, the Mind Nurture Palace, or **Yangxindian**, was where the emperors spent most of their time. Several of these palaces retain their furniture from the Manchu times, most of it eighteenth century; in one, the **Changchungong** (Palace of Eternal Spring), is a series of paintings illustrating the Ming novel, *The Story of the Stone*.

## Nine Dragon Wall

Over on the east side of the complex, the **Nine Dragon Wall** is a relatively recent addition to the Forbidden City (1772). This 30m-long screen of dragons, each toying with a pearl, is composed of 270 pieces of coloured glaze. Note that the third white dragon has a mysterious wooden replacement piece to its jigsaw pattern: just before presentation of the screen to the emperor, the ceramic tile was damaged and, to save the lives of the designers, the inconspicuous replacement was quickly carved from wood.

## The Imperial Garden

From the Inner Court, the Kunningmen (Gate of Terrestrial Tranquillity) opens north onto the **Imperial Garden**, by this stage something of a respite from the elegant buildings. There are a couple of **cafés** here amid a pleasing network of ponds, walkways and pavilions, designed to be reminiscent of southern Chinese landscapes. In the middle of the garden, the **Qin'andian**, or Hall of Imperial Tranquillity, was where the emperor came to worship a Taoist water deity, Xuan Wu, who was responsible for keeping the palace safe from fire. You can exit here into Jingshan Park (see p.58), which provides an overview of the complex.

# Tian'anmen

天安门, tiānānmén • Daily 8.30am–4.30pm • Entrance at junction of Xichang'an Jie and Dongchang'an Jie • ¥15; tickets available from the Forbidden City ticket offices (see p.43) • Tian'anmen East or Tian'anmen West subway (both line 1)

**Tian'anmen**, the Gate of Heavenly Peace, is the main entrance to the Forbidden City. An image familiar across the world, it occupies an exalted place in Chinese iconography, appearing on policemen's caps, banknotes, coins, stamps and most pieces of official paper. As such it's a prime object of pilgrimage, with many visitors milling around and taking pictures of the large **portrait of Mao** (the only one still on public display), which hangs over the central passageway. Once reserved for the sole use of the emperor, but now standing wide open, the entrance is flanked by the twin slogans "Long Live the People's Republic of China" and "Long Live the Great Union between the Peoples of the World".

The entry ticket allows you to climb up onto the **viewing platform** above the gate. Security is tight: all visitors have to leave their bags and go through a metal detector before they can ascend. Inside, the fact that most people cluster around the souvenir stall – which sells official certificates to anyone who wants their visit here documented – reflects the fact that there's not much to look at.

# The parks

Tian'anmen gate is flanked by two parks – **Zhongshan** to the west, and the grounds of the **Working People's Culture Palace** to the east. These are great places to escape the rigorous formality of Tian'anmen Square, not to mention the crowds of the Forbidden City; they also double as a highly pleasant alternate means of access to the latter.

## Zhongshan Park

中山公园, zhōngshān gōngyuán • Entrances on Xichang'an and Nanchang Jie • **Park** Daily 6am–9pm • ¥3 • **Flower exhibition and Huifang Garden** Daily 9am–4.30pm • ¥5 • ⓦ www.zhongshan-park.cn • Tian'anmen West subway (line 1)

Delightful **Zhongshan Park** boasts the ruins of the **Altar of Land and Grain**, a site of biennial sacrifice during the Qing and Ming dynasties. It was built during Yongle's reign in 1420, and hosts harvest-time events closely related to those of the Temple of Heaven (see p.80). Elsewhere in the park you'll find a series of pavilions and a concert hall (see p.153); somewhat incongruously, you'll also be able to have a go on the **bumper cars** (¥10), each of which sports pictures of the American flag and the Statue of Liberty – these, perhaps, compensate for the removal of *Starbucks* from the neighbouring Forbidden City. You'll also have to pay extra for the **flower exhibition** and the **Huifang Garden**; the former is a so-so flower collection located in a greenhouse of sorts, while the latter is a beautiful, bamboo-strewn section of the park.

---

### THE EMPEROR SPEAKS TO HIS PEOPLE

During the Ming and Qing dynasties, Tian'anmen was where the **ceremony** called "the golden phoenix issues an edict" took place. The minister of rites would receive an imperial edict inside the palace and take it to Tian'anmen on a silver "cloud tray", he and his charge under a yellow umbrella. Here, the edict was read aloud to the officials of the court who knelt below, lined up according to rank. Next, the edict was placed in the mouth of a gilded wooden phoenix, which was lowered by rope to another cloud tray below. The tray was then put in a carved, wooden dragon and taken to the Ministry of Rites to be copied out and sent around the country.

Mao too liked to address his subjects from here. On October 1, 1949, he delivered the **liberation speech** to jubilant crowds below, declaring that "the Chinese people have now stood up"; in the 1960s, he spoke from this spot to massed ranks of Red Guards and declared that it was time for a "cultural revolution" (see p.174).

**1**

## Working People's Cultural Palace

劳动人民文化宫, láodòng rénmín wénhuàgōng • Entrances on Dongchang'an Jie and Nanchizi Dajie • Daily 6.30am–7.30pm • ¥2, or ¥15 including Front Hall • ⊕ www.bjwhg.com.cn • Tian'anmen East subway (line 1)

The wonderful **Working People's Cultural Palace** is *so* much more interesting than its name may suggest – it was symbolically named in deference to the fact that ordinary Chinese were only allowed within this central sector of their capital following the communist takeover in 1949. Though far smaller than the Forbidden City, it's also far more manageable, infinitely less crowded, and equally beautiful in parts – proof of which (of sorts) is provided by its status as Beijing's number-one venue for wedding photos. The park is centred on the **Ancestral Temple** (太庙, tài miào), today a sort of Forbidden City annexe; this is a stupendously beautiful place, though you'll need an extra ticket to peek inside the first of its three halls (the other two are, sadly, closed off). Surrounding these are a number of exhibition halls, often worth checking out for their temporary art shows.

## Tian'anmen Square

天安门广场, tiānānmén guǎngchǎng • Daily sunrise to sunset • Free • Tian'anmen East, Tian'anmen West (both line 1) or Qianmen subway (line 2)

For many Chinese tourists, gigantic **Tian'anmen Square** is a place of pilgrimage. Crowds flock to gaze at Chairman Mao's portrait on **Tian'anmen gate** (see p.49), then head south to see the fellow himself (maybe) in his **mausoleum**, quietly bowing their heads by the **Monument to the People's Heroes** en route. The square itself is plain, and rather dull considering – or, perhaps because of – its colourful recent history (see box below). It's sometimes better to look upwards, where you'll often see incredibly long chains of kites disappearing into Beijing's often soup-like sky. It's worth popping by at **sunrise** or

---

### DISSENT IN TIAN'ANMEN SQUARE

Though it was designed as a space for mass declarations of loyalty, Tian'anmen Square has as often been a venue for expressions of popular **dissent**. The first mass protests here occurred on May 4, 1919, when students gathered in the area to demonstrate against the disastrous terms of the Treaty of Versailles, under which the victorious Allies granted several former German concessions in China to the Japanese. The protests, and the movement they spawned, marked the beginning of the painful struggle for Chinese modernization. In 1925, the inhabitants of Beijing again occupied the square, to protest over the massacre in Shanghai of Chinese demonstrators by British troops. Angered at the weak government's capitulation to the Japanese, protesters marched on government offices the following year, and were fired on by soldiers.

The first time the square became the focus of outcry in the communist era was in 1976, when thousands assembled here, without government approval, to voice their dissatisfaction with their leaders; in 1978 and 1979, large numbers came to discuss new ideas of democracy and artistic freedom, triggered by writings posted along "Democracy Wall" on the edge of the Forbidden City. People gathered again in 1986 and 1987, demonstrating against the Party's refusal to allow limited municipal elections to be held. But it was in **1989** that Tian'anmen Square became the venue for the largest expression of popular dissent in China in the twentieth century; from April to June of that year, nearly a million protesters demonstrated against the slow pace of reform, lack of civil liberties and widespread corruption. The government, infuriated at being humiliated by their own people, declared martial law on May 20, and on June 4 the military moved into the square. The ensuing **killing** was indiscriminate; tanks ran over tents and machine guns strafed the avenues. No one knows exactly how many demonstrators died in the massacre – probably thousands. Hundreds were arrested afterwards and some remain in jail, though others have since joined the administration.

These days the square is occasionally the venue for small protests by foreigners or members of the cultish, religious sect **Falun Gong** – hence the many closed-circuit TV cameras and large numbers of Public Security Bureau men, not all in uniform.

## CHAIRMAN MAO

*A revolution is not a dinner party.*

Mao Zedong

**Mao Zedong** (毛泽东, Máo Zédōng), the son of a well-off Hunnanese farmer, believed that social reform lay in the hands of the peasants. Having helped found the Chinese Communist Party, on the Soviet model, in Shanghai in 1921, he quickly organized a peasant workers' militia – the Red Army – to take on the Nationalist government. A cunning guerrilla leader, Mao was said to have learnt his tactics from studying the first tyrant Emperor Qin Shihuang, Sun Tzu's *Art of War*, and from playing the East Asian game of Go. In 1934 Mao's army was pushed from its Jiangxi base by the Kuomintang; the epic retreat that followed, the **Long March** – 80,000 men walking 10,000km over a year – solidified Mao's reputation and spread the message of the rebels through the countryside. They joined another rebel force at Yan'an, in northern China, and set up the first soviets, implementing land reform and educating the peasantry.

In 1949, now at the head of a huge army, Mao finally vanquished the Nationalists and became the "Great Helmsman" of the new Chinese nation – and here the trouble started. The chain-smoking poet rebel indulged what appeared to be a personal need for permanent revolution in catastrophes such as the **Great Leap Forward** of the 1950s and the **Cultural Revolution** of the 1960s. His policies caused enormous suffering; some estimate Mao was responsible for the deaths of over 38 million people – mostly from famine as a result of incompetent agricultural policies. Towards the end of his life Mao became increasingly paranoid and out of touch, surrounded by sycophants and nubile dancers – a situation vividly described by his physician, Zhisui Li, in his book *The Private Life of Chairman Mao*.

Today the official Chinese position on Mao is that he was "70 percent right, 30 percent wrong". Although public images of him have largely been expunged, the personality cult he fostered lives on, particularly in taxis where his image is hung like a lucky charm from the rear-view mirror, and he's often included among the deities in peasant shrines. Today his **Little Red Book**, source of political slogans such as "Power grows from the barrel of a gun", is no longer required reading but English translations are widely available in Beijing – though from souvenir vendors rather than bookshops.

**sunset**, when the national flag at the northern end of the square is raised in a military ceremony. Crowds are usually large for both.

## Monument to the People's Heroes

Towards the northern end of the square is the **Monument to the People's Heroes**, a 38m-high obelisk commemorating the victims of the revolutionary struggle. Its foundations were laid on October 1, 1949, the day that the establishment of the People's Republic was announced. Bas-reliefs illustrate key scenes from China's revolutionary history; one of these, on the east side, shows the Chinese burning British opium (see p.171) in the nineteenth century. The calligraphy on the front is a copy of Mao Zedong's handwriting and reads "Eternal glory to the Heroes of the People". The platform on which the obelisk stands is guarded, and a prominent sign declares that commemorative gestures, such as the laying of wreaths, are banned. In 1976, riots broke out when wreaths honouring the death of the popular politician Zhou Enlai were removed; and the demonstrations of 1989 began here with the laying of wreaths to a recently deceased liberal politician.

## The Chairman Mao Memorial Hall

毛主席纪念堂, máozhǔxí jìniàntáng • Tues–Sun 8.30am–noon • Free (bring ID); bags & cameras forbidden (can be put into lockers for ¥2–15 each depending on size) • ☎ 010 65132277, ⓦ cpc.people.com.cn

Mao's **mausoleum**, constructed in 1977 by an estimated million volunteers, is an ugly building that looks like a drab municipal facility. It contravenes the principles of *feng shui* (see box, p.41) – presumably deliberately – by interrupting the line from the

**1**

palace to Qianmen and by facing north. Mao himself wanted to be cremated, and the erection of the mausoleum was apparently no more than a power assertion by his would-be successor, Hua Guofeng. In 1980 Deng Xiaoping, then leader, said it should never have been built, although he wouldn't go so far as to pull it down.

Much of the interest of a visit here lies in witnessing the sense of awe of the Chinese confronted with their former leader, the architect of modern China who was accorded an almost god-like status for much of his life. The atmosphere is one of reverence, though once through the marble halls, you're herded past a splendidly wide-ranging array of tacky Mao souvenirs; the flashing Mao lighter that plays the national anthem is a perennial favourite, as is the waving-Mao wristwatch (shoddy batteries mean that Mao usually stops waving within the week).

### Viewing the Chairman

After depositing your bag and camera at the bag check across the road to the east, join the orderly queue of Chinese – almost exclusively working-class out-of-towners – on the northern side. The queue advances surprisingly quickly, and takes just a couple of minutes to file through the chambers. Mao's pickled **corpse**, draped with a red flag within a crystal coffin, looks unreal, which it may well be; a wax copy was made in case the preservation went wrong. Mechanically raised from a freezer every morning, it is said to have been embalmed with the aid of Vietnamese technicians who had previously worked on the body of Ho Chi Minh. Apparently, 22 litres of formaldehyde went into preserving his body; rumour has it that not only did the corpse swell grotesquely when too much fluid was used, but that Mao's left ear fell off during the embalming process, and had to be stitched back on.

### Zhengyangmen

正阳门, zhèngyángmén • Daily 8.30am–4pm • ¥20

For a great view over the square head to **Zhengyangmen**, its south gate, which once marked the boundary between the imperial city and the commoners outside. A squat, 40m-high structure with an arched gateway through the middle, it's similar in design to its northern counterpart, Tian'anmen. Avoid the tacky souvenir stands and head to the top; you'll get a good idea of how much more impressive the square looked before Mao's mausoleum was stuck in the middle of it. There's also a small **museum** here, featuring a dull smattering of historical exhibits.

## Around Tian'anmen Square

More interesting than Tian'anmen Square itself are the various sights lying on its periphery. Most notable are the **Great Hall of the People** and the huge **National Museum of China**, which lie to the west and east of the square respectively. A little further south are the less vaunted **Railway Museum** and **Museum of Urban Planning**, each of which merit a visit if you have some time. The Police Museum (see p.65), just to the east, is also worth a look.

### The Great Hall of the People

人民大会堂, rénmín dàhuìtáng • Entrance off Tian'anmen Square • Daily 8.15am–4pm when not in session • ¥30 (bring ID) • Tian'anmen West (line 1) or Qianmen subway (line 2)

Taking up almost half the west side of Tian'anmen Square is the monolithic **Great Hall of the People**, one of ten Stalinist wedding-cake-style buildings constructed in 1959 to celebrate "ten years of liberation" (others include Beijing Station and the Military Museum; see p.74 and p.89). This is the venue of the **National People's Congress**, the Chinese legislature, and the building is closed to the public when in session – you'll know whether it's accessible by the hundreds of black limos with darkened windows parked outside. It's not really a sight as such, but you can take a turn around the building; what you see on the roped-off route through is a selection of the 29

1

cavernous, dim reception rooms, each named after a province of China (the extra one, if you're wondering, is Taiwan). These are decorated in the same pompous but shabby style seen in the lobbies of cheap Chinese hotels – badly fitted red carpet, lifeless murals and armchairs lined up against the walls.

This venue has long been a place for high-level meet-and-greets. Nixon dropped by in 1972, then when Margaret Thatcher came here in 1982 she tripped on the steps – this was regarded in Hong Kong as a terrible omen for the negotiations she was having over the territory's future. In 1989, the visiting Mikhail Gorbachev had to be smuggled in through a side entrance to avoid the crowds of protesters outside.

## The National Museum of China

中国历史博物馆, zhōngguó lìshǐ bówùguǎn • Entrance off Tian'anmen Square • Daily 9am–5.30pm • Free (bring ID) • ☎ 010 65116400, ⓦ en.chnmuseum.cn • Tian'anmen East subway (line 1)

The monumental building to the east of Tian'anmen Square is now home to the **National Museum of China**, one of the world's largest museums. Once a shabby affair giving a Marxist reading of history ("primitive", "slave", "feudal" and "semi-colonial"), it has recently been thoroughly renovated and is now well worth a visit. The main attraction is the **Ancient China** exhibition in the basement, which traces China's history from Neolithic to pre-Communist times, bouncing through the various dynasties in a spellbinding succession of relics. Keep an eye out for two **bronze animal heads**, part of a set of twelve plundered from China's old Summer Palace (see p.99); a Chinese man won the bid for the rabbit and rat at auction in 2009, but refused to pay as a "patriotic act", though in 2013 they were purchased by a French family and donated to the Chinese government. Other things to look out for here include bronze wine vessels from the Western Zhou; a jade shroud and mini Terracotta Army from the Liao; and a bronze acupuncture statue (and, inevitably, some great porcelain vases) from the Ming. Forget the ironically tiring **Road of Rejuvenation** exhibit on the second floor – a collection of bombastic national messages, paintings of Japanese imperial evil deeds and innumerable photos of red-tied delegations, this one's aimed squarely at the locals. Instead, head upstairs to the third and fourth floors, where you'll find small exhibitions of bronze, jade, porcelain, fans, money and more.

## Qianmen

前门, qiánmén • South of Tian'anmen Square • Qianmen subway (line 2)

Just south of Tian'anmen Square is one of Beijing's most famous gates – **Qianmen**, an imposing, double-arched edifice dating back to the fifteenth century. Before the city's walls were demolished, this controlled the entrance to the inner city from the outer, suburban sector, and in imperial days the shops and places of entertainment banned from the interior city were concentrated around here.

## The Museum of Urban Planning

规划博物馆, guīhuà bówùguǎn • Qianmen Dongdajie • Tues–Sun 9am–5pm • ¥30 • ⓦ www.bjghzl.com.cn • Qianmen subway (line 2)

The quirky **Museum of Urban Planning** is little visited: for some reason, displays on solid-waste management and air quality have failed to galvanize the public. Given its focus on the future, it's also laughably old-fashioned – and, on occasion, unintentionally hilarious. Head up the escalators, manned by bored staff, and you'll find the "interactive" area; here you can sit in a boat in a mirrored room, where a giant TV screen will attempt to convince you that you're navigating Beijing's waterways and (weirdly, given the nature of boats, and of Beijing's air) flying through azure-blue skies.

The non-ironic highlights of the museum are all map-based. First, and visible on a wall from the escalator, is a fascinating bronze model showing the city as it used to look in imperial times, back when every significant building was part of an awesome, grand design. Then comes another TV screen, which slowly spools through a digitized version

**1**

of an ancient scroll, heading through Old Beijing from south wall to north wall, via the Forbidden City. The star attraction, though, is an enormous and fantastically detailed underlit model of the city that takes up the entire top floor. At a scale of 1m:1km it covers more than three hundred square metres, and illustrates what the place will look like once it's finished being ripped up and redesigned in 2020.

## 23 Ch'ienmen

前门东大街二十三号, qiánmén dōngdàjiē èrshísān hào • 23 Qianmen Dongdajie • Open 24hr • Free • Ⓦ chienmen23 .com • Qianmen subway (line 2)

If you have time it's well worth popping in to the **23 Ch'ienmen** complex, which used to be the American legation, and has now been redeveloped as a fine-dining complex. Splash out at *Maison Boulud* (see p.136) or get Yunnanese-style food on the cheap at *Lost Heaven* (see p.136).

## Beijing Railway Museum

北京铁路博物馆, běijīng tiělù bówùguǎn • Off Qianmen Dongdajie • Tues–Sun 9am–5pm • ¥20, high-speed cabin an extra ¥10 • ☎ 010 67051638, Ⓦ china-rail.org • Qianmen subway (line 2)

Appropriately located in the old Qianmen Railway Station, itself a fantastic structure constructed in 1906, the **Beijing Railway Museum** – officially the Zhengyangmen branch of the China Railway Museum, which is based at Chaoyang in the northeast of the city – details the advance of China's national rail system, and the vehicles using it. Train buffs will love it for sure, while others may find the various photos and models only mildly interesting; the highlight is a full-size replica of the driver's cabin on a high-speed train.

BEIHAI PARK

# North of the centre

The area north of the Forbidden City has a good collection of sights you could happily spend days exploring. Just beyond the palace are two of Beijing's finest parks – centred on a small hill, Jingshan offers superlative city views from its peak, while a little further north, Beihai is set around a magnificent lake. North of here, the peripheries of two further lakes – Qianhai and Houhai – are filled with bars, restaurants and cafés, and form one of Beijing's most enduringly popular nightlife zones. Around the lakes you'll find a charmingly old-fashioned *hutong* district, which was once the home of princes, dukes and monks. Its alleys are labyrinthine, with something of interest around every corner; some regard them as the final outpost of a genuinely Chinese Beijing.

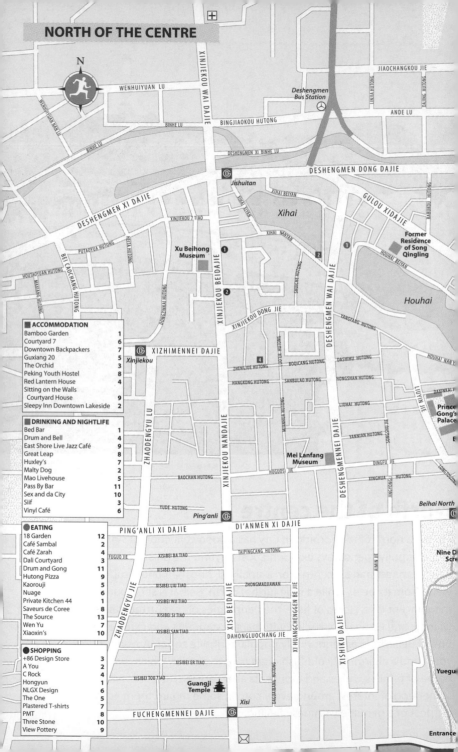

# NORTH OF THE CENTRE

N

WENHUIYUAN LU

XINJIEKOU WAI DAJIE

JIAOCHANGKOU JIE

Deshengmen
Bus Station

ANDE LU

BINGJIAOKOU HUTONG

BINHE LU

BINHE LU

DESHENGMEN XI BINHE LU

DESHENGMEN DONG DAJIE

GULOU XIDAJIE

Jishuitan

XIHAI BEIYAN

Xihai

Former
Residence
of Song
Qingling

DESHENGMEN XI DAJIE

XINJIEKOU 7 TIAO

XIHAI NANYAN

HOUHAI BEIYAN

PUTAOYUA HUTONG

Xu Beihong
Museum

Houhai

HOUTAOYUAN HUTONG

BEI CAOCHANG HUTONG

MAXIANG HUTONG

XINJIEKOU BEIDAJIE

XINJIEKOU DONG JIE

DESHENGMEN WAI DAJIE

YANGFANG HUTONG

HOUHAI NAN Y

XIZHIMENNEI DAJIE

Xinjiekou

THENJIUE HUTONG

BOQICANG HUTONG

DASHIHU HUTONG

LIUYIN JIE

DAXINKAI H

Prince
Gong's
Palace

HANGKONG HUTONG

SANBULAO HUTONG

HONGSHAN HUTONG

ZHAODENGYU LU

XINJIEKOU NANDAJIE

LIUHAI HUTONG

DESHENGMENNEI DAJIE

YANNIAN HUTONG

BAOCHAN HUTONG

Mei Lanfang
Museum

HUGUOSI JIE

DINGFU JIE

XINGHUA HUTONG

LONGTOU JIE

YUDE HUTONG

Ping'anli

Beihai North

DI'ANMEN XI DAJIE

PING'ANLI XI DAJIE

FUGUO JIE

TAIPINGCANG HUTONG

Nine D
Scre

ZHAODENGYU JIE

XISIBEI BA TIAO

XISIBEI QI TIAO

ZHONGMAQJIAWAN

XISI BEIDAJIE

XISIBEI LIU TIAO

XI HUANGCHENGGEN BEI JIE

XISIBEI WU TIAO

XISHIKU DAJIE

XISIBEI SI TIAO

XISIBEI SAN TIAO

DAHONGLUOCHANG JIE

Yuegu

XISIBEI ER TIAO

XISIBEI TOU TIAO

Guangji
Temple

Xisi

FUCHENGMENNEI DAJIE

Entrance

## ◼ ACCOMMODATION
| | |
|---|---|
| Bamboo Garden | 1 |
| Courtyard 7 | 6 |
| Downtown Backpackers | 7 |
| Guxiang 20 | 5 |
| The Orchid | 3 |
| Peking Youth Hostel | 8 |
| Red Lantern House | 4 |
| Sitting on the Walls Courtyard House | 9 |
| Sleepy Inn Downtown Lakeside | 2 |

## ◼ DRINKING AND NIGHTLIFE
| | |
|---|---|
| Bed Bar | 1 |
| Drum and Bell | 4 |
| East Shore Live Jazz Café | 9 |
| Great Leap | 8 |
| Huxley's | 7 |
| Malty Dog | 2 |
| Mao Livehouse | 5 |
| Pass By Bar | 11 |
| Sex and da City | 10 |
| Siif | 3 |
| Vinyl Café | 6 |

## ● EATING
| | |
|---|---|
| 18 Garden | 12 |
| Café Sambal | 2 |
| Café Zarah | 4 |
| Dali Courtyard | 3 |
| Drum and Gong | 11 |
| Hutong Pizza | 9 |
| Kaorouji | 5 |
| Nuage | 6 |
| Private Kitchen 44 | 1 |
| Saveurs de Coree | 8 |
| The Source | 13 |
| Wen Yu | 7 |
| Xiaoxin's | 10 |

## ● SHOPPING
| | |
|---|---|
| +86 Design Store | 3 |
| A You | 2 |
| C Rock | 4 |
| Hongyun | 1 |
| NLGX Design | 6 |
| The One | 5 |
| Plastered T-shirts | 7 |
| PMT | 8 |
| Three Stone | 10 |
| View Pottery | 9 |

Buried deep within the *hutongs* is beautiful **Prince Gong's Palace**, one of the area's must-sees, with the **Bell** and **Drum towers**, once used to mark dawn and dusk, standing on the eastern edge of the district. To the west of the towers, you'll find a number of little **museums**, including the former homes of two twentieth-century cultural icons, **Guo Moruo** and **Xu Beihong**, which now hold exhibitions of their works. There are yet more places to eat and drink just to the east of the towers, on and around Nanluogu Xiang, an artsy, renovated *hutong* area that has proven wildly popular with young locals and foreign visitors alike. It's a great place for people-watching over a coffee, and boasts some terrific places to stay.

## Jingshan and Beihai parks

These two wonderful parks are a great way to round off a visit to the Forbidden City. Directly to its north, the hill of **Jingshan** provides superb views of the city's orange-roofed buildings; you'll be better able to appreciate their formation from this wonderful vantage point. From here, it's a short walk west to **Beihai Park**, essentially a lake surrounded by walking paths, and punctuated by its own small hill. Exiting the park to the north will bring you to the southernmost point of Qianhai Lake (see p.60); it's quite a way from the south gate of the Forbidden City (a minimum of 5km), but with regular water breaks you'll be surprised at how easily this distance can be covered.

### Jingshan Park

景山公园, jīngshān gōngyuán • Daily: April–Oct 6.30am–9pm; Nov–March 6.30am–8pm • ¥2 • Nanluoguxiang subway (line 6)

A visit to **Jingshan Park** is a natural way to round off a trip to the Forbidden City, which most visitors exit from the North Gate, just across the road from the park. An artificial mound, the park was a by-product of the digging of the palace moat, and served as both a windbreak and a barrier to keep malevolent spirits (believed to emanate from the north) from entering the imperial quarter of the city. Its history, most momentously, includes the suicide in 1644 of the last Ming emperor, **Chong Zhen**, who hanged himself here from a tree after rebel troops broke into the imperial palace. The site, on the eastern side of the park, is easy to find – English-language signs for it appear everywhere (beneath those pointing the way to a children's playground) – but the tree that stands here is not the original. Though he was a dissolute opium fiend, the suicide note pinned to his lapel was surprisingly noble:

*My own insufficient virtue and wretched nature has caused me to sin against heaven above. I die knowing I am wholly unworthy to stand before my sacred ancestors… Let the rebels tear my miserable body to pieces but let them touch not a single hair on the head of the least of my subjects.*

Afterwards, the tree was judged an accessory to the emperor's death and, as punishment, was manacled with an iron chain. The **views** from the top of the hill make this park a compelling target: they take in the whole extent of the Forbidden City and (if the weather cooperates) a fair swath of the city outside, a great deal more attractive than seen from ground level. To the west is Beihai Park and its lake; to the north the Bell and Drum towers; and to the northeast the Yonghe Gong (see p.68).

### Beihai Park

北海公园, běihǎi gōngyuán • South gate accessed by Wenjin Jie; north gate via Di'anmen Xidajie • Daily: April–Oct 6.30am–9pm; Nov–March 6.30am–8pm; sights close 5pm • Park entry ¥10; ¥20 including entry to all buildings; pedaloes/rowing boats ¥40–50/hr • North entrance near Beihai North subway (line 6)

Just a few hundred metres west of Jingshan Park, **Beihai Park**, most of which is taken up by a lake, is a favourite spot for many locals. Supposedly created by Kublai Khan, long before any of the Forbidden City structures were conceived, the park is of an ambitious scale: the lake was man-made, the island in its midst created with the excavated earth. Qing Emperor Qianlong oversaw its landscaping into a classical Chinese garden in the eighteenth century. Featuring willows and red-columned galleries, it's still a grand place to retreat from the city and recharge.

### The Round and the island

Just inside the main gate, which lies on the park's southern side, is the **Round**, an enclosure of buildings behind a circular wall, which has at its centre a courtyard where there's a large jade bowl said to have belonged to Kublai Khan. The white-jade Buddha in the hall behind was a present from Burmese Buddhists.

From here, a walkway provides access to the island, which is dotted with buildings – including the **Yuegu Lou**, a hall full of steles (stone slabs carved with Chinese characters); and the giant **dagoba** sitting on the crown of the hill, built in the mid-seventeenth century to celebrate a visit by the Dalai Lama. It's a suitable emblem for a park that contains a curious mixture of religious constructions, storehouses for cultural relics and imperial garden furniture. Nestling inside the dagoba is a shrine to the demon-headed, multi-armed Lamaist deity, Yamantaka.

### North of the lake

On the north side of the lake stands the impressive **Nine Dragon Screen**, its purpose to ward off evil spirits. An ornate wall of glazed tiles, depicting nine stylized, sinuous dragons in relief, it's one of China's largest at 27m in length, and remains in good condition. Nearby are the **Five Dragon Pavilions**, supposedly in the shape of a dragon's spine. Even when the park is crowded at the weekend, the gardens and rockeries over the other side of the lake remain tranquil and soothing – it's easy to see why the area was so favoured by Qianlong. It's popular with courting couples today, some of whom like to dress up for photos in period costume (there's a stall outside the Nine Dragon Screen) or take boats out on the lake.

## Around the Shicha lakes

The area north of Beihai Park is a tangle of **hutongs** – cluttered, grey alleyways which show Beijing's other, private, face. Here you'll see poky courtyards and converted palaces, and come across small open spaces where old men sit with caged pet birds. The network of *hutongs* centres on the two artificial **Shicha lakes**, Qianhai and Houhai. Created during the Yuan dynasty, they were once the terminus for a canal network that served the capital.

There are a few notable sights in the area to the west of Qianhai, including the wonderful **Prince Gong's Palace** and the former residences of celebrated writer, **Guo Moruo**, and **Mei Lanfang**, China's most famous twentieth-century opera singer; further west again is a museum dedicated to esteemed artist **Xu Beihong**, while off Houhai's north side is the former residence of **Song Qingling**, the wife of Sun Yatsen. You're unlikely to want to see every single one of these sights; the palace plus one should suffice.

Much of the district has been recast as a heritage area and is full of restaurants, bars and cafés. All the public toilets have been spruced up, and though they're still fairly rancid, many (amazingly) now have disabled facilities. Still, stray away from the lakeside and the showcasing vanishes quickly.

| ARRIVAL AND INFORMATION | AROUND THE SHICHA LAKES |
| --- | --- |

**By subway** Your best bets are Beihai North and Nanluoguxiang stations (both line 6), which bring you out near Qinghai Lake's south end; Jishuitan (line 2) is close to Xihai, a smaller lake just to the northwest of Houhai.

**Getting around** The best way to get around is by bike. Traffic within the *hutongs* is relatively light, and you're free to dive into any alley you fancy, though you're almost certain to get lost – in which case cycle around until you come to a lake.

**Tours** Regular *hutong* tours leave from the courtyard between the Bell and Drum towers. Visitors are biked about in rickshaws, which initially sounds great, though in reality it's hard not to feel a bit of a plum. Private drivers are hard to avoid – they'll pressurize you to go with them. Be sure to barter; you should pay around ¥60 for an hour, and expect to be taken to a few shops where the driver gets commission. You'd be better off, however, booking a tour from the booking office on the west side of the Drum Tower (¥80/hr). Best of all, take one of the tours run by agencies such as The Hutong or Bike Beijing (see p.26).

## Qianhai and Houhai

24hr • Free; pedaloes from ¥40 per person per hour • Beihai North, Nanluoguxiang (both line 6) or Jishuitan subway (line 2)

Just north of Beihai Park is pretty **Qianhai** (前海, qiánhǎi) lake, an appealing, easygoing place away from the city traffic. Having been dredged and cleaned up, the area around it has become a drinking and dining hotspot, though be warned that the lakeside bars and restaurants are overpriced and rather tacky, and their staff rather pushy; some

---

### COURTYARD HOUSES

Beijing's *hutongs* are lined with **siheyuan** (四合院, sìhéyuàn), traditional single-storey **courtyard houses**. These follow a plan that has hardly changed since the Han dynasty, and is in essence identical to that of the Forbidden City.

A typical courtyard house has its entrance in the south wall. Just outside the front door stand two flat stone blocks – sometimes carved into lions – for mounting horses and to demonstrate the family's wealth and status. Step over the threshold and you are confronted with a freestanding wall; this is to keep out evil spirits, which can only travel in straight lines. Behind it is the outer courtyard, with the servants' quarters to the right and left. The entrance to the inner courtyard, where the family lived, would be in the north wall. The most important rooms, used by the elders, are those at the back, facing south.

With the government anxious to turn Beijing into a showcase for Chinese modernity, and barely a thousand *hutongs* left however, it seems unlikely that many of these houses will survive; the most extensive remaining areas are around the **Shicha lakes** and in the **Dazhalan** area, southwest of Tian'anmen Square (see p.77). A wander around the latter area will show the houses in their worst light: the dwellings are cramped and poorly maintained, the streets dirty, the plumbing and sanitation inadequate; it's only a matter of time before their inhabitants are rehoused in the new suburbs. Responding to increasingly vocal complaints about the destruction of Beijing's architectural heritage, city planners point out that *hutongs* full of courtyard houses are unsuitable for contemporary living: besides the plumbing issues, the houses are very cold in winter, and with only one storey they're an inefficient use of land. Anyway, they argue, the population of a modern city ought to live outside the centre. For all this, in the *hutongs* you'll also see how the system creates a neighbourliness absent from the new high-rises – here, you can't help knowing everyone else's business.

While the *hutongs* around Dazhalan Lu may be under attack, in the last decade some areas around the Shicha lakes have undergone something of a best-of-both-worlds transformation. It all started with a scheme on and around **Nanluogu Xiang**, under which residents were sold a deal by the government – with both sides paying half each, properties were smartened up, roof tiles replaced, walls mended, and public toilets improved. The financial burden was offset, in many cases, by tenants leasing out the front rooms of their *hutongs* – these are the shops, cafés, galleries and bars you see lining Nanluogu Xiang today. While not a perfect solution, it has been wonderful to see Beijing moving forward with some of its own tradition in mind, and the scheme has been successfully employed elsewhere – Wudaoying Hutong, near Yonghe Gong (see map, pp.66–67) is another good example.

East of the Forbidden City, property restoration has followed a different pattern, with housing bashed down and rebuilt in a faux-traditional style – notably, you'll see many so-called *hutong* buildings with more than one storey. This has become a fashionable district for high-ranking cadres to live, and some properties here have sold for more than US$1 million. In addition, a number of new luxury housing estates – very popular with foreigners – have also been built in courtyard-house style; the best examples are around **Deshengmen** in the north of the city.

favour renting a pedal- or rowing boat and drinking on that instead. For the really pleasant places, you'll have to head in from the shore (see p.146).

As you head north along Qianhai, look out for the hardy folk who swim here every day; it may be tempting to join in, but foreigners who do so often end up getting sick. You can hire boats from several jetties around the lake, while in wintertime it becomes a gigantic ice-skating rink. From the top of the cute humpback **Yinding Bridge** (银锭桥, yíndìng qiáo), which spans the lake's narrowest point and marks the divide between Qianhai and **Houhai** (后海, hòuhǎi), you can see the western hills on (very rare) clear days. Turn right, and you're on **Yandaixie Jie** (烟袋斜街, yāndài xiéjiē), an alley of little jewellery and trinket shops that's one of the best places in Beijing to buy contemporary souvenirs (see p.156).

## Guo Moruo's Residence

郭末若故居, guōmòruò gǔjū · Qianhai Xijie (second left from exit B of Beihai North station) · Tues–Sun 9am–4.30pm · ¥20 · ☏ 010 83225392 · Beihai North subway (line 6)

Just west of Qianhai Lake's Lotus Lane, though a little tricky to access, you'll find **Guo Moruo's Residence**. Guo (1892–1978) was a revered writer in his day, though now he's considered a little stuffy. His elegantly furnished and spacious house is worth a peek around – less for the exhibits of dusty books and bric-a-brac than for an insight into how snug courtyard houses could be.

## Prince Gong's Palace and around

恭王府, gōngwáng fǔ · Qianhai Xijie · Daily: March–Nov 7.30am–4.30pm; Dec–Feb 8am–4pm · ¥40 · ☏ 010 66186628 · Beihai North subway (line 6); turn left up Sanzuoqiao Hutong from exit B, then left at the crossroads

The charming **Prince Gong's Palace** was once the residence of Prince Gong, the brother of Emperor Xianfeng and father of the last Qing emperor, Pu Yi. Its many courtyards, joined by covered walkways, have been restored to something like their former elegance. In the very centre is the Yin'an Dian, a hall where the most important ceremonies and rites were held; also look out for the sumptuously painted ceiling of Xi Jin Zhai, used as a studio by Prince Gong, then as a bedroom by He Shen. The northern boundary of the courtyard area is marked by a 151m-long wall; sneak around this and you'll be on the southern cusp of a gorgeous garden area, set around an attractive lake. One hall here was once used for opera performances, though these had sadly been discontinued at the time of writing; it's worth asking to see if they've resumed.

There are plenty of other old palaces in the area, for this was once something of an imperial pleasure ground, and home to a number of high officials and distinguished eunuchs. Head north up Liuyin Jie and you pass the former **Palace of Tao Beile**, now a school, after about 200m. It's one of a number of converted buildings in the area, some of which are identified by plaques.

## Mei Lanfang Museum

梅兰芳博物馆, méilánfāng bówùguǎn · Huguosi Jie, off Deshengmennei Dajie · Tues–Sun 9am–4pm · ¥10 · ☏ 010 66183598 · Ping'anli (lines 4 & 6) or Beihai North subway (line 6)

Some 600m west of Prince Gong's Palace, the small **Mei Lanfang Museum** was once the home of the greatest opera singer of the twentieth century, Mei Lanfang, whose tragic life was the basis for Chen Kaige's opulent movie *Farewell My Concubine* (see p.180). It's a pretty place, featuring plenty of pictures of Mei Lanfang famously dressed as a woman, playing female roles.

## Song Qingling's Former Residence

宋庆龄故居, sòngqìnglíng gùjū · 46 Houhai Beiyan · Daily 9am–4pm · ¥20 · ☏ 010 64044205 · Jishuitan (line 2) or Guloudajie subway (lines 2 & 8)

On the northern shore of Houhai, **Song Qingling's** former residence is a Qing mansion with an agreeable, spacious garden. The wife of Sun Yatsen, leader of the short-lived republic that followed the collapse of imperial China (see p.173), Song commands great respect in China, and the exhibition inside details her busy life. It's all pretty dry, but check out the revolver Sun Yatsen – obviously not a great romantic – gave his wife as a wedding gift.

More interesting, perhaps, is the chance to take a rare glimpse at a typical Chinese mansion from the beginning of the twentieth century – all the furnishings are pretty much as they were when she died, and her personal effects, including letters and cutlery, are on display. It's not much of a diversion from here to head west to the Xu Beihong Museum (see below), about 1km from Deshengmennei Dajie.

## Xu Beihong Museum

徐悲鸿纪念馆, xúbēihóng jìniànguǎn • 53 Xinjiekou Beidajie • Tues–Sun 9–11am & 1.30–4.30pm • ¥5 • ☎ 010 62252042, ⓦ www.xubeihong.org/English/museum.htm • Jishuitan subway (line 2)

Just outside the *hutong* quarter, but easily combined with a visit to the Shicha lakes, is the **Xu Beihong Museum**; though closed for repair at the time of writing, it should have reopened by the time you read this. The son of a wandering portraitist, Xu (1895–1953) did for Chinese art what his contemporary Lu Xun (see p.91) did for literature – modernize an atrophied tradition. Xu had to look after his entire family from the age of 17 after his father died, and spent much of his early life labouring in semi-destitution and obscurity before receiving the acclaim he deserved. His extraordinary talent is well in evidence here in seven halls, which display a huge collection of his works. These include many ink paintings of horses, for which he was most famous, and Western-style oil paintings, which he produced while studying in France (and which are now regarded as his weakest works); the large-scale allegorical images also on display allude to tumultuous events in modern Chinese history. However, the pictures it's easiest to respond to are his delightful sketches and studies, in ink and pencil, often of his infant son.

# The Drum and Bell towers

These two architecturally stunning towers stand directly to the north of the Forbidden City, providing yet more evidence that Beijing was once laid out according to a single, great scheme. Today's city planners have, belatedly, decided to go for something similar; the stretch from here to Jingshan is currently being gentrified, and the wonderful *hutong* area around the towers – which has been living on borrowed time for years – might well have disappeared by the time you read this. It's easy to get to the towers from the lakes; they stand high above the surrounding buildings, so you can't really miss them.

## The Drum Tower

鼓楼, gǔlóu • Junction of Gulou Xidajie, Gulou Dongdajie and Di'anmen Waidajie • Daily 9am–5pm; drumming hourly 9.30–11.30am & 1.30–5pm • ¥20, or ¥30 combined ticket with the Bell Tower • Guloudajie subway (lines 2 & 8), or accessible on many bus routes

The formidable two-storey **Drum Tower**, a squat, wooden, fifteenth-century Ming creation set on a red-painted stone base, is the southern member of the pair of towers. In every city in China, drums like these were banged to mark the hours of the day, and to call imperial officials to meetings. Nowadays, at regular intervals throughout the day, a troupe of drummers in traditional costume whack cheerfully away at the giant drums inside. They're not, to be blunt, terribly artful, but seeing them in action is still an impressive sight; so too is the working replica of an ancient Chinese water clock, a *kelou*. Views from the top are fantastic, particularly after the steep slog up, but unfortunately only the southern end – the one facing the Bell Tower – is open.

## The Bell Tower

钟楼, zhōnglóu • Junction of Gulou Xidajie, Gulou Dongdajie and Di'anmen Waidajie • Daily 9am–5pm • ¥20, or ¥30 combined ticket with the Drum Tower • Guloudajie subway (lines 2 & 8), or accessible on many bus routes

The **Bell Tower**, at the other end of the small plaza from the Drum Tower, is somewhat different in appearance, being made of stone and a bit smaller. The original structure was of Ming vintage, though the tower was destroyed by fire and rebuilt in the eighteenth century. It still, however, boasts its original iron bell, which, until 1924, was rung every evening at 7pm to give an indication of the time. A sign by the bell relates the legend of its creation: the bell-maker was struggling to meet his deadline and sure to be killed, when at the last moment his daughter jumped into the molten mix; with added girl, the bell sounded just fine. Even better than the bell are the views from the top (again, it's a short but tough pant up) – unlike the Drum Tower, you're able to see vistas in all directions.

# Nanluogu Xiang

南锣鼓巷, nánluógǔ xiàng • Nanluoguxiang subway (line 6)

There aren't too many streets in Beijing that could be called cute, so the pedestrianized north–south *hutong* of **Nanluogu Xiang** is like a little urban oasis. Dotted with cafés, boutiques and restaurants, it has become a playground for the city's bo-bos (bourgeois-bohemians). Though some expats sneer at this "Disney hutong", in the alleys shooting off to the east and west there are enough open-air mah jong games, rickety mom-and-pop stores and old men sitting out with their caged birds to maintain that ramshackle, backstreet Beijing charm. If there seems to be a surfeit of bright and beautiful young things, that's because of the drama school just around the corner. All in all, it's a great place to idle over a cappuccino, tuck into a meal (see p.137) or head to for an evening drink (see p.146); there's also some good accommodation in the area (see p.128).

## Mao Dun's Former Residence

茅盾故居, máodùn gùjū • 13 Yuanensi Hutong • Tues–Sun 9am–4pm • ¥5 (not always levied)

The only sight in the Nanluogu Xiang area is **Mao Dun's Former Residence**, a charming little courtyard house. Mao Dun was the pen name of Shen Dehong, writer, communist and ex-minister of culture, whose best work is *Midnight*, a tale of cosmopolitan Shanghai. His house today has been preserved since he died in 1981, and is full of manuscripts and knick-knacks, with some elegant period furniture.

CCTV BUILDING

# East of the centre

Central Beijing's eastern districts make up the city's most cosmopolitan and fashionable area. Just east of Tian'anmen Square, the madcap area of Wangfujing buzzes by day and evening – Beijing's shrine to shopping, it's home to a couple of the city's most popular night markets. North of Wangfujing in an increasingly trendy part of town sit Yonghe Gong and the Kong Miao, two of Beijing's most beguiling temple complexes. Some way to the east is Sanlitun; most famous as a bar district, it's raucous and gaudy by night but engagingly civilized during the daytime, with its many small cafés and restaurants good for people-watching. It's also a great place to shop, with several architecturally adventurous malls. Further east still is lake-filled Chaoyang Park, Beijing's largest, the periphery of which is scattered with various clubs.

South of Sanlitun, things take a more serious turn, and buildings get a *lot* taller. This is Beijing's **Central Business District (CBD)**, the heart of which stretches from **Ritan Park**, a leafy spot that's a hugely popular hangout place, to **Guomao** subway station. In recent years, a whole troupe of superstar architects have been given *carte blanche* to bring their fantasies to life – the most famous example, by far, is the jaw-dropping **CCTV Tower**, though new buildings are sprouting up on what can often seem like a daily basis. All in all, the CBD is about as far away from traditional China as you can get, but there are a few interesting historical sights on its periphery: the **Ancient Observatory**, a section of Ming-dynasty **city wall**, and the unusual **Dongyue Temple** all offer respite from the rampant modernity.

# Wangfujing

王府井, wángfǔjǐng • Wangfujing subway (line 1)

**Wangfujing Dajie** (王府井大街, wángfǔjǐng dàjiē) is where the capital gets down to the business of shopping in earnest. The haunt of quality stores for over a century, it was called Morrison Street before the communist takeover. There are some giant malls here (see p.161), including the **Oriental Plaza**, an upscale shopping mall which stretches east for nearly a kilometre – its entrance has, of late, joined the Forbidden City area as a prime hotspot for Beijing's tearoom scams.

Bar the shopping, and the opportunity to eat scorpions, testicles and the like at two fantastic **night markets**, Dong'anmen and Xiaochi Jie (see box, p.138), there's little to see in Wangfujing bar the occasionally grisly **Police Museum**, a series of colonial-era buildings in the curious **legations quarter**, and the **National Art Museum of China**, a huge exhibition hall showcasing state-approved artworks.

## The old legations quarter

Qianmen (line 2) and Chongwenmen subway (lines 2 & 5)

Scurry into the backstreets between Tian'anmen Square and Chongwenmennei Dajie, and almost within sight of the Great Hall of the People, the National Museum and other Soviet-inspired symbols of Chinese power, you'll come to an odd area that shows very different influences. This was the **legations quarter**, created at the behest of foreign officials in 1861, and run as an autonomous district with its own postal system, taxes and defences; initially, Chinese were not permitted entry without a pass. By the 1920s more than twenty countries had legations here, most built in the style of their home countries, with imported fittings but using local materials, and today you'll see plenty of Neoclassical facades and wrought-iron balconies. Most of the buildings are now used by the police and are therefore politically sensitive – the area was left blank on maps until the 1980s.

You won't be allowed into most of these old concession buildings, though there are a few exceptions. The old **Yokohama Specie Bank** (横滨正金银行, héngbīn zhēngjīn yínháng) off Zhengyi Lu is a Gothic Revival building constructed by the Japanese in the 1930s. Much of the opulent interior, including the chandeliers, tiled floor and balustrades, is original; you'll arouse curiosity, but should be allowed in. Along the road is the Gothic Revival **St Michael's Church** (圣弥额尔天主堂, shèngmí é'ěr tiānzhǔtáng), which is worth a poke about if you find it open. Yielding to local taste, the pillars are painted red as in Chinese temples, and the statues of the saints are labelled in Chinese characters.

## Police Museum

警察博物馆, jǐngchá bówùguǎn • Dongjiaomin Xiang • Tues–Sun 9am–4pm • ¥5 • ☎ 010 85225001 • Qianmen subway (line 2)

Anything vaguely related to crime or public order is exhibited on the four floors of the **Police Museum**, including plenty of uniforms and weapons, forensics tools and an ingenious Qing-dynasty fire engine. It's not for the squeamish: there's a skull that's been caved in by an axe, some horrific crime-scene photos and ancient execution tools – and

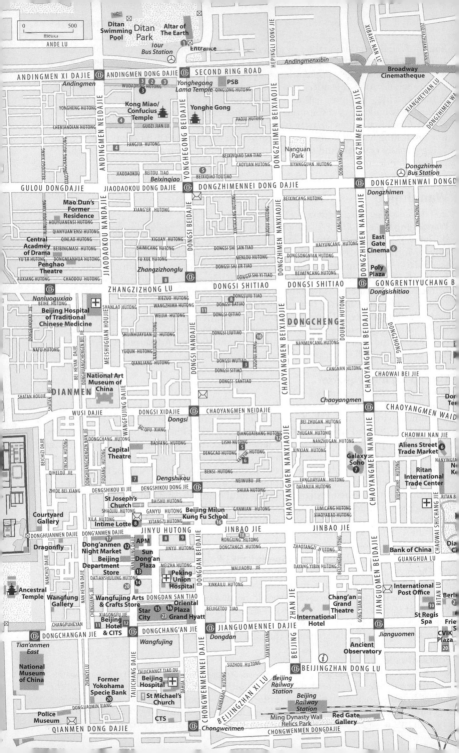

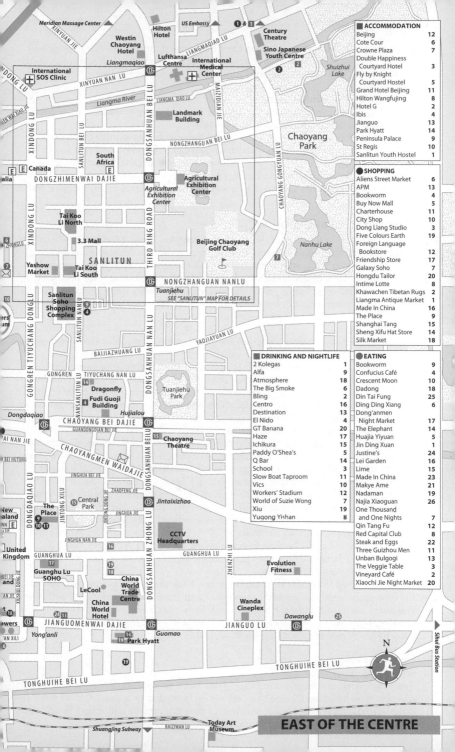

you can cap off a visit with a blast on the firing range on the fourth floor, though all you get to shoot is, alas, a laser gun. Check out the gift shop tat – all sorts of authority figure key-ring dolls are on offer, including one of the internet censor.

## National Art Museum of China

中国美术馆, zhōngguó měishùguǎn • 1 Wusi Dajie • Daily 9am–5pm • Free (bring ID); occasional charges for special exhibitions • ☎ 010 84033500, ⓦ namoc.org • Dongsi subway (lines 5 & 6)

Once regarded as a stuffy academy, the grand **National Art Museum of China** now embraces modern trends such as installation and video art. There's no permanent display and it usually holds a couple of shows at once; past subjects have included women and minority peoples, and there's even been a show of Socialist Realist propaganda – put up not to inspire renewed zeal but as a way to reconsider past follies.

# Yonghe Gong and around

The most famous and ornate of Beijing's many temples, **Yonghe Gong** is a delight to behold – it's quite possible to spend hours admiring the rich decoration of the complex. Just over the road, the **Kong Miao**, or Confucius Temple, is as restrained as the Yonghe Gong is gaudy, and a wonderfully relaxed place to visit – hit both and choose your favourite. Lastly, just to the north is **Ditan Park**, a great place for strolling, and historically significant to boot.

## Yonghe Gong

雍和宫, yōngghé gōng • Yonghegong Beidajie • Daily 9am–4pm • ¥25 • ☎ 010 64044499, ⓦ yonghegong.cn • Yonghegong Lama Temple subway (lines 2 & 5)

You won't see many bolder or brasher temples than the **Yonghe Gong** Lama Temple, built towards the end of the seventeenth century as the residence of Prince Yin Zhen. In 1723, after the prince became Emperor Yong Zheng and moved into the Forbidden City, the temple was retiled in imperial yellow and restricted thereafter to religious use. It became a **lamasery** in 1744, housing monks from Tibet and Inner Mongolia. After the civil war in 1949, it was declared a national monument and closed for the following thirty years. Remarkably, it escaped the ravages of the Cultural Revolution, when most of the city's religious structures were destroyed or turned into factories and warehouses.

Today the lamasery also functions as an active **Tibetan Buddhist** centre. It's used basically for propaganda purposes, to show that China is guaranteeing and respecting the religious freedom of minorities, though it's questionable how genuine the state-approved monks you see wandering around are. After all, this was where the Chinese state's choice for Panchen Lama – the Tibetan spiritual leader, second only to the Dalai Lama in rank – was officially sworn in, in 1995. Just prior to that, the Dalai Lama's own choice for the post, the then 6-year-old Gedhum Choekyi Nyima, had "disappeared" – becoming the youngest political prisoner in the world. Neither he nor his family have been heard of since.

Visitors are free to wander through the prayer halls and pretty, ornamental gardens, the experience largely an aesthetic rather than a spiritual one nowadays. As well as the amazingly intricate mandalas hanging in side halls, the temple contains some notable statuary. There are five main **prayer halls**, arranged in a line from south to north, and numerous side buildings housing Bodhisattva statues and paintings.

### The Yonghe Hall

雍和殿, yōnghédiàn

The **Yonghe Hall**, the second one along as you move north through the complex, is the temple's main building, though this may not be immediately apparent. Here you'll find three large statues – gilded representations of the past, present and future Buddhas, respectively standing to the left, centre and right.

The Pavilion of Eternal Blessings

永佑殿, yǒngyòudiàn

Buddhas of longevity and medicine stand in the third hall, the **Pavilion of Eternal Happiness**, though they're far less interesting than the *nandikesvras*, representations of Buddha having sex, in a side room. Once used to educate emperors' sons, the statues are now covered by drapes. The chamber behind, the **Hall of the Wheel of Law**, has a gilded bronze statue of Gelugpa, the founder of the Yellow Hats (the largest sect within Tibetan Buddhism), and paintings that depict his life, while the thrones at its side are for the Dalai Lama (each holder of the post used to come here to teach).

The Hall of Boundless Happiness

万福殿, wànfúdiàn

In the last, grandest hall, the **Wanfu Pavilion**, stands an 18m-high statue of the Maitreya Buddha, the world's largest carving made from a single piece of wood – in this case, the trunk of a Tibetan sandalwood tree. Gazing serenely out, the giant reddish-orange figure looms over you; details, such as his jewellery and the foliage fringing his shoulders, are beautifully carved. It took three years for the statue, a gift to Emperor Qianlong from the seventh Dalai Lama, to complete its passage to Beijing.

# Kong Miao

孔庙, kǒngmiào • Guozijian Jie • Daily: May–Oct 8.30am–6pm; Nov–April 8.30am–5pm • Performances hourly 9–11am & 2–5pm • ¥30 • Yonghegong Lama Temple subway (lines 2 & 5)

Entered from a quiet *hutong* lined with shops selling incense, images and tapes of religious music, the **Kong Miao**, or **Confucius Temple**, is up there with Beijing's most pleasant sights. One of the best things to do here is sit on a bench in the peaceful courtyard among the ancient, twisted trees and enjoy the silence, though there's plenty to look at inside, too. The complex is split into two main areas: the temple proper to the east, and the easy to miss but equally large old imperial college, Guozi Guan, to the west; in between the two sits a hall containing the **Qianlong stone scriptures**, a Buddhist text consisting of 630,000 characters written between 1726 and 1738.

---

## CONFUCIUS

**Confucius** was born in 552 BC into a declining aristocratic family in an age of petty kingdoms where life was blighted by constant war and feuding. An itinerant scholar, he observed that life would be much improved if people behaved decently, and he wandered from court to court teaching adherence to a set of moral and social values designed to bring the citizens and the government together in harmony. Ritual and propriety were the system's central values, and great emphasis was placed on the five "**Confucian virtues**": benevolence, righteousness, propriety, wisdom and trustworthiness. An arch-traditionalist, he believed that society required strict hierarchies and total obedience: a son should obey his father, a wife her husband, and a subject his ruler.

Nobody paid Confucius much attention during his lifetime, and he died in obscurity. But during the Han dynasty, six hundred years later, **Confucianism** became institutionalized, underscoring a hierarchical system of administration that prevailed for the next two thousand years. Seeing that its precepts sat well with a feudal society, rulers turned Confucianism into the state religion, and Confucius became worshipped as a deity. Subsequently, officials were appointed on the basis of their knowledge of the Confucian texts, which they studied for half their lives.

The great sage only fell from official favour in the twentieth century with the rise of the egalitarian communists, and today there are no functioning Confucian temples left in China. Ironically, however, those temples that have become museums or libraries have returned to a vision of the importance of learning, which is perhaps closer to the heart of the Confucian system than ritual and worship.

### The temple complex

Constructed in 1302–06, the temple is a charming place filled with carved steles, red-lacquered wood and gnarled cypresses, some of which are over 700 years old; one, to the southwest of the complex, is now a mulberry tree too, the ambitious mulberry seed apparently dropped into the trunk by a bird. The buildings themselves are pretty ancient, too; parts of the colossal **Dacheng Hall** date back to 1411. The halls to its east and west were once sacrificial venues, but are now employed as **museums** of sorts; these hold a diverse range of objects from every dynasty, though the Tang pottery, which includes images of pointy-faced foreigners, is most diverting. Small performances, featuring dancing girls in costume, take place to the rear of the complex – the Confucius connection is rather weak, but they're enjoyable to watch nonetheless.

### Guozi Jian

国子监, guózǐ jiàn

To the west of the temple complex is **Guozi Jian**, the old imperial college, the temple's junior by only two years and equally beautiful. After walking through the gigantic main gate, you'll be confronted by the **Memorial Arch**, clad with orange and green tiles and featuring the (slightly tatty) calligraphy of Emperor Qianlong. Behind this is the **Biyong Hall**, set in a circular lake filled with carp; Qianlong used to give speeches here, backed by an elaborate folding screen, and replicas of both are now in place.

## Ditan Park

地坛公园, dìtán gōngyuán • Hepingli Xijie • Daily 6am–9.30pm • ¥2, ¥5 extra for altar and museum • Yonghegong Lama Temple subway (lines 2 & 5)

Just north of Yonghe Gong is **Ditan Park**, the northern member in the imperial city's original quartet of four parks; there was one for each cardinal direction, with Tiantan (to the south; see p.80), Ritan (east; see p.73) and Yuetan (west). Each park was the location for an annual sacrificial ritual; as befits this park's name (*dì* means "ground" or "earth"), this was where the emperor once performed sacrifices to the earth god, using the huge, tiered stone platform just up from the south entrance as an **altar**. A small **museum** next to it holds the emperor's sedan chair – covered, of course, so that no commoner could glimpse the divine presence on his journey here. Wandering among the trees is probably the most diverting way to spend time in the park; at weekends the place is busy with old folk playing croquet, kids playing fishing games and *tai ji* practitioners hugging trees and the like. The park is at its liveliest during Chinese New Year, when it hosts a temple fair (see box, p.177).

## Sanlitun and around

三里屯, sānlǐtún

The most famous **nightlife district** in Beijing, if not all China, **Sanlitun** has come a long way since its first few bars opened up on "Bar Street"– still a popular name in both English and Chinese (酒吧街, jiǔbā jiē) for Sanlitun Lu, the north–south road that bisects the area. Many said bars are, amazingly, still there, their dated live-music sessions almost laughable in comparison with the area's relentless, forward-looking energy – Sanlitun is now full to the brim with fancy boutiques and shopping malls (see p.155), a wonderfully cosmopolitan array of excellent cafés and restaurants (see p.140) and some of Beijing's trendiest bars (see p.146). For all this, there are virtually no tourist sights in the area – nearby **Dongyue Temple** and the bronze treasures in the **Poly Art Museum** are the only real exception.

The Sanlitun area is centred on **Tai Koo Li** (太古里, tàigǔlǐ), a visually splendid mix of upper-class shops, bars and restaurants formally known as "The Village", and still often referred to as such. To the southwest is the **Workers' Stadium** (工人体育场, gōngrén

tǐyùchǎng), colloquially known to Beijingers by the abbreviated term "Gongti", and itself surrounded by bars and clubs.

## Poly Art Museum

保利大厦, bǎolì dàshà • Poly Plaza, Dongzhimen Nandajie • Mon–Sat 9.30am–4.30pm • ¥50 • ☏ 010 65008117, Ⓦ en.polypm.com.cn/english/bwge.php • Dongsishitiao subway (line 2)

Within the **Poly Plaza**, a boring-looking office block, lies a small **museum** that has one of the most select collections of antiquities in the capital. In the hall of ancient bronzes you'll find four of the twelve bronze animals that were looted from the old Summer Palace (see p.99); the pig, tiger, ox and monkey were bought in the West by patriotic businessmen, and their return was much heralded. Another two were returned in 2013, and now take pride of place in the National Museum of China (see p.53); the four here may follow in due course. The second hall displays ancient Buddha statues.

## Dongyue Temple

东岳庙, dōngyuè miào • Chaoyangmenwai Dajie • Tues–Sun 8am–5pm • ¥40 • Ⓦ dongyuetemple.com • Dongdaqiao subway (line 6)

The **Dongyue Temple** is an intriguing place, in pointed contrast to all the shrines to materialism outside. It dates back to the Ming dynasty, and though it's been restored and rebranded as the "Beijing Folk Arts Museum" it's essentially still the same place,

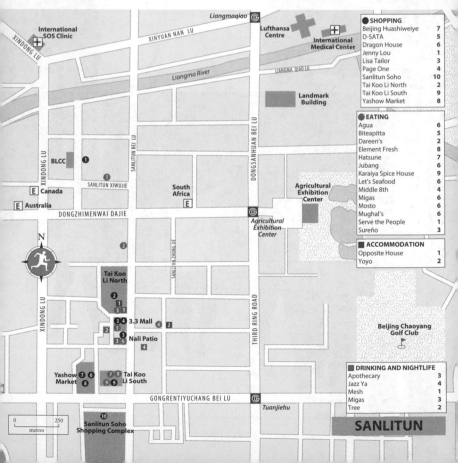

with a few vaguely diverting exhibitions. Pass under the Zhandaimen archway – originally constructed in 1322 – and you enter a courtyard holding around thirty annexes, each of which deals with a different aspect of Taoist life, the whole making up a sort of surreal spiritual bureaucracy. There's the "Department of Suppressing Schemes", "Department of Wandering Ghosts", even a "Department for Fifteen Kinds of Violent Death". In each, a statue of Taoist deity Lao Zi holds court over brightly painted figures, many with monstrous animal heads, too many limbs and the like. The temple shop sells red tablets for worshippers to sign and leave outside the annexes as petitions to the spiritual officials. Departments dealing with longevity and wealth are unsurprisingly popular, but so, tellingly, is the "Department for Official Morality".

# The Central Business District

Bristling with glassy skyscrapers, Beijing's **CBD** is a ritzy area with an international flavour and an affluent, though surprisingly relaxed, atmosphere. Forget traditional tourist sights and activities, bar gawping at an acrobatic show at the excellent Chaoyang Theatre (see p.153) – this area's all about eating (see p.140), drinking (see p.147) and admiring some striking modern architecture.

Other than the zany CCTV building, notable structures include **Central Park** and **The Place**, two complexes facing each other over Jintong Xilu. A mix of office space, apartment blocks, shops and restaurants centred on a mound-like park, the former is an admirable piece of urban engineering; the latter comprises a pair of shopping malls linked underground, and separated above ground by the **world's longest LED screen** (120m), which sparkles into life come sundown. Also in the area is the famed Silk Market, a giant six-storey mall of fake goods (see p.160).

### CCTV Headquarters

央视大楼, yāngshì dàlóu • Guanghua Lu • Closed to visitors • Jintaixizhao subway (line 10)

By far the most distinctive of the CBD's many weird and wonderful structures is the headquarters of **CCTV**, the national state broadcaster. Designed by Dutch architect Rem Koolhaas and completed in 2012, the 230m-high building's extraordinary Escheresque shape – its two leaning towers are joined at top and bottom with horizontal letter Vs, the point of the uppermost "V" seeming to defy gravity – has quickly made it a world-famous symbol of the city.

In true *yin–yang* style, the building just to the north is steeped in infamy: before its completion, it was gutted by fire in 2009, thanks to a stray firework from CCTV's own Chinese New Year party – a huge event, though one mysteriously absent from the news on state television. Sharing foundations with the CCTV building, it couldn't be torn down, and sat as a rusting eyesore for years. It was still under renovation at the time of writing.

# Ritan Park and around

日坛公园, rìtán gōngyuán • 24hr • Free • Yong'anli subway (line 1)

Just west of the CBD is **Ritan Park**, one of the imperial city's original four. Each park was the location for an annual sacrificial ritual performed by the emperor, but today's Ritan Park is popular with embassy staff and courting couples, who make use of its numerous secluded nooks. It's a very attractive park, with paths winding between groves of cherry trees, rockeries and ponds.

### Jianguomenwai diplomatic compound

The area surrounding Ritan Park has a casual, affluent, cosmopolitan atmosphere thanks to its large contingent of foreigners, many of them staff from the **Jianguomenwai diplomatic compound**, an odd place with neat buildings in ordered courtyards, and frozen sentries on plinths. Though their embassy lies elsewhere, you'll see plenty of Russians (and Cyrillic script) here; many have set up shop in this area, most notably in the weird **Ritan International Trade Center**, most of whose shops have closed doors and no customers, and seem to be fronts. Perhaps more interesting is the **North Korean embassy**; though their grouchy staff are unlikely to give you a visa, you can eat North Korean food with them at the fantastic *Unban Bulgogi* restaurant nearby (see p.141).

## The Beijing station area

First things first – the area surrounding **Beijing station** (北京站, běijīng zhàn) is bloody horrible. Crowded and smoky, it's a place to get away from as soon as your train arrives, even though they've finally turned off the Kenny G sax muzak which blared over the square for several years (continuously, or so it felt). Mercifully, there are two nice historical sights within walking distance – Beijing's old **astronomical observatory**, and a section of the old city wall, preserved in the **Ming Dynasty Wall Relics Park**. Also in the area is the wonderful **Red Gate Gallery**, while for fans of kitsch architecture north of Beijing station stands the **International Hotel**, which resembles a toy robot in all but scale.

### The Ancient Observatory

古观象台, gǔguānxiàngtái • Off Jianguomennei Dajie • Tues–Sun 9am–5pm • ¥20 • ☎ 010 65242202, ⊕ www.bjp.org.cn • Jianguomen subway (lines 1 & 2)

An unexpected survivor marooned amid the high-rises beside the concrete knot that is the intersection between Jianguomennei Dajie and the Second Ring Road, the **Ancient Observatory** comes as a delightful surprise. The first observatory on the site was founded in the thirteenth century on the orders of Kublai Khan; the astronomers were commissioned to reform the inaccurate calendar then in use. Subsequently the observatory was staffed by Muslim scientists, as medieval Islamic science enjoyed pre-eminence, but, strangely, in the early seventeenth century it was placed in the hands of Jesuit missionaries (see box below). Led by one Matteo Ricci, they proceeded to astonish the emperor and his subjects by making a series of precise astronomical forecasts. The Jesuits re-equipped the observatory and remained in charge until the 1830s.

The squat, unadorned building was built in 1442. Today it lies empty, and visitors aren't allowed inside – there'd be little point, really, since Beijing's present-day skies often make it impossible to see the *Marriott* down the road, let alone Mars. The best features of the complex are, however, accessible: its **garden**, a placid retreat; and the eight Ming-dynasty **astronomical instruments** sitting on the roof – stunningly

---

### THE JESUITS IN CHINA

**Jesuit missionaries** began to arrive in China in the sixteenth century. Though they weren't allowed to preach freely at first, they were tolerated for their scientific and astronomical skills, and were invited to stay at court: precise astronomical calculations were invaluable to the emperor who, as master of the calendar, was charged with determining the cycle of the seasons in order to ensure good harvests, and observing the movement of celestial bodies to harmonize the divine and human order. Some Jesuits rose to high positions in the imperial court, and in 1692 they finally won the right to preach in China.

**Matteo Ricci** (1552–1610) was the most illustrious of the early Jesuit missionaries to China. A keen Chinese scholar, he translated the Confucian Analects (see p.185) into Portuguese and created the first system for romanizing Chinese characters. He began studying the Chinese language in 1582, when he arrived in Macau. In 1603 he moved to Beijing and won the respect of the local literati with his extensive knowledge of cartography, astronomy, mathematics and the physical sciences.

sculptural armillary spheres, theodolites and the like, all beautifully ornamented with entwined dragons, lions and clouds, looking for all the world like gigantic Art Nouveau trinkets. The attached **museum**, displaying pottery decorated with star maps, and arrayed around a courtyard featuring navigational equipment dating from the Yuan dynasty onwards, is well worth a wander round.

## Red Gate Gallery

红门画廊, hóngmén huàláng • Dongbianmen watchtower, Chongwenmen Dongdajie • Daily 10am–5pm • Free • ☎ 010 65251005, ⓦ redgategallery.com • Jianguomen subway (lines 1 & 2)

Housed within one of the last remnants of the old city wall, the Western-run **Red Gate Gallery** opened up in 1991, in the process becoming Beijing's first private contemporary gallery. However, the curators have steadfastly refused to rest on their laurels, and their venue remains a little more adventurous than its city-centre competition; a continuous procession of cutting-edge Chinese work has cultivated a good reputation overseas.

## Ming Dynasty Wall Relics Park

明城墙遗址公园, míngchéngqiáng yízhǐ gōngyuán • Off Chongwenmen Dongdajie • Daily 8am–5pm • ¥10 • Chongwenmen or Beijing Railway Station subway (both line 2)

Rising up above Beijing's main train station is the last remaining section of the city's old wall, which now forms part of the **Ming Dynasty Wall Relics Park**. The skinny stretch of parkland is a grand place to be in the spring, when blossom bursts from its many plum and cherry trees, but the wall itself makes for a fine diversion at any time of year. From its uppermost vantage points, you can peer down to see trains coursing in and out of the railway station; also make time to ascend the main tower, whose innards are a temple-like feast of vermillion-painted columns.

# Today Art Museum

今日美术馆, jīnrì měishùguǎn • Building 4, Pingod Community, 32 Baiziwan Lu • Daily 10am–5pm • Free • ☎ 010 58621100, ⓦ todayartmuseum.com • Shuangjing subway (line 4)

Housed in an abandoned brewery, the **Today Art Museum** was the first not-for-profit privately owned gallery in the city. They focus on promoting contemporary Chinese art, though each year sees a few top-notch exhibitions roped in from overseas.

DAZHALAN LU

# South of the centre

Visitors usually head south of Tian'anmen Square for one main reason – the ravishing Temple of Heaven, a visually arresting ancient building that counts as an example of Beijing's imperial architecture at its best. However, there's plenty to distract you in the Qianmen district on your way. Of most interest is the earthy, old-fashioned *hutong* area (see box, p.60) surrounding the famed Dazhalan Lu shopping street, which has been Beijing's prime backpacker base for decades, and remains the city's best area for aimless browsing, snacking and wandering. Close to the Temple of Heaven lies another site of imperial ritual, the Temple of Agriculture, which is now the engrossing Museum of Ancient Architecture. West of here, Niu Jie – at the heart of the city's Muslim quarter – and the Fayuan Temple are both well worth a look.

# Qianmen Dajie

前门大街, qiánmén dàjiē • Qianmen subway (line 2) • Trams 9am–6pm; ¥25

Stretching immediately south of Qianmen (see p.53), **Qianmen Dajie** was once the Imperial Way. The newly pedestrianized street was gentrified to within an inch of its life in preparation for the 2008 Olympics, though wasn't completed until well over a year after the games had finished. Formed of a pleasing pastiche of dynastic styles, it's now one of the trendiest parts of Beijing. Many choose to travel its length in a restored **tram**; the two grinding up and down the street are relics from the days when the city had a full network, but it's a lot to pay for an 800m-long trip, and it's faster to walk.

# Dazhalan Lu and around

大栅栏路, dàzhàlánlù • Qianmen subway (line 2)

There were fears for **Dazhalan Lu**, one of Beijing's most famous old shopping streets, during the Qianmen area's pre-Olympic round of renovation. Mercifully, this street – pronounced "Dashilar" by any good Beijinger – was spared the wrecking ball, and it remains one of the city's best places to shop. At its eastern extremity, on the junction with Qianmen Dajie, are flagship branches of Beijing's two biggest tea chains, Ten Fu (see p.162) and Zhang Yiyuan (see p.162). Heading west, and hidden in a maze of souvenir shops, you'll soon come across Ruifuxiang, a venerable fabric retailer (see p.160); Tongrentang, a vaunted Chinese pharmacy with an international reputation (see p.34); the Beijing Silk Store (see p.158); and Neiliansheng shoe shop (see p.160).

At the end of the pedestrianized area, Dazhalan Lu narrows and you enter a district of **hutongs**, many destined for the wrecking ball (see box, p.60). A stroll here offers a glimpse of the bustle and shabbiness that remains typical of Chinese metropolitan life but is vanishing from Beijing; you'll come across cobblers, knife sharpeners and dubious masseurs, stone lions flanking sagging courtyard doors, and furtive fruit vendors keeping an eye out for the police. You'll notice, with nose as well as eyes, the profusion of **public toilets** – the old *hutong* buildings have terrible plumbing. If you keep going straight, you'll eventually rejoin the traffic at Nanxinhua Jie. Head off either side and you're likely to get lost – not an unpleasant experience if you're not in a hurry.

# Liulichang Jie

琉璃厂街, liúlíchǎng jiē

If you need something to aim for at the end of your walk, you could do worse than aim for **Liulichang Jie**, a street to the west of Dazhalan Lu. Literally meaning "glaze factory street", after the erstwhile factories here that made glazed tiles for the roofs of the Forbidden City, it has been rebuilt as a heritage street, using Ming-style architecture; today it's full of curio stores (remember to bargain hard, and that every antique is fake). Though there is nothing to distinguish it outwardly from the shops, no. 14 is a small and rather charming **museum** of folk carving (daily

---

**BEIJING'S UNDERGROUND CITY**

On Dongdamochang Jie, a narrow alley just southeast of Qianmen, lies an interesting window into Beijing's not-so-distant days of communist paranoia. A faded English sign is all there is to show that this was one entrance to the **Underground City**, a warren of bunkers constructed under Beijing during the 1960s. Built by "volunteers" at the behest of Chairman Mao in response to the perceived nuclear threat from the Soviet Union, it once had entrances all over the city, a control centre in the Western Hills and supply arteries big enough for trucks to drive down. Fortunately it was never put to use, and wouldn't have been much use even if it were – it was too close to the surface to offer protection against any but the smallest conventional bombs. Today the tunnels have all fallen into disrepair, and their entrances sealed off.

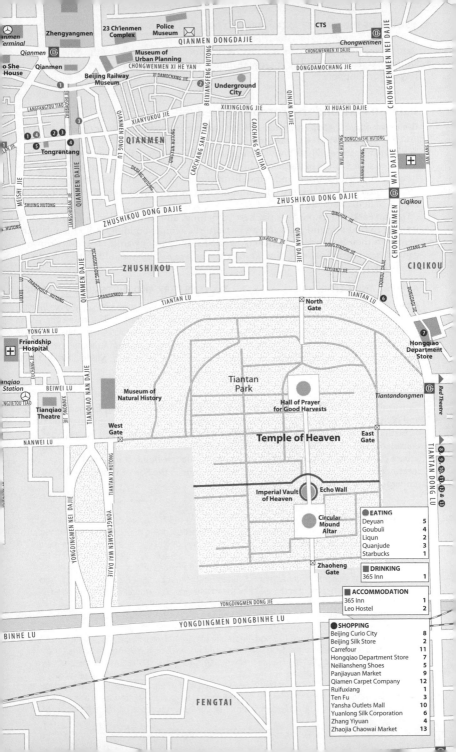

9am–6pm; free), full of screen doors, woodblocks and the like, with some very skilfully crafted pieces. The *Ji Guge* teahouse on the main road offers welcome respite for shoppers.

## Tiantan Park and the Temple of Heaven

**Tiantan Park** 天坛公园, tiāntán gōngyuán · Daily 6am–9pm **Temple of Heaven** 天坛, tiāntán · Daily 8am–6pm · ¥35, park only ¥15 · ☎ 010 67028866, ⓦ en.tiantanpark.com · Tiantandongmen subway (line 5)

Set in a large, tranquil park about 2km south of Tian'anmen, the **Temple of Heaven** is widely regarded as the pinnacle of Ming design. For five centuries it was at the very heart of imperial ceremony and symbolism, and for many modern visitors its architectural unity and beauty remain more appealing – and on a much more accessible scale – than the Forbidden City.

**Tiantan Park** itself is possibly the best in Beijing, and worth a visit in its own right; it's easy to find peaceful seclusion away from the temple buildings. Old men gather here with their pet birds and crickets, while from dawn onwards, *tai ji* practitioners can be seen lost in concentration among the groves of 500-year-old thuja trees (see box below).

### ARRIVAL AND DEPARTURE                    TIANTAN PARK AND THE TEMPLE OF HEAVEN

**Access** The temple is easiest to access through Tiantan Park's east gate, which is the only one close to a subway station (Tiantandongmen). Walking, cycling or coming by bus, you're more likely to enter the park from the north or west. If you're coming from the Qianmen area, you'll be able to eat up some of the distance to the temple on the cute (and expensive) trams which clunk down Qianmen Dajie (see p.77). Exiting the park via its west gate, you can head a little north to the Museum of Natural History (see p.82). The Museum of Ancient Architecture (see p.82) lies just about within walking distance, further to the southwest.

### Brief history

Construction of the Temple of Heaven was begun during the reign of Emperor Yongle, and completed in 1420. The temple complex was conceived as the prime meeting point of earth and heaven, and symbols of the two are integral to its design. Heaven was considered round, and the earth square; thus the round temples and altars stand on square bases, while the park has the shape of a semicircle beside a square. The intermediary between earth and heaven was, of course, the Son of Heaven – the emperor, in other words.

---

### TAI JI

In the early morning, in every park in the city, you'll see folk going through the mesmerizing, precise moves of **tai ji quan** (太极拳, tàijíquán). It may not look it, but *tai ji* is actually a martial art, developed by Taoist monks. It's all about augmenting the body's natural energy, or *qi* (气, qì), which supposedly circulates around the body along particular channels – the same idea lies behind acupuncture and traditional Chinese medicine. *Qi gong* – breath skills – are used to build up an awareness of *qi* and the ability to move it around, eventually replacing excess muscular movements and rendering all actions fluid and powerful.

**Forms** – pre-arranged movement sets – are used to develop speed and power. Acute sensitivity is cultivated, allowing the martial artist to anticipate attacks and strike first; counterattacks are made with the body in a state of minimal tension, creating *tai ji's* characteristic soft appearance. Students are taught not to directly resist but to redirect the attacker's energy, applying a principle from the Taoist *Tao de Qing*, "the soft and the pliable will defeat the hard and the strong".

*Tai ji* was codified in 1949 to make it easier to teach, and so bring it to the masses. The original Chen form is closely related to kung fu, but the form that you'll most often see is a slowed down and simplified version, stripped of explicit martial content and used to promote health.

The temple was the site of the most important ceremony of the imperial court calendar, when the emperor prayed for the year's harvests at the **winter solstice**. Purified by three days of fasting, he made his way to the park on the day before the solstice, accompanied by his court in all its magnificence. On arrival at Tiantan, the emperor would meditate in the Imperial Vault, ritually conversing with the gods on the details of government, before spending the night in the Hall of Prayer for Good Harvests. The following day he sacrificed animals before the Circular Mound Altar. It was forbidden for commoners to catch a glimpse of the great annual procession to the temple, and they were obliged to bolt their windows and remain in silence indoors. Indeed, the Tiantan complex remained sacrosanct until it was thrown open to the people on the first Chinese National Day of the Republic, in October 1912. The last person to perform the rites was General Yuan Shikai, the first president of the Republic, on December 23, 1914. He planned to declare himself emperor but his plans were thwarted by his opponents, and he died a broken man in 1916.

## Hall of Prayer for Good Harvests

At the north end of the park, the principal temple building, the **Hall of Prayer for Good Harvests**, amply justifies all the hype. Made entirely of wood, without the aid of a single nail, the circular structure rises from another tiered marble terrace and has three blue-tiled roofs. Four compass-point pillars, representing the seasons, support the vault, enclosed in turn by twelve outer pillars (one for each month of the year and hour of the day). The dazzling colours of the interior, surrounding the central dragon motif on the coffered ceiling, give the hall an ultramodern look; it was in fact rebuilt, faithful to the Ming design, after the original was destroyed by lightning in 1889. The official explanation for this appalling omen was that it was divine punishment meted out on a sacrilegious caterpillar, which was on the point of crawling to the golden ball on the hall's apex when the lightning struck. Thirty-two court dignitaries were executed for allowing this to happen.

## Imperial Vault of Heaven and the Echo Wall

Directly south of the Hall of Prayer for Good Harvests, the **Imperial Vault of Heaven** is an octagonal tower made entirely of wood, with a dramatic roof of dark blue, glazed tiles, supported by eight pillars. This is where the emperor would change his robes and meditate. The shrine and stone platforms inside held stone tablets representing the emperor and his ancestors, and the two chambers either side carried tablets representing the elements. The tower is encircled by the **Echo Wall**, said to be a perfect whispering gallery, although the unceasing cacophony of tourists trying it out makes it impossible to tell.

## Circular Mound Altar

Heading south again from the Imperial Vault of Heaven, you'll soon be upon the **Circular Mound Altar**, consisting of three marble tiers representing (from the top down) heaven, earth and man. The tiers are comprised of blocks arranged in various multiples of nine, cosmologically the most powerful number, symbolizing both heaven and emperor. The centre of the altar's bare, roofless top tier, where the Throne of Heaven was placed during ceremonies, was considered to be the middle of the Middle Kingdom – the very centre of the earth. Various acoustic properties are claimed for the altar; from this point, it is said, all sounds are channelled straight upwards to heaven. To the east of the nearby fountain, which was reconstructed after fire damage in 1740, are the ruins of a group of buildings used for the preparation of sacrifices.

4

## Museum of Natural History

自然博物馆, zìrán bówùguǎn • Tianqiao Nandajie • Tues–Sun 10am–5pm • ¥10 • ☎ 010 67027702, ⓦ bmnh.org.cn • Qianmen subway (line 2); the museum is a 10min walk from the southern end of Qianmen Dajie

Just north of Tiantan Park's west gate, the **Museum of Natural History** is highly popular with local and foreign kids alike – they never fail to be impressed by the dinosaur skeletons, set amid an array of local fossils. On the upper levels of the building, China's prodigious wealth of animal life is portrayed in stuffed form, while sharks, manta rays and the like zip above your head in the basement **aquarium**.

## Museum of Ancient Architecture

古代建筑博物馆, gǔdài jiànzhù bówùguǎn • South of Nanwei Lu (look for the red arch) • Tues–Sun 9am–5pm • ¥15 • ☎ 010 63172150, ⓦ bjgjg.com • Qianmen subway (line 2), then taxi; just off bus routes #15 and #803; or a 15min walk from the Museum of Natural History

One of Beijing's most underrated attractions, the **Museum of Ancient Architecture** is housed in the former Xiannong Temple. The twin of the nearby Temple of Heaven, it was dedicated to the god of earth, and every year the emperor ritually ploughed a furrow to ensure a good harvest. The buildings and the flat altar are refined, though not spectacular. The **Hall of Worship** holds oddments such as the gold-plated plough used by the emperor, as well as a display explaining the building's history.

More diverting is the main **Hall of Jupiter**, with its beautifully ornate ceiling and an enlightening collection of architectural exhibits showing how China's traditional buildings were put together. There are wooden models, many with cutaways, of famous and distinctive buildings, including Yingxian pagoda (west of Beijing in Shanxi province), and a stilt house of Yunnan province's Dong people. Also on hand are samples of *dougongs*, interlocking, stacked brackets, as complex as puzzle boxes. The giant floor model of how Beijing looked in 1949 – before the communists demolished most of it – is informative, revealing how all the surviving imperial remnants are fragments of a grand design, with a precise north–south imperial axis and sites of symbolic significance at each of the cardinal points. For those who prefer spectacle, there's a great sinuous wooden dragon on show, once part of a temple ceiling.

## The Muslim quarter

Access via the arch at the north end of Niu Jie

Some 3km southwest of Qianmen, Beijing's shabby **Muslim quarter** is focused on congested **Niu Jie** (牛街, niújiē; Ox Street). It's a chaotic, congested thoroughfare lined with offal stalls, steamy little restaurants and hawkers selling fried dough rings, rice cakes and *shaobing*, Chinese-style muffins with a meat filling. The white caps and the beards sported by the men distinguish these people of the Muslim **Hui minority** – of which there are nearly 200,000 in the capital – from the Han Chinese.

### Niu Jie mosque and around

牛街清真寺, niújiē qīngzhēnsì • Niu Jie • Daily from first to last prayers • ¥10, free for Muslims • ☎ 010 63532564 • Caishikou subway (line 4) or bus #6 from the north gate of Tiantan Park

Niu Jie's focus is the **mosque** on its eastern side, an attractive, colourful marriage of Chinese and Islamic design, with abstract and flowery decorations and text in Chinese and Arabic over the doorways. You won't get to see the handwritten copy of the Koran, dating back to the Yuan dynasty, without special permission, or be allowed into the main prayer hall if you're not a Muslim, but you can inspect the courtyard, where a copper cauldron, used to cook food for the devotees, sits near the graves of two Persian imams who came here to preach in the thirteenth century. Also in the courtyard is the "tower for viewing the moon", which allows imams to ascertain the beginning and end of Ramadan, the Muslim period of fasting and prayer.

# Fayuan Temple

法源寺, fǎyuán sì • Fayuansi Qianjie • Daily 8.30am–5pm • ¥5 • ☎ 010 63534171 • Caishikou or Taoranting subway (both line 4), or a short walk from Niu Jie mosque

One of Beijing's oldest temples, though the present structures are in fact Qing and thus relatively recent, **Fayuan Temple** is a striking Buddhist place of worship. A long way from tourist Beijing, it's appealingly ramshackle and authentic, with the well-worn prayer mats and shabby fittings of a working temple. Monks sit outside on broken armchairs counting prayer beads, or bend over books in halls that stink of butter – burned in lamps – and incense. There are two great Ming bronze lions in the first courtyard, resembling armoured were-puppies, and more fine bronzes of the four Heavenly Guardians and a chubby Maitreya in the hall beyond. The halls behind are home to a miscellany of Buddhist sculpture, the finest of which is a 5m-long wooden reclining Buddha in the back hall.

4

# West of the centre

The area west of the Forbidden City is rarely visited by Western tourists, partly because Beijing's best restaurants and places to stay lie elsewhere. However, there's enough tucked away here to entertain the curious for a few days: look around and you'll find a number of wonderful temples, a top-class museum and a pair of appealing parks, as well as the city's principal zoo and aquarium. There's quirky architecture aplenty here too, with a real mishmash of styles: postmodern whimsy and Stalinist brutalism sit side by side, amid swaths of traditional *hutongs*. The area's principal sights come in three main bands, each of which can, if you get your skates on, be eaten up in a single day; the northernmost can also be combined with a boat trip to the Summer Palace (see p.95).

The first band of sights lies on the main road west from Tian'anmen; before long you'll be outside the superb **Capital Museum**, a visit to which can be combined with a trip south to **Baiyun Guan**, a pleasant Taoist temple that seems worlds away from its earthy surroundings. West of the Capital Museum is the old-school, gung-ho **Military Museum**; bank north here and you'll find the **World Art Museum** and **Yuyuantan Park**.

The second main batch of sights lies one block to the north, between Xisi and Fuchengmen subway stations. Here lie the **Guangji and Baita temples**, as well as a museum dedicated to **Lu Xun**, China's most famous writer. The third band of sights lies north again, stretching west of Xizhimen station. The architecturally fascinating **Beijing Exhibition Hall** marks the eastern perimeter of the city **zoo**, which itself borders the absorbing **Wuta Temple**. West again is another temple, **Wanshou**, which sits next to charming **Zizhuyuan Park**.

## West along Xichang'an Jie

From Tian'anmen, traffic fires along **Xichang'an Jie**, a gigantic thoroughfare which mutely morphs through several different names on its way out west. Close to Tian'anmen is the hectic **Xidan** (西单, xīdān) shopping district; though it has few sights, it does boast a few points of interest to travellers among the mammoth malls. The area's main sights are, indeed, a fair way west, clustered around the Muxidi and Military Museum subway stations (both on line 1). Of greatest interest are the **Capital Museum** and **Baiyun Guan** Taoist temple, which are within easy walking distance of each other; in between the two runs a small stream, whose banks are a favourite with local fishermen. It's quite possible to walk along (and, in some places, above) the creek to lovely **Yuyuantan Park**, on the periphery of which are the **Military Museum** and **World Art Museum**.

### Zhongnanhai

中南海, zhōngnánhǎi • Tian'anmen West subway (line 1)

Closest to Tian'anmen is the large **Zhongnanhai** complex, much of it parkland, which functions as the Communist Party headquarters – armed sentries ensure that only invited guests get inside. Once home to the Empress Dowager Cixi (see box, p.96), since 1949 it's been the base of the party's Central Committee and the Central People's Government; Mao Zedong and Zhou Enlai both worked here. In 1989, pro-democracy protesters camped outside hoping to petition their leaders, and a decade later a similarly large protest was held by Falun Gong practitioners, whose quasi-religious sect remains proscribed by a government fearful of its still sizeable following and resultant potential threat to the Party.

Further west, the present-day Aviation Office stands on the site of the **Democracy Wall**, which received its name during the so-called "Beijing Spring" in 1978 when posters questioning Mao and his political legacy were pasted here.

### National Center for the Performing Arts

中国国家大剧院, zhōngguó guójiā dàjùyuàn • 2 Xichang'an Jie • ☎ 010 66550000, ⓦ chncpa.org • Tian'anmen West subway (line 1)

Designed by French architect Paul Andreu and nicknamed – for obvious reasons – the "Egg", the **National Center for the Performing Arts**, off Zhongnanhai's southeastern corner, opened up in 2007. This glass-and-titanium dome houses a concert hall, two theatres and a 2500-seat opera house (see p.151). Visitors enter through a tunnel under the surrounding moat, the park-like banks of which are the best vantage point for this wonderful specimen of modern architecture – look east to the po-faced monumentalism of the Great Hall of the People (see p.52) to see how far China's architecture has come in a few short decades.

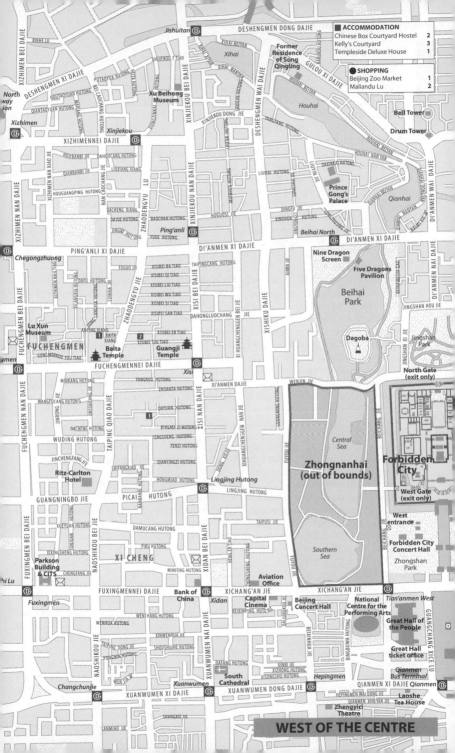

WEST OF THE CENTRE

**5**

## Bank of China
中国银行, zhōngguó yínháng · Fuxingmen Neidajie · Xidan subway (lines 1 & 4)

Overlooking Xidan station is the huge headquarters of the **Bank of China**, built in 2002. It was designed by superstar Chinese architect I.M. Pei, who was also responsible for the Louvre's pyramid in Paris; there are glass pyramids here too, easily visible from the giant atrium.

## Capital Museum
首都博物馆, shǒudū bówùguǎn · Fuxingmenwai Dajie · Tues–Sun 9am–5pm · Free (bring ID) · ☎ 010 63370491, ⓦ capitalmuseum.org.cn/en · Muxidi subway (line 1)

The gigantic **Capital Museum** is a real beauty, both inside and out, whose most interesting feature is a giant bronze cylinder, which shoots diagonally down through the roof as if from heaven. It's a huge place, and walking between the various exhibits will take some time, but despite this the layout is actually quite simple: displays on Beijing are in the **cube**, cultural relics in the **cylinder**. If you're short on time or energy, skip the cube and head for the rarer pieces in the cylinder instead.

### The cylinder

The cylinder's ground-floor gallery holds **Ming and Qing paintings**, mostly landscapes – well presented, but not as comprehensive as the display in the Forbidden City (see p.48). The calligraphy upstairs can be safely missed unless you have a special interest, but the **bronzes** on level three are pretty interesting: a sinister third-century-BC owl-headed dagger, for example, or the strangely modern-looking (though actually more than 3000 years old) three-legged cooking vessels decorated with geometric patterns. The display of **jade** on the fourth floor is definitely worth lingering over. The qualities that combine to create the best jade is an esoteric subject – it's all about colour, lustre and clarity – but anyone can appreciate the workmanship that has gone into the buckles, boxes and knick-knacks here; the white quail-shaped vessels are particularly lovely.

### The cube

The cube of exhibition halls on the building's west side can be navigated rather more quickly. The bottom level hosts a confusing and disappointing show on the **history of Beijing**: exhibits are jumbled together – a modern lathe is displayed next to a stele, for example – without enough English captions to make any sense of the showcase at all. The next level up displays models of historical buildings, which can be skipped in favour of the show-stealing **Buddhist figurines** on the top floor. As well as depictions of serene long-eared gentlemen, there are some very esoteric Lamaist figures from Tibet; the goddess Marici, for example, comes with her own pig-drawn chariot and other fierce deities have lion heads or many arms.

## Baiyun Guan
白云观, báiyún gùan · Off Baiyun Lu · Daily 8.30am–4.30pm · ¥10 · ☎ 010 63463531 · Muxidi subway (line 1)

Once the most influential Taoist centre in the country, **Baiyun Guan** (White Cloud Temple) is well worth hunting down. It was renovated after a long spell as a barracks during communist times, and now houses China's national Taoist association (see box opposite). A popular place for pilgrims, with a busy, thriving feel, it's at its most colourful during the Chinese New Year temple fair.

Though laid out in a similar way to a Buddhist temple, Baiyun Guan has a few distinctive features, such as the three gateways at the entrance, symbolizing the three states of Taoism – desire, substance and emptiness. Each hall is dedicated to a different deity, whose respective domains of influence are explained in English outside; the thickest plumes of incense emerge from the hall to the gods of wealth. The eastern and western halls hold a great collection of Taoist relics, including some horrific **paintings**

## TAOISM

*Humans model themselves on earth*
*earth on heaven*
*heaven on the way*
*and the way on that which is naturally so*

Lao Zi, *Daodejing*

Taoism is a religion deriving from the *Daodejing* or "Way of Power", an obscure, mystical text (see p.185) comprising the teachings of the semi-mythical **Lao Zi**, who lived around 500 BC. The Tao (道, dào), which literally means "Way", is defined as being indefinable; accordingly the book begins: "The Tao that can be told/is not the eternal Tao/The name that can be named/is not the eternal name". But it is the force that creates and moves the natural world, and Taoists believe that the art of living lies in understanding it and conforming to it. Taoism emphasizes contemplation, meditation, eschewal of dogma, and going with the flow. Its central principle is that of **wu wei**, literally non-action, perhaps better understood as "no action which goes against nature".

Taoism developed, at least in part, in reaction to the rigour and formality of state-sponsored Confucianism (see box, p.69). Taoism's holy men tend to be artisans and workmen rather than upright advisers, and in focusing on the relationship of the individual with the natural universe, Taoism represents a retreat from the political and social. The communists, accordingly, regard Taoism as fatalistic and passive.

**of hell** showing people being sawn in half. In the western courtyard a shrine houses twelve deities, each linked with a different animal in the Chinese version of the zodiac; here, visitors light incense and kowtow to the deity that corresponds to their birth year. Also in the courtyard is a **shrine to Wen Cheng**, the deity of scholars, with a 3m-high bronze statue of him outside. Rubbing his belly is supposed to bring success in academic examinations.

Worship in China can be a lively affair, and there are a number of on-site amusements. Three **monkeys** depicted in relief sculptures around the temple are believed to bring you good luck if you can find, and stroke, them all. One is on the gate, easy to spot as it's been rubbed black, while the other two are in the first courtyard. Another playful diversion is trying to ding the bell under the courtyard bridge by throwing a coin at it. In the back courtyard, devotees close their eyes and try to walk from a wall to an incense burner.

### Military Museum

军事博物馆, jūnshì bówùguǎn • Fuxing Lu • Tues–Sun 8.30am–5pm • Free (bring ID) • ☎ 010 66866244, ⊛ eng.jb.mil.cn • Military Museum subway (lines 1 & 9)

Now that all the communists have been to marketing school, it's almost refreshing to be confronted with the old-fashioned Soviet-style brutalism of the **Military Museum**, which is as subtle as a cattle prod. The entrance hall is full of big, bad art, including photo-collages of Mao inspecting his army and soldiers performing an amphibious landing (a hint at Taiwan's fate?). The last Chinese public image of Marx hung here until 1999. The hall beyond has a wealth of Russian and Chinese weaponry on show, including tanks and rockets, with – in case martial feelings have been stirred – an air-rifle shooting gallery at the back. In the rear courtyard a group of miscellaneous old aircraft includes the shells of two American spy planes (with Nationalist Chinese markings) shot down in the 1950s.

### The upper halls

From the lobby, turn west and climb the dim, unsigned staircase to the much more engaging **upper halls**. The exhibition on the third floor commemorates the **Korean War**;

**5**

its chief interest for foreign visitors lies in the fact that it's one of those places that isn't meant for them – captions are only in Chinese and there is much crowing over what is presented as the defeat of American power. There are also more paintings of lantern-jawed soldiers charging machine-gun posts and the like.

The fourth floor holds a large exhibition on **historical warfare**, this time with English captions. Arranged in chronological order, it presents Chinese history as a series of bloody conflicts between rival warlords – which is, actually, not far from the truth. The suits of armour worn by Qing soldiers and Japanese pirates are intimidating even when empty. Also on display are mock-ups of ingenious Chinese siege weapons, Ming-dynasty gunpowder-driven devices for firing eighty arrows at a time, and the world's earliest handgun, dating from the fifteenth century. Opposite this hall lies another treat for connoisseurs of kitsch – the "**Friendship Hall**", containing gifts given to representatives of the Chinese military abroad. Competition for the most tasteless item is fierce, but the gold sub-machine gun from Lebanon and the silver model tractor from Romania certainly deserve a mention.

## Millennium Monument and World Art Museum

Off Fuxing Lu, directly north of Beijing West railway station • Both Tues–Sun 9am–5pm • Free (bring ID); occasional charges for special exhibitions • ☎ 010 59802222, ⊛ worldartmuseum.cn • Military Museum subway (lines 1 & 9)

A fenced-off avenue off Fuxing Lu leads up to the grandiose **China Millennium Monument** (中华世纪坛, zhōnghuá shìjì tán), a sterile public work and "Centre for Patriotic Education". This is also the home of the **World Art Museum** (世界艺术馆, shìjiè yìshùguǎn), a space intended to foster cultural understanding by displaying visiting exhibitions from abroad; there's no permanent collection, and though many exhibitions are actually local (and nationalistic) rather than global, most are very impressive.

## Yuyuantan Park

玉渊潭公园, yùyuāntán gōngyuán • South entrance off Fuxing Lu • Daily: April, May, Sept & Oct 6am–8.30pm; June–Aug 6am–9.30pm; Nov–March 6.30am–7pm • ¥2, pedal boats ¥10/hr • ⊛ www.yytpark.com • Military Museum (lines 1 & 9), Muxidi (line 1) and Xidiaoyutai subway (line 4)

Giant **Yuyuantan Park**, low on grass but studded with trees, offers pleasing respite from the area's honking traffic. It's centred on a large, pleasant lake where you can take out pedal boats; the lake is bisected by a long, skinny walking path, which also provides the park's best vistas.

## Central Radio & TV Tower

中央广播电视塔, zhōngyāng guǎngbō diànshì tǎ • Off the Ring Road • Daily 8.30am–10pm • ⊛ beijingtower.com.cn • ¥50 • Xidiaoyutai subway (line 4)

Accessible by footbridge from the northwest corner of Yuyuantan Park, Beijing's 405m-high **Central Radio & TV Tower** is (for now, at least) also the city's tallest building. A giant, needle-like structure, the tower stands on the foundation of the Altar of the Moon, a Ming-dynasty sacrificial site. You ride up to the top in a lift; the outdoor viewing platform, 238m above ground, offers stunning views of the city on a clear day. Telescopes are dotted around for closer examination, though unfortunately the view into Zhongnanhai (see p.85) is blocked by some judiciously placed buildings.

# Fuchengmennei Dajie

阜城门内大街, fùchéngménnèi dàjiē

A few interesting sights – two **temples** and the **Lu Xun Museum** – lie north of **Fuchengmennei Dajie**, a road zipping between Fuchengmen and Xisi subway stations. You can arrive at one station and depart from the other, walking to all three sights in between; most of this area is rather earthy, but appealing in an old-Beijing kind of way. It also features a few intriguing places to stay (see pp.130–131).

## Guangji Temple

广济寺, guǎngjì sì • Fuchengmennei Dajie • Daily 6am–4.30pm • Free • Xisi subway (line 4)

A quiet complement to the Baita Temple further west, the working Buddhist **Guangji Temple** is the headquarters of China's Buddhist Association. Though an unassuming place, it boasts an important collection of painting and sculpture, as well as a Ming-dynasty Tripitaka; these are, however, only on view to academics with a specialist interest in the art. Visitors can look around, though; keep an eye out for Trikala Buddhas made of yellow sandalwood.

## Baita Temple

白塔寺, báitǎ sì • Fuchengmennei Dajie • Fuchengmen (line 2) or Xisi subway (line 4)

Under renovation at the time of writing, the massive white **dagoba** of the famous **Baita Temple** is visible from afar, rising over the rooftops of the labyrinth of *hutongs* that surround it. Shaped like an upturned bowl with an inverted ice-cream cone on top (the work of a Nepali architect), the 35m-high dagoba was built in the Yuan dynasty; it's a popular spot with Buddhist pilgrims, who ritually circle it clockwise. The temple is worth visiting not least for the collection of thousands of small statues of Buddha – mostly Tibetan – housed in one of its halls, very impressive en masse. Another hall holds bronze *luohans* – Buddha's original group of disciples – including one with a beak, small bronze Buddhas and other, outlandish Lamaist figures. The silk and velvet priestly garments on display here were unearthed from under the dagoba in 1978. A shop beside it sells religious curios, such as Buddha images printed on dried leaves.

## Lu Xun Museum

鲁迅博物馆, lǔxùn bówùguǎn • Xisantiao Hutong, off Fuchengmennei Dajie • Tues–Sun 8am–5pm • Free (bring ID) • ☎ 010 66164080, ⓦ www.luxunmuseum.com.cn • Fuchengmen subway (line 2)

A large and extensively renovated courtyard house, this was once home to **Lu Xun** (1881–1936), widely accepted as the greatest Chinese writer of the modern era. Lu Xun gave up a promising career in medicine to write books, with the aim, so he declared, of curing social ills with his pithy, satirical stories. He bought this house in 1924, but as someone who abhorred pomp, he might feel a little uneasy here nowadays. His possessions have been preserved like treasured relics, giving a good idea of what Chinese interiors looked like at the beginning of the twentieth century, and there's a photo exhibition lauding his achievements. Unfortunately there are no English captions, though a bookshop on the west side of the compound sells English translations of his work.

# Xizhimen

西直门, xīzhímén

The area around **Xizhimen** is one of the city's transport hubs, and many pass through it on their way to the Summer Palace. However, there are a few interesting sights along the road heading west of the railway station; these include two great **temples**, and the city **zoo**.

---

### THE TRUE STORY OF AH Q

One of the most appealing and accessible of **Lu Xun**'s tales is **The True Story of Ah Q**, a lively tragicomedy written in the plain style he favoured as an alternative to the complex classical language of the era. Set in 1911, during the inception of the ill-fated republic, it tells the life story of a worthless peasant, Ah Q, who stumbles from disaster to disaster, believing each outcome to be a triumph. He epitomized every character flaw of the Chinese race as seen by his creator; Ah Q dreams of revolution and ends up being executed, having understood nothing.

**5**

## Beijing Exhibition Hall and around

北京展览馆, běijīng zhǎnlǎn guǎn • Xizhimenwai Dajie • ☎ 010 68316677, ⓦ bjexpo.com • Beijing Zoo subway (line 4)

Built by the Russians in 1954, and easily distinguishable by its slim, star-topped spire, the giant **Beijing Exhibition Hall** is by far the city's best overtly communist construction – a work of grandiose Socialist Realism with fine details, including heroic workers atop columns carved with acorns. It's certainly worth inspection; though its cavernous halls are usually closed, the architecture can be appreciated from side-roads to the east and west.

The road on the east side leads to the dock for boats to the Summer Palace (see box, p.95). Head up the alley on the west side and you'll come to the city's oldest Western restaurant, the *Moscow* – the food is mediocre, but check out the grand decor if you're passing.

### The zoo and the aquarium

动物园, dòngwùyuán • Xizhimenwai Dajie • **Zoo** Daily April–Oct 7.30am–6pm; Nov–March 7.30am–5pm **Aquarium** Daily 10am–4.30pm; dolphin shows daily 10am & 2.30pm • All-inclusive tickets ¥130, children ¥70, children under 1.2m free; zoo-only tickets ¥40 • ☎ 010 68390274, ⓦ www.bjzoo.com • Beijing Zoo subway (line 4)

Beijing's city **zoo** is most worth visiting for its panda house. Here you can join the queues to have your photo taken sitting astride a plastic replica of the creature, then push your way through to glimpse the living variety – kept in relatively palatial quarters and familiar through the much-publicized export of the animals to overseas zoos for mating purposes. While the pandas lie on their backs in their luxury pad waving their legs in the air, other animals (less cute or less endangered) slink, pace or flap around their miserable cells. The children's zoo, with plenty of farmyard animals and ponies to pet, is rather better, and the new **Beijing Aquarium**, in the northeast corner of the compound, is surprisingly good. As well as thousands of varieties of fish, including sharks, it has a twice-daily **dolphin show**.

### Wuta Temple

五塔寺, wútǎ sì • Wutasi Lu, off Zhongguancun Nandajie • Daily 9am–4.30pm • ¥20; free to first 300 visitors on Wed • National Library subway (lines 4 & 9)

The canalside **Wuta Temple** boasts a central hall radically different from any other sacred building you'll see in the capital. Completed in 1424, it's a stone cube decorated on the outside with reliefs of animals, Sanskrit characters and Buddha images – each has a different hand gesture – and topped with five layered, triangular spires. It's visibly Indian in influence, and is said to be based on a temple in Bodhgaya, where the Buddha gained enlightenment. There are 87 steps to the top, where you can inspect the spire carvings at close quarters – including elephants and Buddhas, and, at the centre of the central spire, a pair of feet. The new halls behind the museum are home to statues of bulbous-eyed camels, docile-looking tigers, puppy-dog lions and the like, all collected from the spirit ways of tombs and long-destroyed temples. Outside is a line of seventeenth-century tombstones of Jesuit priests made in traditional Chinese style, with turtle-like dragons at the base and text in Chinese and Latin.

### Zizhuyan Park

紫竹院公园, zǐzhúyuàn gōngyuán • Best accessed via east gate on Zhongguancun Nandajie • Daily 6am–8pm • Free • National Library subway (lines 4 & 9)

Centred on a huge lake, pretty **Zizhuyan Park** is worth popping into if you're visiting either of the two nearby temples, Wuta or Wanshou. Paths lead though gorgeous groves of bamboo, some bisecting the lake itself, while others merely skirt the waters. Note that it's possible to board ferries from here to the Summer Palace (see box, p.95).

## Wanshou Temple

万寿寺, wànshòu sì · Guangyuanjia Lu · Daily 9am–4pm · ¥20; free to first 300 visitors on Wed · National Library (lines 4 & 9) or Weigongcun subway (line 4), then taxi

Dating from the Ming era and a favourite of the Dowager Empress Cixi (see box, p.96), **Wanshou Temple** is the last survivor of the several dozen that once lined the canalsides all the way up to the Summer Palace. It's now a small **museum of ancient art**, with five exhibition halls of Ming and Qing relics, mostly ceramics. There's nothing spectacular on view but it's worth a look if you are in the area. If you want to meet some locals, head for the "English corner" where students go to practise speaking English.

SEVENTEEN-ARCH BRIDGE, KUNMING LAKE

# The far north

In the far northwest corner of Beijing is the wonderful Summer Palace; an imperial retreat which has retained the charm of centuries gone by, it's an excellent place to get away from the smog of the city, and deservedly one of Beijing's most-visited sights. Though rather eclipsed by its newer neighbour, the "old" Summer Palace of Yuanmingyuan also merits a visit, if only for the contrast provided by the ruins. Beijing's main university district lies nearby, with student life revolving around the party hub of Wudaokou. From here, it's not too far to Dazhong Temple, or by bus to the Botanical Gardens, Xiangshan Park and other excursions to the west of Beijing (see p.114). Continuing east will bring you to area redeveloped for the 2008 Olympics, though somewhat neglected since that heady summer. East again, and on the way to the airport, is the superb 798 Art District – tough to get to, but certainly worth it.

# The Summer Palace

颐和园, yíhé yuán • Daily 8am–7pm, buildings close at 5pm • Park entry ¥20, including access to buildings ¥50 • ☎ 010 62881144 • Xiyuan or Beigongmen subway (both line 4); also accessible by boat (see box below)

One of Beijing's must-see attractions, the **Summer Palace** is a lavish imperial playground whose grounds are large enough to have an almost rural feel. Once the private haunt of the notorious Empress Cixi (see box, p.96), it functions today as a lovely public park, two-thirds of which is taken up by **Kunming Lake**. During the hottest months of the year, the imperial court would decamp to this perfect hillside location, cooled by the lake and sheltered by judicious use of garden landscaping.

The palace buildings, many connected by a suitably majestic gallery, are built on and around **Wanshou Shan** (Longevity Hill), north of the lake and just in from the East Gate. Many of the palace edifices are intimately linked with Cixi – anecdotes about whom are the stock output of the numerous tour guides – but to enjoy the site, you need know very little of its history: like Beihai (see p.58), the park, its lake and pavilions form a startling visual array, akin to a traditional Chinese landscape painting brought to life.

## Brief history

There have been imperial summer pavilions at the Summer Palace since the eleventh century, although the present park layout is essentially eighteenth-century, created by the Manchu Emperor Qianlong. However, the key character associated with the palace is the **Dowager Empress Cixi**, who ruled over the fast-disintegrating Chinese empire from 1861 until her death in 1908. The Summer Palace was very much her pleasure ground; it was she who built the palaces here in 1888 after the original palace was destroyed by Western forces during the Opium Wars, and determinedly restored them after another bout of European aggression in 1900.

## The palace compound

City buses, most tours and those coming via Xiyuan subway station will enter via the **East Gate**, which is overlooked by the main palace compound; a path leads from the gate, past several halls (all signposted in English), to the lakeside. Those arriving at Beigongmen subway station will enter through the **North Gate**, on the other side of Wanshou Shan; from here, it's a lovely walk of just over 1km to the palace compound.

### Renshoudian

The strange bronze animal in the first courtyard is a *xuanni* or *kylin*, with the head of a dragon, deer antlers, a lion's tail and ox hooves. It was said to be able to detect disloyal subjects. The building behind is the **Renshoudian** (Hall of Benevolence and Longevity), a majestic, multi-eaved hall where the empress and her predecessors gave audience; it retains much of its original nineteenth-century furniture, including an imposing red sandalwood throne carved with nine dragons and flanked by peacock feather fans. The inscription on the tablet above reads "Benevolence in rule leads to long life". Look out, too, for the superbly well-made basket of flowers studded with precious stones.

### Deheyuan

A little way further along the main path, to the right, the **Deheyuan** (Palace of Virtue and Harmony) is dominated by a three-storey theatre, complete with trap doors in

---

### BOAT SERVICES TO THE SUMMER PALACE

The fastest route to the Summer Palace is to take the subway, but there's also a **boat service** that leaves from Zizhuyuan Park and behind the Beijing Exhibition Hall (hourly 10am–5pm; ¥70 including park ticket to palace). The route follows the old imperial approach along the now dredged and prettified Long River, passing attractive bridges and willow groves en route. Your vessel will either be a large, dragon-shaped cruiser or a smaller four-person speedboat.

**6**

### THE DOWAGER EMPRESS CIXI

The notorious Cixi entered the imperial palace at 15 as the **Emperor Xianfeng's concubine**, quickly becoming his favourite and bearing him a son. When the emperor died in 1861 she became regent, ruling in place of her infant boy, Tonghzi. For the next 35 years she, in effect, ruled China, displaying a mastery of intrigue and court politics. When her son died of syphilis in 1875, she installed another puppet infant, her nephew, and retained her authority. Her fondness for extravagant gestures (every year she had ten thousand caged birds released on her birthday, for example) drained the state's coffers, and her deeply conservative policies were inappropriate for a time when the nation was calling for reform.

With foreign powers taking great chunks out of China's borders on and off during the nineteenth century, Cixi was moved to respond in a typically misguided fashion. Impressed by the claims of the xenophobic **Boxer Movement** (whose Chinese title translated as "Righteous and Harmonious Fists") that their members were invulnerable to bullets, in 1899 Cixi let them loose on all the foreigners in China. The Boxers laid siege to the foreign legation's compound in Beijing for nearly two months before a European expeditionary force arrived and, predictably, slaughtered the agitators. Cixi and her nephew, the emperor, only escaped the subsequent rout of the capital by disguising themselves as peasants and fleeing the city. On her return, Cixi clung on to power, attempting to delay the inevitable fall of the dynasty. One of her last acts, the day before she died in 1908, was to oversee the murder of her puppet emperor, Guangxu.

the stage for surprise appearances and disappearances by the actors. Theatre was one of Cixi's main passions – she even took part in performances sometimes, playing the

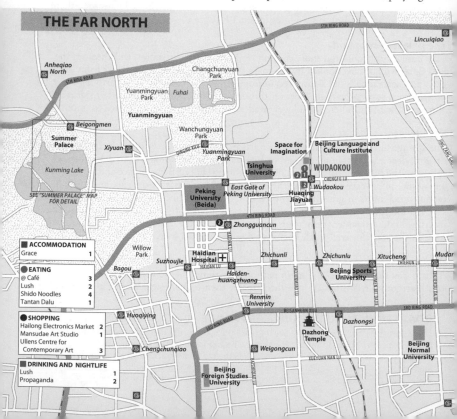

role of Guanyin, the goddess of mercy. Today some of the halls function as a **museum** of theatre, with displays of costumes, props and waxworks of Cixi and attendants. The most unusual exhibit is a vintage Mercedes-Benz, a gift to the warlord Yuan Shikai (see p.173) in the early twentieth century and the first car to appear in China.

### Yulangtang

The next major building along the path is the lakeside **Yulangtang** (Jade Waves Palace). This is where the Emperor Guangxu, then still a minor, was kept in captivity for ten years while Cixi exercised his powers. A pair of decorative rocks in the front courtyard, supposed to resemble a mother and her son, were put there by Cixi to chastise Guangxu for insufficient filiality. The main hall contains a tablet of Cixi's calligraphy reading "The magnificent palace inspires everlasting moral integrity". One character has a stroke missing; apparently no one dared tell her.

### Leshoutang

North of here, behind Renshoudian, are Cixi's private quarters, three large courtyards connected by a winding gallery. The largest, the **Leshoutang** (Hall of Joy and Longevity), houses Cixi's hardwood throne. The large table in the centre of the main hall was where she took her infamous meals of 128 courses. The chandeliers were China's first electric lights, installed in 1903 and powered by the palace's own generator.

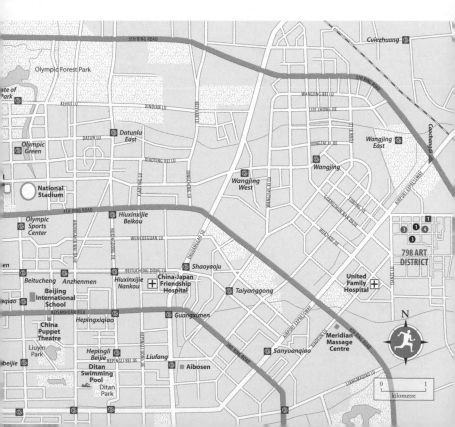

## The north shore of Kunming Lake

From Leshoutang, the **Long Corridor** leads to the northwest corner of Kunming Lake. Flanked by various temples and pavilions, the corridor is actually a 700m covered way, its inside walls painted with more than eight thousand restored images of birds, flowers, landscapes and scenes from history and mythology. Near its western end is Cixi's ultimate flight of fancy, a magnificent lakeside pavilion in the form of a 36m-long **marble boat**, boasting two decks. Completed using funds intended for the Chinese navy, it was regarded by Cixi's acolytes as a characteristically witty and defiant snub to her detractors. Her misappropriations helped speed the empire's decline, with China suffering heavy naval defeats during the 1895 war with Japan. Close to the marble boat is a jetty – the tourist focus of this part of the site – with **rowing boats** for hire (see box opposite).

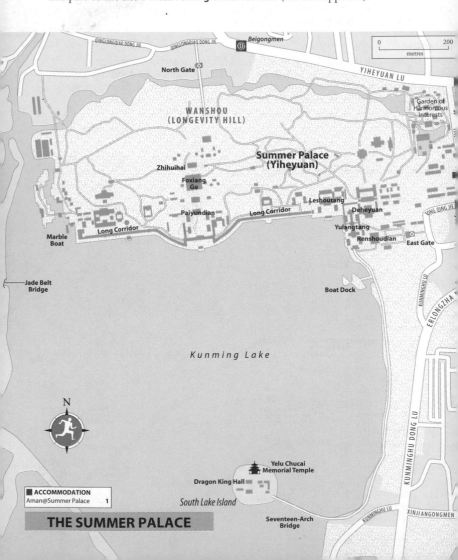

> **BOATING AND SKATING ON KUNMING LAKE**
>
> **Boating** on Kunming Lake is a popular pursuit and well worth the money (boats can be hired at any of the jetties for ¥40/hr). In addition to the jetty by the marble boat, you can dock over below Longevity Hill, on the north side of the lake by the gallery. You can row out to the two bridges spanning narrow stretches of water – the gracefully bowed Jade Belt on the western side and the long, elegant Seventeen-Arch Bridge on the east. In winter, the Chinese **skate** on the lake here – a spectacular sight, as some of the participants are really proficient. Skates are available for rent by the lakeside (10/hr).

**6**

## Wanshou Shan

About halfway down the Long Corridor you'll see an archway and a path that leads uphill away from the lake. Head up the path and through two gates to the **Paiyundian** (Cloud Dispelling Hall), which was used by Cixi as a venue for her infamously extravagant birthday parties. The elegant objects on display here are twentieth-birthday presents to her from high officials (the rather flattering oil painting of her was a present from the American artist Hubert Vos). The largest building here, near the top of the hill, is the **Foxiang Ge** (Tower of Buddhist Incense), a charming three-storey octagonal pagoda built in 1750. It commands a panoramic view of the whole park, and deservedly the area around it is a popular picnic spot. The **Zhihuihai** (Sea of Wisdom Hall), on top of the hill, is strikingly different in style from the other buildings: there's not a single beam or column, and it's tiled in green and yellow ceramic tiles and dotted with niches holding Buddha statues.

### Garden of Harmonious Interests

At the foot of the hill on the far (north) side lies a souvenir market and the little-visited but very attractive back lake. Walk east along the side of this lake for 500m and you arrive at the **Garden of Harmonious Interests**, a pretty collection of lotus-filled ponds and pavilions connected by bridges. Cixi used to fish from the large central pavilion; to keep her sweet, eunuchs dived in and attached fish to her hook. The bridge up to the pavilion is called "Know the Fish Bridge" after an argument that took place here between two Ming-dynasty philosophers: one declared that the fish he could see were happy; the other snorted, "How could you know? You're not a fish", whereupon the first countered, "You're not me, so how do you know I don't know?"

## The south of the park

The scenery is wilder and the crowds thinner at the southern part of Kunming Lake, a pleasant fifteen-minute walk. Should you need a destination, the main attraction to head for is the white **Seventeen-Arch Bridge**, 150m long and topped with 544 cute, vaguely canine lions, each with a slightly different posture. The bridge leads to **South Lake Island**, where Qianlong used to review his navy, and which holds a brace of fine halls, most striking of which is the **Yelu Chucai Memorial Temple**. Yelu, an adviser to Genghis Khan during the Yuan dynasty, is entombed next to the temple, in the company of his wives and concubines, slaughtered for the occasion. The small, colourful **Dragon King Hall** nearby was used to pray for rain.

# Yuanmingyuan

圆明园, yuánmíng yuán • Two entrances on Qinghua Xilu • Daily 7am–7pm, buildings close at 5pm • Park entry ¥10, ticket including entry to buildings ¥25 • Ⓦ yuanmingyuanpark.com • Yuanmingyuan Park subway (line 4)

Beijing's original summer palace, the **Yuanmingyuan** was built by the Qing Emperor Kangxi in the early eighteenth century. Once nicknamed China's Versailles for its elegant, European-influenced design, the palace boasted the largest royal gardens in the

**6**

world, containing some two hundred pavilions and temples set around a series of lakes and natural springs. Today there is precious little left; in 1860, the entire complex was burnt and destroyed by British and French troops, who were ordered by the Earl of Elgin to make the imperial court "see reason" during the Opium Wars (see p.171). The troops had previously spent twelve days looting the imperial treasures, many of which found their way to the Louvre and the British Museum; this includes the famed "twelve bronzes", a series of cast animal heads which have been making their way back to Beijing in dribs and drabs. This unedifying history is described in inflammatory terms on signs all over the park and it's a favoured site for brooding nationalists. Still, don't let that put you off, as the overgrown ruins are rather appealing and unusual.

There are actually three parks here, the Yuanmingyuan (Park of Perfection and Brightness), **Wanchunyuan** (Park of Ten Thousand Springs) and **Changchunyuan** (Park of Everlasting Spring), all centred around the lake, **Fuhai** (Sea of Happiness). All together this forms an absolutely gigantic area, but the best-preserved structures are the fountain and the **Hall of Tranquillity** in the northeastern section. The stone and marble fragments hint at how fascinating the original must once have been, with its marriage of European Rococo decoration and Chinese motifs.

## Peking University

北京大学, běijīng dàxúe • Haidian • Free, though you may be asked for ID • ⓦ english.pku.edu.cn • East Gate of Peking University subway (line 4)

On the way to or from the Summer Palace, you may care to stop by China's most prestigious university. Nobody at all calls this Peking University, or even **Beijing Daxue** – the contraction "Beida" is used by all and sundry. Its campus is undeniably conducive to learning; in fact its old buildings and quiet, well-maintained grounds make it nicer than most of the city's parks. The **lake** is a popular place to skate in the winter – you can rent skates for ¥10 an hour.

Originally established and administered by Americans at the beginning of the twentieth century, the university stood on the hill in Jingshan Park before moving to its present site in 1953. Now busy with new contingents of students (including many from abroad), it was half-deserted during the Cultural Revolution (see p.174), when students and teachers alike, regarded as suspiciously liberal, were dispersed for "re-education". Later, in 1975–76, Beida was the power base of the radical left in their campaign against Deng Xiaoping, the pragmatist who was in control of the day-to-day running of the Communist Party's Central Committee during Mao's twilight years. The university's intake suffered when new students were required to spend a year learning Party dogma after 1989; now it's once again a centre for challenging political thought.

## Wudaokou

Wudaokou subway (line 13)

The **Wudaokou** district sits close to the Peking and Tsinghua university complexes. As you'd expect of an area featuring thousands and thousands of China's best students (and an ever-growing number from abroad, particularly South Korea), it puts forward a youthful, cosmopolitan air. Wudaokou is regarded as the home of Beijing's alternative culture; for the casual visitor, it's best used as a place to eat (see p.142) or to catch the local rock bands (see p.148).

## Dazhong Temple

大钟寺, dàzhōng sì • Beisanhuan Lu • Tues–Sun 8.30am–4.30pm • ¥15 • ⓦ dazhongsi.org • Dazhongsi subway (line 13)

Deriving its name from the enormous bell hanging in the back, the **Dazhong Temple**'s halls (*dazhong* means big bell) now house one of Beijing's most interesting little exhibitions, showcasing several hundred bronze bells from temples all over the country. The bells here are considerable works of art, their surfaces enlivened with embossed texts in Chinese and Tibetan, abstract patterns and images of storks and dragons. The odd, scaly, dragon-like creature shown perching on top of each bell is a *pulao*, a legendary animal supposed to shriek when attacked by a whale (the wooden hammers used to strike the bells are carved to look like whales). The smallest bell here is the size of a goblet; the largest, a Ming creation called the **King of Bells**, is as tall as a two-storey house. Hanging in the back hall, it is, at fifty tonnes, the biggest and oldest surviving functional bell in the world, and can reputedly be heard up to 40km away. You can climb up to a platform above it to get a closer look at some of the 250,000 Chinese characters on its surface, and join visitors in trying to throw a coin into the small hole in the top. The method of its construction and the history of Chinese bell-making are explained by displays, with English captions, in side halls. The shape of Chinese bells dampens vibrations, so they only sound for a short time and can be effectively used as instruments: you can buy CDs of the bells in action.

## Olympic Green

奥林匹克公园, àolínpǐkè gōngyuán • Olympic Sports Center or Olympic Green subway (both line 8)

China used the 2008 Olympics to make an impact on the world stage, and facilities built for the occasion were accordingly lavish. The **Olympic Green** was placed on the city's north–south axis, laid down during the Yuan dynasty – so it's bang in line with the Forbidden City. In addition, subway line 8, a highly auspicious number in Chinese, was built for the occasion. Several of the venues used for the Games are still standing, but most come here to bear witness to two masterpieces of modern architecture, the astonishing **National Stadium** and the **National Aquatics Center**.

### BEIJING 2008: THE LEGACY

In a nation so obsessed with the number eight that SIM cards or apartments bearing that number cost more, it was unimaginable that the Chinese would not be selected to host the **Olympics** in 2008. And so it was that the city duly won the vote in 2001, and prepared for the Games to end all Games – some put the final cost at over US$40 billion, making it by far the most expensive sporting event in history. The Games were an extraordinary success, from the utterly compelling opening ceremony to the results of the home nation, who won 51 gold medals – far ahead of the USA in second place.

The legacy of the Games has, however, been more mixed. Increased participation across a wide range of sports has been the most positive aspect of the Games' legacy (though China still fell behind the USA again in the medals table at London 2012). And there were substantial improvements to infrastructure and public transport, though these would have happened anyway, and were merely accelerated by the event. In fact, the effect on the local economy was, in the end, minimal, with increased takings from international tourists offset by losses from enforced factory closures in the Beijing area.

The biggest losers, however, have been the wonderful Olympic **venues**, which were built with no real future plan in mind. The main stadium has seen little use since the Olympics, hosting a couple of concerts and football games, and a short-lived theme park; the Water Cube continues to haemorrhage money, despite the new income stream from its new on-site water park (see p.102); and other venues have fared even worse. Ironically, in seeking to show Chinese might to the world, the ongoing cost of the Olympics has angered a fair chunk of Beijing's population – lessons to be taken on board in advance of China's inevitable bid for a forthcoming edition of football's World Cup.

**6**

### National Stadium

奥林匹克体育馆, àolínpǐkè tǐyùguǎn • Daily 8am–5pm • ¥50

Centrepiece of the Olympic Park is the 90,000-seat National Stadium, nicknamed the "**Bird's Nest**" on account of its exterior steel lattice. It was built at a cost of over US$400m by Herzog & de Meuron, with input from Ai Weiwei, China's greatest living self-publicist. The stadium made a grand stage for many memorable events, including the spectacular opening display, but since the Olympics hasn't seen much use and is eventually expected to become part of a larger shopping and event complex. A few hundred people visit every day, mostly out-of-towners; you can join them in wandering round the empty shell for an extortionate entry fee. For ¥120 you can even mount the winner's podium and be handed a fake medal.

### National Aquatics Center

国家游泳中心, guójiā yóuyǒng zhōngxīn • ⓦ water-cube.com • Daily 10am–9.30pm • ¥200

Next door to the National Stadium, the National Aquatics Center quickly became known as the **Water Cube**, thanks to its bubble-like exterior membrane. Part of it is now occupied by the **Beijing Watercube Waterpark**, which – though expensive – is a lot of fun, pulling in visitors with wave machines, water slides and the occasional inflatable jellyfish.

## 798 Art District

798艺术区, qījiǔbā yìshùqū • Daily 24hr, though many galleries close on Mon • Free • ⓦ 798district.com • Bus #915, #918 or #934 from Dongzhimen subway (lines 2 & 13), or ¥35–50 by taxi

Though it's way out on the way to the airport (take a cab, it's *so* much easier), the **798 Art District** – a collection of more than a hundred art galleries (see box opposite) plus boutiques (see p.160) and cafés (see p.142) – is a hotspot for the arty crowd, and one of Beijing's most interesting attractions. The area is particularly lively during the **798 Art Festival** – though the size of the festival, its dates, and, indeed, whether it happens at all, are dependent on the precarious political climate. It should be scheduled for the autumn.

Originally this huge complex of Bauhaus-style buildings was an electronics factory, built by East Germans; when that closed down in the 1990s, artists moved in and converted the airy, light and, above all, cheap spaces into studios. As the Chinese art market blossomed, galleries followed, then boutiques and cafés – a gentrification that would take fifty years in the West happened here in about five. Though the city government – terrified of unhindered expression – initially wanted to shut the area down, the future of the place finally looks secure. It has grown rather commercial of late, though most of the shops, cafés and restaurants at least suit the vibe of the place.

Today, 798 has the feel of a campus, with a grid of pedestrianized, tree-lined streets dotted with wacky sculptures – a caged dinosaur, a forlorn gorilla – and the gnarliness of the industrial buildings (those in "Power Square" are particularly brutal) softened by artsy graffiti. It's surprisingly large, but there are maps throughout. Exhibitions open every week, and every art form is well represented – though with such a lot of it about, it varies in quality. Note that unlike all other Beijing sites, it's actually better on the weekend, when there's a real buzz about the place; on weekdays it can feel a little dead – particularly on **Mondays** when almost all the galleries are closed.

## 798'S BEST GALLERIES

**Beijing Commune** 北京公社 běijīng gōngshè ☎010 86549428, Ⓦbeijingcommune.com. Small place renowned for its imaginatively curated shows. Tues–Sun 10am–6pm.

**Galleria Continua** 常青画廊 chángqīng huàláng ☎010 64361005, Ⓦgalleriacontinua .com. Shows international and home-grown art stars across three floors' worth of space – head up to the top for a nuts-and-bolts view (literally) of the former factory. They tend to choose artists "with something to say", and rotate exhibitions 3–5 times per year. Tues–Sun 11am–6pm.

**Long March Space** 长征空间 chángzhēng kōngjiān ☎010 64387107, Ⓦlongmarchspace .com. This space is popular for its attempts to reach out to the masses with education programmes (as its name hints). Tues–Sun 11am–7pm.

**Mansudae Art Studio** 万寿台创作社美术馆 wànshòutái chuàng zuòshè měishùguǎn ☎010 59789317, Ⓦmyinweb.com/mansudae. Small studio displaying North Korean painting – every bit as fascinating as you might imagine, with pieces ranging from misty mountain scenes to brave Socialist Realism. There's also a small shop on site, where you can buy North Korean goodies (see p.156). Tues–Sun 10am–6pm.

**Tokyo Gallery+** 东京艺术工程 dōngjīng yìshùgōngchéng ☎010 84573245, Ⓦtokyo-gallery.com. The first gallery to set up shop here, and still one of the best, with a large, elegant space for challenging shows. Tues–Sun 10am–5.30pm.

**Ullens Centre for Contemporary Art** 尤伦斯当代艺术中心 yóulúnsī dāngdài yìshùzhōngxīn ☎010 64386675, Ⓦucca.org.cn. This huge non-profit space is more of a museum than a gallery; nothing is for sale and it is the only place that charges an entrance fee. There are three exhibition halls and a programme of regular events (all detailed on the website), which mainly focus on Asian artists. Tues–Sun 10am–7pm; free on Thurs, otherwise ¥15.

**White Space** 空白空间 kòngbái kōngjiān ☎010 84562054, Ⓦalexanderochs-galleries.de. This well-run space, owned by a German curator, has a reputation for putting on challenging shows by up-and-coming artists. Tues–Sat 10am–6pm.

6

# Caochangdi

曹场地, cǎochǎngdì • Ⓦcaochangdi.org • Off the Airport Expressway, near the Fifth Ring Rd • ¥45–60 by taxi from the centre, or ¥10 from 798

If the 798 Art District is just too commercial for you, take a cab to **Caochangdi**, a couple of kilometres towards the airport. This overspill gallery area, away from the tourists and boutiques, is where the hardcore avant-gardists escaped to when 798 became too mainstream for them – though it's increasingly becoming the place for parties and hype. Many of the spaces here were designed by artsy provocateur Ai Weiwei.

# Around Beijing

Some inviting destinations, offering both countryside and culture, lie within a few hours of the capital. Most compelling is the Great Wall, whose remains, either crumbling or spruced up, can be seen in a number of places in the hills a few hours north and east of the city. The undulating, wooded landscape to the west of Beijing, called the Western Hills, is the most attractive countryside in the city's vicinity, and easily accessible from the centre. The Botanical Gardens, Xiangshan Park and Badachu – the last of these a collection of eight temples – make for an excellent day-retreat. A little further out, the striking Fahai, Tanzhe and Jietai temples stand in superb rural isolation. All are at their quietest and best on weekdays.

Though less scenic than the Western Hills, the area north of the city also contains the vast **Aviation Museum** and the much-visited **Ming Tombs**. Further afield, and well worth at least a couple of days, the city of **Chengde** is within easy travelling distance, and boasts some of the finest imperial architecture in the country. There are fewer places of interest south of the city, but the "wilderness valley" of **Shidu** is worth exploring.

## The Great Wall

长城, chángchéng

*This is a Great Wall, and only a great people with a great past could have a great wall, and such a great people with such a great wall will surely have a great future.*

Richard M. Nixon

Stretching from Shanhaiguan, by the Yellow Sea, to Jiayuguan Pass in the Gobi Desert, the **Great Wall** is an astonishing feat of engineering. Then again, the Chinese certainly had form in this regard – the practice of building walls along the country's northern frontier began in the fifth century BC and continued until the sixteenth century (see box below). Over time, this discontinuous array of fortifications and ramparts came to be known as **Wan Li Changcheng** (literally, "Long Wall of Ten Thousand Li", *li* being a Chinese measure of distance roughly equal to 500m), or "the Great Wall" to English-speakers. Today, this great monument to state paranoia is big business – the restored sections are besieged daily by rampaging hordes of tourists – and is touted by the government as a source of national pride. Its image adorns all manner of products, from wine to cigarettes, and is even used – surely rather inappropriately – on visa stickers.

For all this, even the most-visited section at **Badaling**, constantly overrun by Chinese and foreign tourists, is still easily one of China's most spectacular sights. The section at **Mutianyu** is somewhat less crowded; distant **Simatai** much less so, and far more beautiful. To see the wall in its crumbling glory, head out to **Jingshanling**,

---

### THE WALL'S LONG HISTORY

The Chinese have walled their cities throughout recorded history, and during the Warring States period (around the fifth century BC) simply extended the practice to separate themselves from rival territories. The Great Wall's origins lie in these fractured lines of fortifications and in the vision of the first Emperor **Qin Shi Huang** who, having unified the empire in the third century BC, joined and extended the sections to form one continuous defence against barbarians.

Under subsequent dynasties, whenever insularity rather than engagement drove foreign policy, the wall continued to be maintained, and in response to shifting regional threats grew and changed course. It lost importance under the **Tang**, when borders were extended north, well beyond it – the Tang was, in any case, an outward-looking dynasty that kept the barbarians in check far more cheaply by fostering trade and internal divisions. With the emergence of the insular **Ming**, however, the wall's upkeep again became a priority: from the fourteenth to the sixteenth centuries, military technicians worked on its reconstruction. The Ming wall is the one you see today.

The 7m-high, 7m-thick wall, with its 25,000 battlements, served to bolster Ming sovereignty for a couple of centuries. It restricted the movement of the nomadic peoples of the distant, non-Han minority regions, preventing plundering raids: signals made by gunpowder blasts, flags and smoke swiftly sent news of enemy movements to the capital. In the late sixteenth century, a couple of huge **Mongol invasions** were repelled, at Jinshanling and Badaling. But a wall is only as strong as its guards, and by the seventeenth century the Ming royal house was corrupt and its armies weak; the wall was little hindrance to the invading Manchu. After they had established their own dynasty, the **Qing**, they let the wall fall into disrepair. Slowly it crumbled away, useful only as a source of building material – demolitions of old *hutongs* in Beijing have turned up bricks from the wall, marked with the imperial seal.

**Jiankou** or **Huanghua**, as yet largely untouched by development. For other trips to unreconstructed sections, check out ⓦwildwall.com or contact China Culture Center (ⓦchinaculturecenter.org).

## Badaling

八达岭, bādálíng • Daily 7am–6pm; museum closed Mon • ¥45, including wall and museum; cable car ¥60/80 one-way/return

The best-known section of the wall is at **Badaling**, 70km northwest of Beijing, which was the first section to be restored (in 1957) and opened up to tourists. Here the wall is 6m wide, with regularly spaced watchtowers dating from the Ming dynasty. It follows the highest contours of a steep range of hills, forming a formidable defence, such that this section was never attacked directly but instead taken by sweeping around from the side after a breach was made in the weaker, low-lying sections.

Badaling may be the easiest part of the wall to get to from Beijing, but it's also the most packaged. At the entrance, a giant tourist circus – a plethora of restaurants and souvenir stalls – greets you. As you ascend to the wall, you pass the cable car's lower terminus and

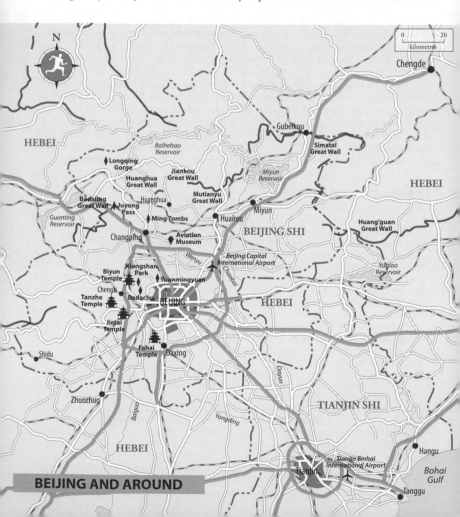

BEIJING AND AROUND

the **Great Wall Museum**. The museum, with plenty of aerial photos, models and construction tools, is worth a browse, though it's more useful visited on the way down.

Once you're up on the wall, flanked by guardrails, it's hard to feel that there's anything genuine about the experience. Indeed, the wall itself is hardly original here, as the "restorers" basically rebuilt it wholesale on the ancient foundations. To get the best out of the experience you need to walk – you'll quickly lose the crowds and, generally, things get better the further you go.

## ARRIVAL AND DEPARTURE                                                        BADALING

If you come with a tour you'll arrive in the early afternoon, when the place is at its busiest, spend an hour or two at the wall, then return, which really gives you little time for anything except the most cursory of jaunts and the purchase of an "I climbed the Great Wall" T-shirt. It's just as easy, and cheaper, to travel under your own steam.

**By bus** The easiest way to get here is on bus #919 from Deshengmen bus station (near Jishuitan subway stop) – there's an ordinary service (2hr; ¥7) and a much quicker a/c luxury bus (1hr; ¥12). Note that private minibuses also call themselves #919 and that you might get scalped on these; the real buses are larger and have "Deshengmen–Badaling" written in the window.

**By train** A nicer ride than the bus is by train from Beijing North station to Badaling (12 daily; 1hr 15min); the station is a 2km walk from the wall entrance. There are five morning services, and the last one back is at 9.30pm.

**By tourist bus** Regular tourist buses to Badaling leave from Qianmen (depart 7–11am; ¥120 return, including wall ticket); some also visit the Ming Tombs (see p.111; ¥180 return, including tickets) on their way around. Returning to Beijing shouldn't be a problem as tourist buses run until about 6pm.

**Tours** As well as CITS (see p.26), all the more expensive Beijing hotels (and a few of the cheaper ones) run tours to Badaling, usually with a trip to the Ming Tombs thrown in. Most such tours hover around the ¥240 mark, including the Ming Tombs and lunch, and will pick up from your hotel.

## ACCOMMODATION

**Commune by the Great Wall** 长城脚下的公社 chángchéng jiǎoxiàde gōngshè 4km east of Badaling ☎010 8118 1888, ⓦwww.commune bythegreatwall.com. For a luxurious break, visit this "lifestyle retreat" by the Shuiguan pass, a particularly precipitous section of the wall. Each of the eleven

striking buildings was designed by a different architect (the complex won an architectural award at the 2002 Venice Biennale) and is run as a small boutique hotel. If you can't afford their rates – it's expensive – you can take a tour of the complex for ¥120, or pop in for lunch (around ¥400). **¥1830**

## Juyong Pass

居庸关, jūyōng guān • Daily 8am–6pm • ¥45

The closest section to Beijing, the wall at **Juyong Pass**, only fifteen minutes' bus ride south of the Badaling section, has been rather over-restored by enthusiastic builders. That said, it's not too popular, and thus not too crowded. Strategically, this was an important stretch, guarding the way to the capital, just 50km away. From the two-storey gate, the wall climbs steeply in both directions, passing through modern copies of the mostly Ming fortifications. The most interesting structure, and one of the few genuinely old ones, is the intricately carved stone base of a long-vanished stupa just beyond here. Access to unreconstructed sections is blocked, but you can walk for about an hour in either direction.

## ARRIVAL AND DEPARTURE                                                     JUYONG PASS

**By bus** You can catch the ordinary (not luxury) bus #919 (2hr; ¥7) from Deshengmen bus station (near Jishuitan subway stop), which stops here on the way to and from Badaling.

**By tourist bus** Tourist buses from Qianmen stop here on their way to Badaling (see above).

## Mutianyu

慕田峪, mùtiányù • Daily 7am–6pm • ¥45 • Cable car ¥80 return; chairlift ¥40 each way

The **Mutianyu Great Wall**, 90km northeast of the city, is the second most popular point on the wall after Badaling, though since it receives relatively few tour buses it's a noticeably quieter place. It's geared towards families, with a cable car, chairlifts and tobogganing facilities. The wall itself passes along a ridge through some lush, undulating hills. Well endowed with guard towers, it was built in 1368 and renovated in 1983.

From the entrance, steep steps lead up to the wall; you can get a cable car up, though it's not far to walk. The stretch of wall you can walk here is about 3km long – barriers in both directions stop you continuing any further.

## ARRIVAL AND INFORMATION                                               MUTIANYU

However you reach Mutianyu, returning by other means shouldn't be a hassle, provided you do so before 6pm: plenty of minibuses wait in the car park to take people back to the city. If you can't find a minibus back to Beijing, get one to the town of **Huairou** (怀柔, huáiróu), from where you can get regular bus #916 back to the capital – the last bus leaves at 6.30pm.

**By bus** Take bus #916 from Dongzhimen to Huairou (1hrs; ¥12); get off at Mingzhu Square, where you can catch a minibus to the wall (¥20 per person).

**Tourist information** ⓦ mutianyugreatwall.net is a good source of up-to-date information.

**Tours** Available from hotels and offices all over Beijing, these tend to cost around ¥280, including a visit to the Ming Tombs (see p.111), lunch and all tickets.

## ACCOMMODATION

**Goose and Duck Ranch** 鹅和鸭农庄 éhéyā nóngzhuāng In Qiaozi, near Huairou ☏ 010 64353778, ⓦ gdclub.net.cn. This chirpy family holiday camp has plenty of outdoor pursuits on offer, including archery, go-karting and horseback riding. Their all-inclusive weekend getaways (around ¥500 per person per day) are popular and convenient – turn up at the bar and they'll look after you from there. You'll have to book three days in advance. Both cabins and bungalows sleep up to four. Cabins **¥300**, bungalows **¥880**

**Mutianyu Great Wall Guesthouse** 慕田峪长城宾馆 mùtiányù chángchéng bīnguǎn Near eastern barrier ☏ 010 69626867. Situated in a reconstructed watchtower 500m before the eastern barrier, this is a good place for a quiet overnight stay, though be aware it has no plumbing. Reservations essential. **¥180**

**Shambhala @ the Great Wall** 新红资避暑山庄 xīnhóngzī bìshǔ shānzhuāng Xiaguandi village, near Huairou, about 2hr north of Beijing ☏ 010 84018886, ⓦ redcapitalclub.com.cn. This former hunting lodge is now an idyllic boutique hotel, set in attractive countryside. Each of the ten traditional courtyard buildings was constructed from local materials, with a mix of Chinese, Tibetan and Manchu themes, and the rooms, each protected by a stone animal, feature Qing-style carved beds. There's also an on-site spa for some serious pampering, and the place is a short walk from the Great Wall. **¥1200**

## Simatai

司马台, sīmǎtái • Daily 8am–4pm • ¥40 • cable car ¥20

Some 110km northeast of the city, **Simatai** has long been famed as the most unspoilt section of the Great Wall around Beijing. With the wall snaking across purple hills that resemble crumpled velvet from afar, and blue mountains in the distance, it fulfils the expectations of most visitors more than the other sections. At the time of writing, though, the whole area was closed for renovation. It is due to reopen in 2014, and will no doubt have been spruced up considerably, so take the information below as provisional.

From the car park, a winding path takes you up to the wall, where most visitors turn right. Most of this section dates back to the Ming dynasty, and sports a few late innovations such as spaces for cannons, and inner walls at right angles to the outer wall to thwart invaders who breached the first defence. Regularly spaced watchtowers allow you to measure your progress uphill along the ridge. If you're not scared of heights you can take the **cable car** to the eighth tower. The walk over the ruins isn't an easy one, and gets increasingly precipitous after about the tenth watchtower. The views are sublime, though. After about the fourteenth tower (two hours on), the wall peters out and the climb becomes quite dangerous, and there's no point going any further.

Turning left when you first reach the wall, you can do the popular hike to Jinshanling in three or four hours (see opposite). Most people, though, do the walk in the other direction, as it's more convenient to finish up in Simatai.

At all the less visited places, each tourist, or group of tourists, will be followed along the wall, for at least an hour, by a villager selling drinks and postcards; if you don't want to be **pestered** make it very clear from the outset that you are not interested in anything they are selling – though after a few kilometres you might find that ¥5 can of Coke very welcome.

## ARRIVAL AND DEPARTURE                                          SIMATAI

The journey out from the capital to Simatai takes about 3hr by private transport. It's easiest to take a tour – you can travel here independently but considering the logistical hassles and expense it's only worth doing if you want to stay for a night or two.

**By bus** To get here under your own steam, take bus #980, #970 or #987 from Dongzhimen to Miyun (¥15), and hunt down a minibus (¥15) to take you the rest of the way; taxis will cost up to ¥100 each way. To get from Simatai back to Beijing, you can either take a taxi back to Miyun, from where the last public bus to Beijing leaves at 4pm, or wait at the Simatai car park for a tourist bus.

**By taxi** A rented taxi will cost about ¥850 return from Beijing, including waiting time.
**Tours** Tours run from the backpacker hotels and hostels for around ¥180, and sometimes offer overnight stays. Most other hotels can arrange transport, too (usually a minibus), though you should expect to pay a little more for these.

## ACCOMMODATION AND EATING

Locals hang around the car park, renting out spare **rooms** in their houses for ¥50–100 (they'll start higher, of course). Facilities will be simple, with only cold water on tap; your host will bring a bucket of hot water to the bathroom for you on request. For **eating**, head to one of the nameless places at the side of the car park, where the owners often whip up some very creditable dishes; if you're lucky, they'll have some locally caught wild game in stock.

## Jinshanling

金山岭长城, jīnshānlǐng chángchéng • Daily 8am–5pm • ¥60

**Jinshanling**, about 135km from Beijing and not far west of Simatai, is one of the least visited and best preserved parts of the wall, with jutting obstacle walls and oval watchtowers, some with octagonal or sloping roofs. Turn left when you hit the wall and it's a three-hour walk to Simatai along an unreconstructed section. You won't meet many other tourists, and will experience something of the wall's magnitude: a long and lonely road that unfailingly picks the toughest line between peaks. Take the hike seriously, as you are scrambling up and down steep, crumbly inclines, and you need to be sure of foot. Watch, too, for loose rocks dislodged by your fellow hikers. When you reach Simatai a toll may be imposed at the suspension bridge. Note that this walk is still possible while Simatai is being renovated – you just can't go any further after the bridge.

Finally, if you head right when you get onto the wall at Jinshanling, you quickly reach an utterly abandoned and overgrown section. After about four hours' walk along here, you'll reach a road that cuts through the wall, and from here you can flag down a passing bus back to Beijing. This route is only recommended for the intrepid.

## ARRIVAL AND DEPARTURE                                       JINSHANLING

**By bus** This is one of those places that's far better reached on a tour. If you really fancy making the trip on public transport, take a bus to Chengde from Liuliqiao or Sihui in Beijing (see p.24); you're usually required to pay for the full ticket to Chengde (¥85). Get off at the Jinshanling intersection, from which minibuses run to the wall for ¥15.
**Tours** Plenty of hostels run tours out here from around ¥180; most drop you off in the morning, then pick you up post-hike at Simatai in the afternoon.

## Huanghua

黄花长城, huánghuā chángchéng • Daily 8am–5pm • ¥25

The section of the wall at **Huanghua**, 60km north of Beijing, is completely unreconstructed. It's a good example of Ming defences, with wide ramparts, intact parapets and beacon towers. If arriving by minibus, you'll be dropped off on a road that cuts through the wall. The section to the left is too hard to climb, but the section on the right, past a little reservoir, shouldn't present too many difficulties for the agile; indeed, the climb gets easier as you go, with the wall levelling off along a ridge.

The wall here is attractively ruined – so watch your step – and its course makes for a pleasant walk through some lovely countryside. Keep walking the wall for about 2km, to the seventh tower, and you'll come to steps that lead south down the wall and onto a stony path. Follow this path down past an ancient barracks to a pumping station, and you'll come to a track that takes you south back to the main road, through a graveyard and orchards. When you hit the road you're about 500m south of where you started. Head north and after 150m you'll come to a bridge where taxis and buses to Huairou congregate.

## ARRIVAL AND DEPARTURE                                    HUANGHUA

**By bus** Take bus #916 from Dongzhimen bus station to Huairou (¥12), and catch a minibus from there (¥10). The last bus from Huairou to Beijing is at 6.30pm.

**Tours** Backpacker hostels occasionally run tours this way, though you'll really have to ask around.

## ACCOMMODATION AND EATING

Locals rent out spare **rooms** in their houses for ¥50–100. Facilities will be simple, with only cold water on tap, but your host will bring a bucket of hot water to the bathroom for you on request. There are a couple of **restaurants** in the village, though nothing to get too excited about.

## Jiankou

箭扣, jiànkòu • Daily 8am–5pm • ¥20

First it was Simatai, then Huanghua; now that these have become entrenched on the tourist trail, the new intrepid destination is **Jiankou**, about 30km north of Huairou. Here you can take tough, jaw-droppingly beautiful hikes along an uncommercialized section of wall, experiencing this winding mountain road in all its ruined glory.

The wall here is white, as it's made of dolomite, and there is a hikeable and very picturesque section, about 20km long, that winds through thickly forested mountains. Whichever part you decide to walk, don't take the trip without a local guide – much of the stonework is loose on the wall, which is a little tricky to find in the first place. You really need to watch your step, and some nerve-wracking sections are so steep that they have to be climbed on all fours.

Only the most determined choose to travel the full 20km hike from west to east; most people do the first 12km or so, or choose to walk the spectacular middle section, which is easier to get to and has no tricky parts (though a guide is still recommended). The far western end of the hike starts at **Nine Eye Tower**, one of the biggest watchtowers on the wall, and named after its nine peepholes. It's a tough 12km from here to the **Beijing Knot**, a watchtower where three walls come together. Around here the views are spectacular, and for the next kilometre or so the hiking is easier, at least until you reach a steep section called "**Eagle Flies Vertically**". Though theoretically you can scale this, then carry on for another 10km to Mutianyu, it is not recommended; the hike gets increasingly dangerous and includes some almost vertical climbs, such as the notorious "sky stairs".

## ARRIVAL AND INFORMATION                                     JIANKOU

It's possible to get to Jiankou and back in a day, if you leave very early, but you'd be better off planning to stay a night at **Xizhazi** village (西栅子, xīzhàzi). From here it takes an hour or so just to reach the wall but without a local to guide you it's easy to get lost.

**By bus** Take bus #916 from Dongzhimen to Huairou (1hr, ¥12), then charter a minibus or taxi to Xizhazi village

(minimum ¥100 one way; 1hr 15min).

## ACCOMMODATION

**Jiankou Zhao's hostel** 赵氏山庄 zhàoshì shān zhuāng Near the car park in Xizhazi village ☎010 8969 6677. Plenty of local farmers rent out rooms, but it's recommended that you call in at this spartan but clean

hostel. Mr Zhao is full of information on the hike, and will either guide you himself or sort out someone else to do it. The home-cooked food, incidentally, is excellent – ask if he has any trout. Rooms from **¥70**, dorms **¥15**

# The Ming Tombs and around

十三陵, shísān líng

After their deaths, all but three of the sixteen Ming-dynasty emperors were entombed in giant underground vaults, the **Shisan Ling** (literally, Thirteen Tombs), usually referred to in English as the **Ming Tombs**. Two of the tombs, Chang Ling and Ding Ling, were restored in the 1950s; the latter was also excavated.

The tombs are located in and around a valley 40km northwest of Beijing. The location, chosen by the third Ming emperor (Yongle) for its landscape of gentle hills and woods, is undeniably one of the loveliest around the capital, the site marked above ground by grand halls and platforms. That said, the fame of the tombs is overstated in relation to the actual interest of their site, and unless you've a strong archeological bent, a trip here isn't worth making for its own sake. The tombs are, however, very much on the tour circuit, being conveniently placed on the way to **Badaling Great Wall** (see p.106). The site also makes a nice place to picnic, especially if you just feel like taking a break from the city. To get the most out of the place, it's better not to stick to the tourist route between the car park and Ding Ling, but to spend a day here and hike around the smaller tombs further into the hills. You'll need a map to do this – you'll find one on the back of some Beijing city maps, or you can buy one at the site (¥2).

On the way to or from the tombs, you may care to stop by at the rather good **Aviation Museum**, a miniature airport's worth of downed planes.

## The Spirit Way

神道, shéndào • Daily 7am–7pm • ¥35

The approach to the Ming Tombs, the 7km **Spirit Way**, is Shisan Ling's most exciting feature, and it's well worth backtracking along from the ticket office. The road commences with the **Dahongmen** (Great Red Gate), a triple-entranced triumphal arch, through the central opening of which only the emperor's dead body was allowed to be carried. Beyond, the road is lined with colossal stone statues of animals and men. Alarmingly larger than life, they all date from the fifteenth century and are among the best surviving examples of Ming sculpture. Their precise significance is unclear, although it is assumed they were intended to serve the emperors in their next lives. The animals depicted include the mythological *qilin* (a reptilian beast with deer's horns and a cow's tail) and the horned, feline *xiechi*; the human figures are stern military mandarins. Animal statuary reappears at the entrances to several of the tombs, though the structures themselves are something of an anticlimax.

## Chang Ling

长陵, cháng líng • Daily 8.30am–5pm • ¥45

At the end of the Spirit Way stands the tomb of Yongle himself: **Chang Ling**, the earliest at the site. There are plans to excavate the underground chamber – an exciting prospect since the tomb is contemporary with some of the finest buildings of the Forbidden City in the capital. At present, the enduring impression above ground is mainly one of scale – vast courtyards and halls, approached by terraced white marble. Its main feature is the

**Hall of Eminent Flowers**, supported by huge columns consisting of individual tree trunks which, it is said, were imported all the way from Yunnan in the south of the country.

## Ding Ling

定陵, dìng líng • Daily 8.30am–5pm • ¥35

The main focus of the Ming Tombs area is **Ding Ling**, the underground tomb-palace of the Emperor Wanli, who ascended the throne in 1573 at the age of 10. Reigning for almost half a century, he began building his tomb when he was 22, in line with common Ming practice, and hosted a grand party within on its completion. The mausoleum, a short distance east of Chang Ling, was opened up in 1956 and found to be substantially intact, revealing the emperor's coffin, flanked by those of two of his empresses, and floors covered with scores of trunks containing imperial robes, gold and silver, and even the imperial cookbooks. Some of the treasures are displayed in the tomb, a huge musty stone vault, undecorated but impressive for its scale; others have been replaced by replicas. It's a cautionary picture of useless wealth accumulation, as the tour guides are bound to point out.

## Aviation Museum

航空博物馆, hángkōng bówùguǎn • Off Shunsha Lu, Daxinshan Village • Tues–Sun 8.30am–5.30pm • ¥50, plus ¥5 for Mao jet • Ⓦ chn-am.com • ¥35 taxi ride from Shahe University Park subway (Changping Line, accessible via Xi'erqi station on line 13), ¥45 taxi ride from Ming Tombs or bus #912 from Andingmen subway stop

Near the Ming Tombs some 60km north of Beijing in the village of Daxinshan, the enormous **Aviation Museum** is a fascinating place containing over three hundred aircraft, displayed in a giant hangar inside a hollow mountain and off a runway-like concourse – it's like being in a small airport. The aircraft on show range from the copy of the Wright brothers' plane flown by Feng Ru, a pioneering Chinese aviator, in 1909, to Gulf War helicopter gunships. As well as plenty of fighter planes, many of which saw action in the Korean War, the bomber that flew in China's first atom bomb test is here, as is **Mao's personal jet** (with his teacup and frilly cushions still inside) and the plane that scattered the ashes of the deceased Zhou Enlai, which is covered with wreaths and tributes. But unless you have a special interest in aircraft, it's the sight of archaic downed machines en masse – like the setting for a J.G. Ballard story – that makes the place memorable.

### ARRIVAL AND DEPARTURE                                    THE MING TOMBS

**By bus** To get to the tombs on ordinary public transport, take bus #872 from Deshengmen (hourly; 1hr; ¥10). You can use this same bus to get from the Spirit Way to the tombs, though you may be waiting a while. Buses drop you at a car park in front of Ding Ling.

**By tourist bus** The easiest way to get to the Ming Tombs is to take a tourist bus that goes to Badaling (see p.106), some of which visit the tombs on the way to and from

Beijing. You can get off here, then rejoin another tourist bus later, either to continue to Badaling or to return to the city.

**By subway** By 2015 the Changping Line, accessible via Xi'erqi station in the far northwest of Beijing on line 13, should have extended out to the tombs.

**Tours** There are few, if any, dedicated tours to the Ming Tombs alone; they're usually included with a visit to Badaling (see p.106).

## Longqing Gorge

龙庆峡, lóngqìng xiá • ¥40 • Tourist bus #8 (mid-April to mid-Oct and during the Ice Festival; 2hr 30min) from the #328 bus terminus near Andingmen subway stop

North from Beijing there are vast swaths of new tree growth – the **Great Green Wall**. Pushing on through the rugged landscape beyond reveals some areas of great natural beauty, most notably **Longqing Gorge**, a local recreation spot at the edge of a reservoir some 90km northwest of the capital. This is known as the place to come for outdoor pursuits such as canoeing, horseriding and rock climbing, all of which can be arranged when you arrive, for ¥60–120. The main attraction, though, is the **Ice Festival** held on the shore of the reservoir (late Jan & Feb, sometimes into March), at which groups of

**FROM TOP** CHANG LING, MING TOMBS (P.111); BISHU SHANZHUANG, CHENGDE (P.119) >

sculptors compete to create the most impressive ice sculpture. The enormous resulting carvings depict cartoon characters, dragons, storks and figures from Chinese popular culture; with coloured lights inside for a gloriously tacky psychedelic effect, they look great at night.

# The Western Hills

西山, xīshān

Like the Summer Palace (see p.95), Beijing's **Western Hills** are somewhere to escape urban life for a while, though they're more of a rugged experience. Thanks to their coolness at the height of summer, the hills have long been favoured as a restful retreat by religious men and intellectuals, as well as politicians in modern times – Mao lived here briefly, and the Politburo assembles here in times of crisis.

The hills are divided into three parks, the nearest to the centre being the **Botanical Gardens**, 6.5km northwest of the Summer Palace. Two kilometres farther west, **Xiangshan** is the largest and most impressive of the parks, but just as pretty is **Badachu**, its eight temples strung out along a hillside 2.5km to the south of Xiangshan. You can explore two of the parks in one day, but each deserves a day to itself. The hills take roughly an hour to reach on public transport. Lastly, some way further west, **Fahai Temple** boasts some fantastic frescoes.

## The Botanical Gardens

植物园, zhíwù yuán • Daily 6am–8pm • ¥10, including conservatory ¥45 • ⓦ www.beijingbg.com

The **Botanical Gardens**, just over 5km west of the Summer Palace as the crow flies, feature over two thousand varieties of trees and plants arranged in formal gardens (and usually labelled in English). They're at their prettiest in summer, though the terrain is flat and the landscaping is not as original as in the older parks. The impressive conservatory has desert and tropical environments and a lot of fleshy foliage from Yunnan.

Behind the Wofo Temple is a bamboo garden, from which paths wind off into the hills; one heads northwest to a pretty cherry valley, just under 1km away, where **Cao Xueqiao** is supposed to have written *Dream of Red Mansions* (see p.185).

### Wofo Temple

卧佛寺, wòfó sì • Daily 8am–4.30pm • ¥5, or free with Botanical Gardens through ticket

The gardens' main path leads after 1km to the **Wofo Si**, whose main hall houses a huge **reclining Buddha**, more than 5m in length and cast in copper. With two giant feet protruding from the end of his painted robe and a pudgy baby-face, calm in repose, he looks rather cute, although he is not actually sleeping but dying – about to enter nirvana. Suitably huge shoes, presented as offerings, are on display around the hall.

| ARRIVAL AND DEPARTURE | THE BOTANICAL GARDENS |
| --- | --- |

**By bus** Bus #331 heads from outside the Yuanmingyuan (see p.99) via the north gate of the Summer Palace, both of which are also on subway line 4. Bus #360 also heads this way from the zoo.

**By taxi** The quickest way here would be to get a cab (¥25)

from Anheqiao North subway (line 4), one stop along from the Summer Palace's Beigongmen station; you're less likely to be ripped off here, though drivers will still need persuading to use the meter.

## Xiangshan Park and around

香山公园, xiāngshān gōngyuán • Daily 7am–6pm • ¥10 • Cable car ¥30 one way, ¥50 return • ⓦ xiangshanpark.com

Two kilometres west of the Botanical Gardens lies **Xiangshan Park**, a range of hills dominated by Xianglu ("Incense Burner") Peak in its western corner. It's at its best in the autumn (before the sharp November frosts), when the leaves turn red in a massive profusion of colour. Though busy at weekends, the park is too large to appear swamped and is always a good place for a hike and a picnic. Take the path up to the peak (1hr) from where, on clear days, there are magnificent views down towards the Summer Palace and as far as distant Beijing. You can hire a horse to take you down again for ¥30, the same price as the **cable car**.

### Zhao Miao

昭庙, zhāo miào • Daily 7am–4pm • Free with park entry

Right next to the north gate of the park is the **Zhao Miao** (Temple of Brilliance), one of the few temples in the area that escaped vandalism by Western troops in 1860 and 1900. It was built by Qianlong in 1780 in a Tibetan style, designed to make visiting Lamas feel at home.

## Biyun Temple

碧云寺, bìyún sì • Daily 8am–5pm • ¥10

Some 400m west of the park's north gate is the superb **Biyun** ("Azure Clouds") **Temple**, a striking building dominated by extraordinary conical stupas. Inside, rather bizarrely, a tomb holds the hat and clothes of **Sun Yatsen** – his body was held here for a while before being moved in 1924. The giant main hall is now a maze of corridors lined with *arhat* statues, five hundred in all, and it's a magical place. The benignly smiling golden figures are all different – some have two heads or sit on animals, one is even pulling his face off – and you may see monks moving among them and bowing to each.

7

---

### ARRIVAL AND DEPARTURE                          XIANGSHAN PARK AND AROUND

**By subway** By the time you read this, the new Western Suburban line should have commenced operations, heading from Bagou (line 10) to the Fragrant Hills station at the end of the line.

**By bus** Bus #331 heads from outside the Yuanmingyuan (see p.99) via the north gate of the Summer Palace, both of which are also on subway line 4. Bus #360 also heads this way from the zoo.

**By taxi** The quickest way here is to get a cab (¥30) from Anheqiao North subway (line 4). You're less likely to be ripped off here, though drivers will still need persuading to use the meter.

---

### ACCOMMODATION

**Fragrant Hills Hotel** 香山饭店 xiāngshān fàndiàn Close to the main entrance to Xiangshan Park ☏ 010 6259 1166, ⊛ xsfd.com. This hotel makes a good base for a weekend escape and some in-depth exploration of the Western Hills. A startlingly incongruous sight, the light, airy hotel looks like something between a temple and an airport lounge. It was designed by I.M. Pei, also responsible for the Pyramid at the Louvre in Paris, and the Bank of China building at Xidan (see p.88). **¥688**

## Badachu

八大处, bādàchù • Daily 8am–5pm • ¥10 • Cable car ¥50, sled ¥40 • Bus #347 from the zoo, or ¥25 by taxi from Pingguoyuan subway (line 1)

A forested hill 10km south of Xiangshan Park, **Badachu** ("Eight Great Sites") derives its name from the presence of eight temples here. Fairly small affairs, lying along the path that curls around the hill, the temples and their surroundings are nonetheless quite attractive, at least on weekdays; don't visit at weekends when the place is swamped.

At the base of the path is a pagoda holding what's said to be one of **Buddha's teeth**, which once sat in the fourth temple, about halfway up the hill. The third temple is a nunnery, and is the most pleasant, with a relaxing teahouse in the courtyard. There's a statue of the rarely depicted, boggle-eyed thunder deity inside the main hall. The other temples make good resting points as you climb up the hill.

Inevitably, there's a **cable car** that you can ride to the top of the hill; you'll see it as you enter the park's main (north) gate. To descend, there's also a metal **sled** that you can use to slide down the hill. You'll whizz to the bottom in a minute.

### Fahai Temple

法海寺, fǎhǎi sì · Daily 9am–5pm · ¥20 · ¥15 by taxi from Pingguoyuan subway (line 1)

Though its exterior is unremarkable, **Fahai Temple**, roughly 25km west of the capital, is worth a visit for its beautiful, richly detailed Buddhist frescoes. The halls where the frescoes are painted are rather dark, so you're issued with a small torch at the entrance, but if you've got a decent one of your own then take it along. The lively, expressive images, painted in the 1440s, depict the pantheon of Buddhist deities travelling for a meeting. Look out for the elegant god of music, Sarasvati, whose swaying form seems appropriately melodic, and the maternal-looking god of children, Haritidem, with her attendant babies. There are plenty of animals, too; as well as the rather dog-like lions, look out for the six-tusked elephant – each tusk represents a quality required for the attainment of enlightenment.

## Tanzhe Temple and Jietai Temple

Due west of Beijing, two splendid temples sit in the wooded country outside the industrial zone that rings the city. Though the **Tanzhe** and **Jietai temples** are relatively little visited by tourists, foreign residents rate them as among the best places to escape the city smoke. Getting there and back can be time-consuming, so take a picnic and take the day to enjoy the clean air, peace and solitude in the wooded hills.

### Tanzhe Temple

潭柘寺, tánzhé sì · Daily 8am–5pm · ¥55 (¥85 combined ticket with Jietai Temple)

About 40km west of Beijing, **Tanzhe Temple** has the most beautiful and serene location of any temple near the city. It's also one of the oldest, having been constructed during the Jin dynasty (265–420 AD), and one of the largest too. The temple is formed from a number of different shrines, all of them accessed by following the labyrinth of alleyways and steps leading up the hillside. The air is crisp and fragrant, punctuated with billows of incense. Although there are no longer any monks living or working at the temple, it once housed a thriving monastic community. These days, a terrace of stupas provides the final resting place for a number of eminent monks.

Wandering through the complex, past said stupas, you reach an enormous central courtyard, with an ancient, towering gingko tree that's over a thousand years old (christened the "King of Trees" by Emperor Qianlong) at its heart. Across the courtyard, a second, smaller gingko, known as "The Emperor's Wife", was once supposed to produce a new branch every time a new emperor was born. From here you can take in the other buildings, arrayed on different levels up the hillside, or look around the lush gardens, whose bamboo is supposed to cure all manner of ailments. Back at the entrance, the spiky *zhe* trees nearby (*Cudrania tricuspidata*, sometimes called the **Chinese mulberry**), after which the temple is named, "reinforce the essence of the kidney and control spontaneous seminal emission". Or so a sign here says.

### Jietai Temple

戒台寺, jiètái sì · Daily 8am–5pm · ¥45 (¥85 combined ticket with Tanzhe Temple)

Sitting on a hillside 12km east of Tanzhe, **Jietai Temple** looks more like a fortress than a temple, surrounded as it is by forbiddingly tall, red walls. First constructed during the Sui dynasty (581–600), it's an extremely atmospheric, quiet place, made slightly spooky by its dramatically shaped pines – eccentric-looking venerable trees growing in odd directions. Indeed one, leaning out at an angle of about thirty degrees, is pushing over a pagoda on the terrace beneath it.

In the main hall is an enormous tenth-century platform of white marble at which novice monks were ordained. At 3m high, it's intricately carved with figures – monks, monsters (beaked and winged) and saints. The chairs on top are for the three masters and seven witnesses who oversaw ordinations. Another, smaller, side hall holds a beautiful wooden altar that swarms with dragon reliefs.

**By public transport** Ride the subway line 1 all the way to its western terminus at Pingguoyuan, then catch bus #931 (¥3; this bus has two routes, so make sure the driver knows where you're going) to Tanzhe Temple; it stops at Jietai too, but this is more easily visited on the return journey. If you don't fancy waiting for a bus, taxis between the two temples will cost around ¥35.

**By taxi** You can save yourself some hassle by hiring a taxi to visit both temples, which should cost around ¥400 if you start from the city centre.

# Shidu

十渡, shídù · Bus #917 from Tianqiaole Theatre (see p.152; 2hr 30min)

The "wilderness area" of **Shidu** ("Ten Bends"), around 90km southwest of the city, is Beijing's equivalent to Guilin; as with southern China's prime tourist trap, the landscape here resembles a classical Chinese painting, with the Juma River twisting between steep karst peaks. As at Longqing Gorge (see p.112), you can go horseriding, boating, fishing and rock climbing – all of which cost ¥150–200, can be organized on your arrival, and are aimed at novices. There's even a bungee jump (¥150). But perhaps it's most rewarding simply as a place to **hike** – pick up a map at the entrance and set off. Though it can get crowded, few visitors seem to get much further than the restaurants that line the only road, so the experience rather improves the further into the resort you go.

**7**

# Chengde

承德, chéngdé

Relatively quiet and small for a Chinese city, unassuming **CHENGDE** boasts a highly colourful history. Though the town itself is bland, on its fringes lie some of the most magnificent examples of imperial architecture in China, remnants from its glory days as the summer retreat of the Manchu emperors. Gorgeous temples punctuate the cabbage fields around town, and a palace-and-park hill complex, **Bishu Shanzhuang**, covers an area nearly as large as the town itself. In recent years Chengde has once more become a summer haven, justly popular with weekending Beijingers escaping the capital.

Bishu Shanzhuang lies in the north of the town, while farther north and to the east, on the other side of the river, stand a series of imposing **temples**. The majority of Chengde's one-million-strong population live in a semi-rural suburban sprawl to the south of the centre, leaving the city itself fairly small-scale – the new high-rises on its traffic-clogged main artery, **Nanyingzi Dajie**, have yet to obscure the view of distant mountains and fields.

### Brief history

Originally called "Rehe", the town was discovered by the Qing-dynasty emperor **Kangxi** at the end of the seventeenth century, while marching his troops to the Mulan hunting range to the north. He was attracted to the cool summer climate and the rugged landscape, and built small lodges here from which he could indulge in a fantasy Manchu lifestyle, hunting and hiking like his northern ancestors. The building programme expanded when it became diplomatically useful to spend time north of Beijing, forging closer links with the troublesome **Mongol tribes**. Chengde was thus a thoroughly pragmatic creation, devised as a means of defending the empire by overawing Mongol princes with splendid audiences, hunting parties and impressive military manoeuvres.

Construction of the first palaces started in 1703. By 1711 there were 36 palaces, temples, monasteries and pagodas set in a great walled park, its ornamental pools and islands dotted with beautiful pavilions and linked by bridges. Craftsmen from all parts of China were invited to work on the project; Kangxi's grandson, **Qianlong** (1736–96), added another 36 imperial buildings during his reign, which was considered to be the heyday of Chengde.

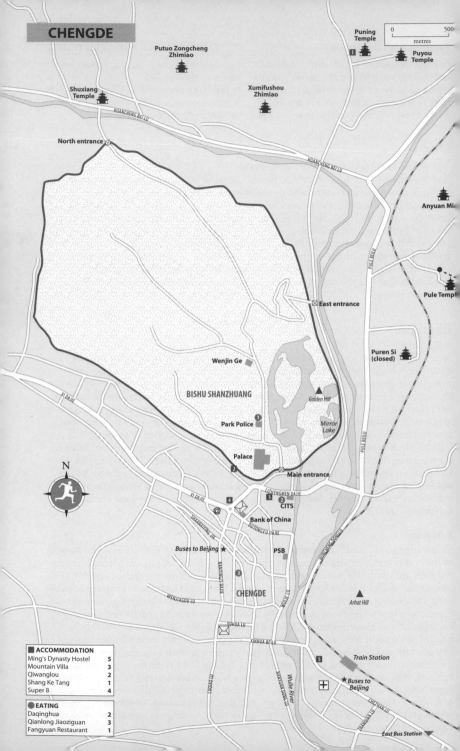

# CHENGDE

Puning Temple

Puyou Temple

Putuo Zongcheng Zhimiao

Shuxiang Temple

Xumifushou Zhimiao

Anyuan Mi

HUANCHENG BEI LU

North entrance

HUANCHENG BEI LU

Pule Temp

PULE BEI LU

East entrance

Pule Temp

Puren Si (closed)

Wenjin Ge

BISHU SHANZHUANG

Golden Hill

Mirror Lake

PULE BEI LU

Park Police

Palace

Main entrance

LIZHENGMEN DAJIE

XI DAJIE

XI DAJIE

SHANGYING JIE

@

Bank of China

CITS

DUTONGFU DAJIE

Buses to Beijing

NANYING DAJIE

PSB

Arhat Hill

WENJIAGOU LU

CHENGDE

LIZHENGMEN DONG LU

YUHUA LU

XINHUA BEILU

Train Station

Buses to Beijing

Wulie River

HAIGUAN DONG LU

CHEZHAN LU

East Bus Station

0     500
metres

N

## THE PANCHEN LAMA IN CHENGDE

In 1786, the **Panchen Lama** was summoned from Tibet by Emperor Qianlong for his birthday celebrations, an adroit political move designed to impress the followers of Lamaist Buddhism. The Buddhists included a number of minority groups who were prominent thorns in the emperor's side, such as Tibetans, Mongols, Torguts, Eleuths, Djungars and Kalmucks. Some accounts (notably not Chinese) tell how Qianlong invited the Panchen Lama to sit with him on the Dragon Throne, which was taken to Chengde for the summer season. He was certainly feted with honours and bestowed with costly gifts and titles, but the greatest impression on him and his followers must have been made by the replicas of the Potala and of his own palace, constructed at Chengde to make him feel at home (see p.122) – a munificent gesture, and one that would not have been lost on the Lamaists. However, the Panchen Lama's visit ended questionably when he succumbed to smallpox, or possibly poison, in Beijing and his coffin was returned to Tibet with a stupendous funeral cortege.

### The British

**7**

The first **British Embassy** to China, under Lord Macartney, visited Qianlong's court in 1793. Having sailed up the river to Beijing in a ship whose sails were painted with characters reading "Tribute bearers from the vassal king of England", they were somewhat disgruntled to diwscover that the emperor had decamped to Chengde for the summer. However, they made the 150km journey there, in impractical European carriages, where they were well received by the emperor, though the visit was hardly a success. Macartney caused an initial stir by refusing to **kowtow**, while Qianlong was disappointed with the gifts the British had brought and, with Manchu power at its height, rebuffed all British trade demands, remarking: "We possess all things. I set no value on objects strange or ingenious, and have no use for your country's manufactures." His letter to the British monarch concluded, magnificently, "O king, Tremblingly Obey and Show No Negligence!"

### Recent times

Chengde gradually lost imperial popularity when it came to be seen as unlucky after emperors Jiaqing and Xianfeng died here in 1820 and 1860 respectively. The buildings were left empty and neglected for most of the twentieth century, but largely escaped the ravages of the Cultural Revolution. Restoration, in the interests of tourism, began in the 1980s and is ongoing.

## Bishu Shanzhuang

避暑山庄, bìshǔ shānzhuāng • Daily 8am–5.30pm • Mid-April to mid-Oct ¥120, mid-Oct to mid-April ¥90 • ☎ 0314 216 1132

Surrounded by a 10km-long wall and larger than the Summer Palace in Beijing, **Bishu Shanzhuang** (also referred to as the Mountain Resort) occupies the northern third of the town's area. This is where, in the summer months, the Qing emperors lived, feasted, hunted, and occasionally dealt with affairs of state. The palace buildings just inside the main entrance are unusual for imperial China as they are low, wooden and unpainted – simple but elegant, in contrast to the opulence and grandeur of Beijing's palaces. It's said that Emperor Kangxi wanted the complex to mimic a Manchurian village, to show his disdain for fame and wealth, though with 120 rooms and several thousand servants he wasn't exactly roughing it.

The principle of idealized naturalness governed the design of the **park**. With its twisting paths and streams, rockeries and hills, it's a fantasy re-creation of the rough northern terrain and southern-Chinese beauty spots that the emperors would have seen on their tours. The whole is an attempt to combine water, buildings and plants in graceful harmony. Lord Macartney noted its similarity to the "soft beauties" of an English manor park of the Romantic style.

Covering the whole park and its buildings takes at least a day, and an early start is recommended. It's at its nicest in the early morning anyway, when a vegetable market sets up just outside the front gate, and old people practise *tai ji* or play Go by the palace. The park is simply too big to get overcrowded, and if you head north beyond the lakes, you're likely to find yourself alone.

### The Palace

The **main gate**, Lizhengmen, is in the south wall, off Lizhengmen Dajie. The **palace quarter**, just inside the complex to the west of the main gate, is built on a slope facing south, and consists of four groups of dark wooden buildings spread over an area of 100,000 square metres. The first, southernmost group, the Front Palace – where the emperors lived and worked – is the most interesting, as many of the rooms have been restored to their full Qing elegance, decked out with graceful furniture and ornaments. Even the everyday objects are impressive: brushes and ink stones on desks, ornate fly whisks on the arms of chairs, little jade trees on shelves. Other rooms house displays of ceramics, books and exotic martial-art weaponry. The Qing emperors were fine calligraphers, and examples of their work appear throughout the palace.

### Front Palace

There are 26 buildings in this group, arranged south to north in nine successive compounds, which correspond to the nine levels of heaven. The main gate leads into the **Outer Wumen**, where high-ranking officials waited for a single peal of a large bell, indicating that the emperor was ready to receive them. Next is the **Inner Wumen**, where the emperor would watch his officers practise their archery. Directly behind, the **Hall of Frugality and Sincerity** is a dark, well-appointed room made of cedarwood, imported at great expense from south of the Yangzi River by Qianlong, who had none of his grandfather Kangxi's scruples about conspicuous consumption. Topped with a curved roof, the hall has nine bays, and patterns on the walls include symbols of longevity and good luck. The **Four Knowledge Study Room** behind was where the emperor worked, changed his clothes and rested. A vertical scroll on the wall outlines the knowledge required of a gentleman: he must be aware of what is small, obvious, soft and strong.

### Rear Palace

The main building in the Rear Palace is the **Hall of Refreshing Mists and Waves**, the living quarters of the imperial family, and beautifully turned out in period style. It was in the west room here that Emperor Xianfeng signed the humiliating Beijing Treaty in the 1850s, giving away more of China's sovereignty and territory after their defeat in the Second Opium War. The **Western Apartments** are where the notorious Cixi, better known as the Dowager Empress (see box, p.96), lived when she was one of Xianfeng's concubines. A door connects the apartments to the hall, and it was through here that she eavesdropped on the dying emperor's last words of advice to his ministers, intelligence she used to force herself into power.

### Outer complexes

The other two complexes are much smaller. The **Pine and Crane Residence**, a group of buildings parallel to the front gate, is a more subdued version of the Front Palace, and was home to the emperor's mother and his concubines. In the **Myriad Valleys of Rustling Pine Trees**, to the north of here, Emperor Kangxi read books and granted audiences, and Qianlong studied as a child. The group of structures southwest of the main palace is the **Ahgesuo**, where male descendants of the royal family studied during Manchurian rule; lessons began at 5am and finished at noon. A boy was expected to speak Manchu at 6, Chinese at 12, be competent with a bow by the age of 14 and marry at 16.

## The lake

Rowing boat rental ¥30–50/hr

The best way to get around the **lake area** of the park – a network of pavilions, bridges, lakes and waterways – is to rent a **rowing boat**. Much of the architecture here is a direct copy of southern Chinese buildings. In the east, the **Golden Hill**, a cluster of buildings grouped on a small island, is notable for a hall and tower modelled after the Golden Hill Monastery in Zhenjiang, Jiangsu Province. The **Island of Midnight and Murmuring Streams**, roughly in the centre of the lake, holds a three-courtyard compound which was used by Kangxi and Qianlong as a retreat, while the compound of halls, towers and pavilions on **Ruyi Island**, the largest, was where Kangxi dealt with affairs of state before the palace was completed.

## Wenjin Ge

Just beyond the lake area, to the west, is the grey-tiled **Wenjin Ge**, or Knowledge Imparting Library, surrounded by rockeries and pools for fire protection. From the outside, the structure appears to have two storeys. In fact there are three – a central section is windowless to protect the books from the sun. Sadly, the building is closed to the public.

## North of the lake

A vast expanse of grassland extends from north of the lake area to the foothills of the mountains, comprising **Wanshun Wan** ("Garden of Ten Thousand Trees") and **Shima Da** ("Horse Testing Ground"). The hilly area in the northwest of the park has a number of rocky valleys, gorges and gullies with a few tastefully placed lodges and pagodas. The deer, which graze on tourist handouts, were reintroduced after being wiped out by imperial hunting expeditions.

## The temples

The **temples** in the foothills of the mountains around Chengde were built in the architectural styles of different ethnic nationalities, so wandering among them is rather like being in a religious theme park. This isn't far from the original intention, as they were constructed by Kangxi and Qianlong less to express religious sentiment than as a way of showing off imperial magnificence, and also to make envoys from anywhere in the empire feel more at home. Though varying in design, all the temples share **Lamaist features** – Qianlong found it politically expedient to promote Tibetan and Mongolian Lamaism as a way of keeping these troublesome minorities in line.

The temples are now in varying states of repair, having been left untended for decades. Originally there were twelve, but the remaining seven that can still be visited stand in two groups: a string of five just beyond the northern border of Bishu Shanzhuang, and two more to the east of the park. If you're short on time the **Puning Si** is a must, if only for the awe-inspiring statue of **Guanyin**, the largest wooden statue in the world.

A good itinerary is to see the northern cluster in the morning, return to town for lunch, and in the afternoon head for the Pule Si and Sledgehammer Rock, a bizarre protuberance that dominates the eastern horizon of the town (see p.123).

## Puning Temple

普宁寺, pǔníng sì • Daily 8am–5.30pm • April–Oct ¥80, Nov–March ¥60 • Bus #6 from centre

**Puning Temple** is the only working temple in Chengde, with shaven-headed Mongolian monks manning the altars and trinket stalls, and though the atmosphere is not especially spiritual – it's usually clamorous with day-trippers, here to see the huge Guanyin statue – the temple and its grounds exude undeniable charm.

Puning Si was built in 1755 to commemorate the Qing victory over Mongolian rebels at Junggar in northwest China, and is based on the oldest Tibetan temple, the

Samye. Like traditional Tibetan buildings, it lies on the slope of a mountain facing south, though the layout of the front is typically Han, with a gate hall, stele pavilions, a bell and a drum tower, a Hall of Heavenly Kings, and the Mahayana Hall.

### Hall of Heavenly Kings and East Hall

In the **Hall of Heavenly Kings**, the statue of a fat, grinning monk holding a bag depicts Qi Ci, a tenth-century character with a jovial disposition, believed to be a reincarnation of the Buddha. In the **East Hall**, the central statue, flanked by *arhat* statues, depicts Ji Gong, a Song-dynasty monk who was nicknamed Crazy Ji for eating meat and being almost always drunk, but who was much respected for his kindness to the poor.

### Mahayana Hall

The rear section of the temple, separated from the front by a wall, comprises 27 Tibetan-style rooms laid out symmetrically, with the **Mahayana Hall** in the centre. Some of the buildings are actually solid (the doors are false), suggesting that the original architects were more concerned with appearances than function. The hall itself is dominated by the 23m-high **wooden statue of Guanyin**, the Goddess of Mercy. She has 42 arms with an eye in the centre of each palm, and three eyes on her face, which symbolize her ability to see into the past, present and future. The hall has two raised entrances, and it's worth looking at the statue from these upper viewpoints as they reveal new details, such as the eye sunk in her belly button, and the little Buddha sitting on top of her head.

### Xumifushou Zhimiao

须弥福寿之庙, xūmífúshòu zhīmiào • Daily 8am–5.30pm • April–Oct ¥80, Nov–March ¥60 (joint ticket with Putuozongcheng Miao) • Bus #118 from Lizhengmen Dajie

The **Xumifushouzhi Temple**, just southwest of Puning Si, was built in 1780 in Mongolian style for the sixth Panchen Lama when he came to Beijing to pay his respects to the emperor. Though he was lavishly looked after, he went home in a coffin, dead from either smallpox or poison (see box, p.119). The temple centrepiece is the **Hall of Loftiness and Solemnity**, its finest features the eight sinuous gold dragons sitting on the roof, each weighing over a thousand kilograms.

### Putuozongcheng Miao

普陀宗乘之庙, pǔtuózōngchéng zhīmiào • Daily 8am–5.30pm • April–Oct ¥80, Nov–March ¥60 (joint ticket with Xumifushou Zhimao) • Bus #118 from Lizhengmen Dajie

Next door to the Xumifushou Zhimao, the magnificent **Putuozongcheng Miao** ("Temple of Potaraka Doctrine") was built in 1771 and is based on the Potala Palace in Lhasa. Covering 220,000 square metres, it's the largest temple in Chengde, with sixty groups of halls, pagodas and terraces. The grand terrace forms a Tibetan-style facade screening a Chinese-style interior, although many of the windows on the terrace are fake, and some of the whitewashed buildings around the base are merely filled-in shapes.

---

#### CATCHING THE GHOST

On the thirteenth day of the first lunar month (January or February), monks at Puning Si's Mahayana Hall observe the ritual of **catching the ghost**, during which a ghost made of dough is placed on an iron rack while monks dressed in white dance around it, then divide it into pieces and burn it. The ritual is thought to be in honour of a ninth-century Tibetan Buddhist, Lhalung Oaldor, who assassinated a king who had ordered the destruction of Tibetan Buddhist temples, books and priests. The wily monk entered the palace on a white horse painted black, dressed in a white coat with a black lining. After killing the king, he washed the horse and turned the coat inside out, thus evading capture from the guards who did not recognize him.

Inside, the **West Hall** is notable for holding a rather comical copper statue of the Propitious Heavenly Mother, a fearsome woman wearing a necklace of skulls and riding side-saddle on a mule. According to legend, she vowed to defeat the evil demon Raksaka, so she first lulled him into a false sense of security – by marrying him and bearing him two sons – then swallowed the moon and in the darkness crept up on him and turned him into a mule. The two dancing figures at her feet are her sons; their ugly features betray their paternity. The **Hall of All Laws Falling into One**, at the back, is worth a visit for the quality of the decorative religious furniture on show. Other halls hold displays of Chinese pottery and ceramics and Tibetan religious artefacts, an exhibition slanted to portray the gorier side of Tibetan religion and including a drum made from two children's skulls. The roof of the temple has a good view over the surrounding countryside.

### Pule Si

普乐寺, pǔlè sì • Daily 8.30am–4.30pm • ¥50 (joint ticket with Anyuan Miao) • Bus #10 from Lizhengmen Dajie

Due northeast of Bishu Shanzhuang, the **Pule Si** ("Temple of Universal Happiness") was built in 1766 by Qianlong as a place for Mongol envoys to worship, and its style is an odd mix of Han and Lamaist elements. The Lamaist back section, a triple-tiered terrace and hall with a flamboyantly conical roof and lively, curved surfaces, steals the show from the more sober, squarer Han architecture at the front. The ceiling of the back hall is a wood-and-gold confection to rival the Temple of Heaven in Beijing. Glowing at its centre is a mandala of Samvara, a Tantric deity, in the form of a cross. The altar beneath holds a Buddha of Happiness, a life-size copper image of sexual congress; more cosmic sex is depicted in two beautiful mandalas hanging outside. Outside the temple, the view from the car park is spectacular, and just north is the path that leads to Sledgehammer Rock and the cable car.

### Anyuan Miao

安远庙, ānyuān miào • Daily 8.30am–4.30pm • ¥50 (joint ticket with Pule Si) • Bus #10 from Lizhengmen Dajie

**Anyuan Miao** ("Temple of Appeasing the Borders") lies within walking distance to the north of the Pule Si, and is decidedly less appealing. It was built in 1764 for a group of Mongolian soldiers who were moved to Chengde by Qianlong, and has a delightful setting on the tree-lined east bank of the Wulie River.

### Sledgehammer Rock

棒钟山, bàngzhōng shān • ¥50 • 2km walk from the Pule Si, or cable car (¥50 return) • Bus #10 from Lizhengmen Dajie

Of the scenic areas around Chengde, the one that inspires the most curiosity is **Sledgehammer Rock**. Thinner at the base than at the top, the towering column of rock is more than 20m high, and skirted by stalls selling little models and Sledgehammer Rock T-shirts. According to legend, the rock is a huge dragon's needle put there to plug a hole in the peak, which was letting the sea through. The rock's obviously phallic nature is tactfully not mentioned in tourist literature, but is acknowledged in local folklore – should the rock fall, it is said, it will have a disastrous effect on the virility of local men.

On the south side of the rock, at the base of a cliff, is **Frog Crag** (蛤蟆石, hámá shí), a stone that vaguely resembles a sitting frog – the 2km walk here is pleasant, if the frog itself disappoints.

## ARRIVAL AND DEPARTURE

### CHENGDE

**By train** Chengde can be accessed from Beijing's main and North stations (8 daily; 5hr 30min–9hr), though unlike elsewhere in northeast China, it's faster to arrive by bus. The train station sits to the south of town; from Beijing you'll chug through rolling countryside, with a couple of Great Wall vistas on the way. Heading back, tickets are easy to buy at the station, though there's a helpfully located ticket office just east of the *Mountain Villa* hotel.

**By bus** Travelling from Beijing to Chengde by bus (3–5hr), you'll pitch up in one of several locations. There's a station of sorts immediately in front of the train station, though more and more services are using the East station, which lies 7km to the south (bus #118 to Bishu Shanzhuang, or ¥20 by taxi). From Beijing, the two best departure points are the Liuliqiao and Sihui bus stations. Heading back to

Beijing you'll find buses in front of the train station. In addition, sleeper-style services (which are, oddly, a little cheaper than the regular buses) leave at 9.30pm from Nanyingzi Dajie, stopping at the train station (10pm) on the way.

## GETTING AROUND

Getting around Chengde can be slow going – public transport is crowded and at peak hours during the summer the main streets are so congested that it's quicker to walk. The town itself is just about small enough to cover on foot. It's easy to walk between the two westernmost temples, and even on to Puning Si, though this last section is busy, tedious and best navigated by taxi.

**By bus** Local buses are infrequent and always crammed. Buses #5 and #11 go from the train station to Bishu

Shanzhuang; bus #6 skirts Bishu Shanzhuang on its way to the Puning Si; bus #118 heads from town to the northern temples; and bus #10 goes from the centre to Pule Si, Anyuan Miao and Sledgehammer Rock.

**By minibus** Hotels will be able to help with chartering a minibus for around ¥300 a day (bargain hard).

**By taxi** Taxis are easy to find, but the drivers are often unwilling to use their meters – flagfall is ¥5, and a ride around town shouldn't cost more than ¥10.

## ACCOMMODATION

There are plenty of hotels in Chengde town itself, plus a couple of expensive places on the fringes of Bishu Shanzhuang. Unfortunately, strict enforcement of local government rules means foreigners are barred from cheaper accommodation. If you're really slumming it, try the side-alleys opposite the *Super 8*. On the plus side, rates at approved hotels are highly negotiable and off-peak discounts of up to two-thirds are available.

★ **Ming's Dynasty Hostel** 明朝国际城市青年酒店 míngcháo guójì chéngshì qīngnián jiǔdiàn Chezhan Lu ☎0314 761 0360, ⓦmingsdynastyhostel .com. Just a few minutes on foot from the train station, this is a great addition to the town, especially for budget travellers. Rooms are simple but kept nice and clean, and staff here are more informative than those at Chengde's most expensive hotels. Dorms ¥100, twins ¥330

**Mountain Villa** 山庄宾馆 shānzhuāng bīnguǎn 127 Xiaonanmen (entrance on Lizhengmen Dajie) ☎0314 202 5588. This grand, well-located complex has huge rooms, high ceilings and a cavernous lobby, and is extremely popular with tour groups. The large rooms in the main building are nicer but a little more expensive than those in the ugly building round the back, and there are some very cheap rooms in the basement. Service can be patchy. ¥550

**Qiwanglou** 倚望楼宾馆 yǐwànglóu bīnguǎn Near Bishu Shanzhuang ☎0314 218 2288, ⓦqiwanglou .com. A well-run (though hugely expensive) hotel in an

imitation Qing-style building around the corner and uphill from the main entrance to Bishu Shanzhuang. Its flower-filled grounds make for an interesting walk even if you're not staying here. Service is excellent, and the staff are among the few people in Chengde who speak some English. ¥1680

★ **Shang Ke Tang** 上客堂宾馆 shàng kè táng bīnguǎn Puning Si ☎0314 205 8888. This interesting hotel's staff wear period clothing and braided wigs befitting the adjoining Puning Temple, and glide along the dim bowels of the complex to lead you to appealingly rustic rooms. You're a little away from the action here, though this is not necessarily a negative, and there are a few cheap restaurants in the area. ¥550

**Super 8** 速八酒店 sùbā jiǔdiàn 2 Lizhengmen Dajie ☎0314 202 8887, ⓦsuper8.com.cn. One of the cheaper places foreigners are allowed to stay in, this is a cheery, well-located place with rooms overlooking the main roundabout. Staff speak no English, but are eager to please. ¥318

## EATING AND DRINKING

Chengde is, unfortunately, not a great place to eat. There are plenty of **restaurants** catering to tourists on Lizhengmen Dajie around the main entrance to Bishu Shanzhuang; on summer evenings, rickety tables are put on the pavement outside, and plenty of diners stay on drinking well into the evening. The best place for a **drink** is busy Shaanxiying Jie, a streamside street stretching west of Nanyingzi Dajie. There are a few quieter places across the road to the east.

**Daqinghua** 大清花 dàqīnghuā 21 Lizhengmen Dajie ☎0314 208 2222. Pine-walled dumpling restaurant that's the best option in the area around the Bishu Shanzhuang entrance. Their dumplings (¥12–20) are great and come

with a variety of fillings, though there's a full menu of tasty Chinese staples to choose from. Daily 11.30am–8.50pm.

**Fangyuan Restaurant** 芳园居 fāngyuánjū. Inside Bishu Shanzhuang ☎0314 216 1132. This snazzy restaurant serves imperial cuisine, including such exotica as "Pingquan Frozen Rabbit". Prices are pretty high, though, and you won't get much change from ¥150 per person, even without drinks. Daily 11am–5pm.

★ **Qianlong Jiaoziguan** 乾隆饺子馆 qiánlóng jiǎoziguǎn. Just off Centre Square ☎0314 207 6377. The best *jiaozi* in town, and far more besides, are served at this restaurant just off a park in the heart of the shopping district. The menu is full of Chinese staples with a few more interesting items such as sauerkraut with lung, braised bullfrog in soy, and battered venison. The more interesting mains clock in at ¥60–100, though penny-pinchers will appreciate the spicy Sichuan noodles (¥8). Daily 11.30am–8.50pm.

7

# Accommodation

Beijing hotels were once largely impersonal concerns, with standardized, rather nondescript modern interiors – a by-product of the early communist years. However, a glut of newer accommodation options has placed more emphasis on design and character, and the established hotels are sprucing themselves up; whatever your budget, it's now possible to stay somewhere that's memorable as well as functional. Beijing now boasts five-star hotels as glitzy as you'd find in any major city, an ever-increasing array of boutique-style mid-rangers and some great cheapies. Most notable, however, is the impressively large number of traditional-as-it-gets courtyard options, set in Beijing's famed *hutongs*; not only are these tremendously atmospheric but you don't have to spend too much for the experience, since many of the city's youth hostels are this way inclined.

## ESSENTIALS

### HOTELS

**Upmarket** The capital's upmarket hotels (from ¥900 per night for a double room in high season) are legion, and more are appearing all the time. They offer amenities such as gyms, saunas, and business centres; annoyingly, while cheap hotels have free internet, you have to pay for it at pricey ones. These establishments are comparable to their counterparts elsewhere in the world, though the finer nuances of service might well be lacking. If nothing else, they make useful landmarks, and some have pretty good restaurants that are, by Western standards at least, inexpensive.

**Mid-range** Mid-range hotels (¥400–900) are well equipped and comfortable, offering spacious double rooms, but are generally anonymous and unstylish – except for a few small hotels converted from old courtyard houses, which have an ambience that is recognizably Chinese, with quiet courtyards and period furniture (see box, p.129). Breakfast apart, it's recommended to eat out rather than in the hotel restaurant: hotel food is pretty mediocre at this level.

**Budget** Budget hotels (up to ¥400) boast little in the way of facilities; you can expect your room to be clean, but it might be poky. There is, however, a lot of choice in this price range, thanks to Chinese chains such as *Home Inn* (ⓦ homeinns.com), *Motel 168* (ⓦ www.motel168.com) and *Jinjiang Inn* (ⓦ jinjianginns.com).

### HOSTELS

If you want a bit of atmosphere, however, go for a hostel instead. Beijing's hostels (¥50–100 for a dorm bed, en-suite doubles for less than ¥250) are clean and professionally run. You can expect them to feature a lounge with a TV and a few DVDs, self-service laundry (¥15 or so) and bike rental (around ¥20/day). They have to be given credit for offering free wi-fi and internet access, something the larger hotels charge for.

Don't be put off if you don't fit the backpacker demographic; there are a few slightly pricier options in which you won't hear Bob Marley or see tables filled with empty Qingdao bottles. All hostels also have inexpensive double and some single rooms, though sometimes with shared bathrooms (from ¥250 or so). An added bonus is that they are actually rather better located than most of the larger mid-range hotels, in quiet neighbourhood *hutongs* not too far from the subway. Note that any place billing itself a "youth hostel" will give you a ¥10 per night discount if you have a youth-hostel (ISIC) card, which they can sell you for ¥50.

### COSTS AND BOOKING

**Room rates** Unless otherwise stated, the prices we quote represent the cost of the cheapest double room in high season (April–Sept). Almost all hotels, certainly all the more upmarket establishments, have high- and low-season rates; some upper-bracket places offer off-season discounts of up to 70 percent. At all but the cheapest hotels, it's possible to bargain the price down; otherwise, you'll find discounted rates on the internet (see below). Bear in mind too that most places have a range of rooms, and staff will usually offer you the more expensive ones – it's always worth asking if they have anything cheaper. Most hotels have a few single rooms, priced slightly cheaper than doubles.

**Reservations and booking websites** It should be fairly straightforward to reserve a room by phone – at higher-end hotels and all hostels someone on reception will speak English, though at mid-range places you might be less lucky. You can also reserve rooms from counters at the airport, and they will usually offer a small discount – though you'll get a much better deal if you book the same room yourself. Online reservations are simple, and often give access to sizeable discounts; ⓦ elong.com is the prime

**8**

---

### WHICH AREA?

**Central Beijing** – anywhere within or just off the Second Ring Road – has plenty of luxury and a few mid-range hotels, while some budget options have also sprung up, including a number of good youth hostels. In addition, Beijing being the size it is, proximity to a subway stop is an enormous advantage – accommodation within the Second Ring Road will almost always be within walking distance of a station. The glitzy, expensive hotels are generally in the **east** of the city; a cosmopolitan area with lively restaurants and nightlife, this is the place to stay if you are looking for international-standard style and comfort. Such places are clustered around shop-heavy **Wangfujing**, bar- and restaurant-heavy **Sanlitun**, and businesslike **Jianguomen Dajie**.

The **north** of the city, south of the Second Ring Road, has some charmingly ramshackle (and newly fashionable) areas, particularly around Nanluogu Xiang and the Drum Tower. Head for this area if you want to stay in traditional Beijing; it's also the best area for budget and mid-range places.

The **west** and **south** of the city are, on the whole, less interesting – though there are plenty of accommodation options here, few are included below for this reason. Lastly, a few **country retreats** are reviewed in the "Around Beijing" chapter (see p.104), while it's also possible to stay in pretty Chengde city, a few hours away (see p.117).

local site, while non-Chinese sites such as ⓦ trivago.com also have plenty of choice. For cheaper options, check out ⓦ hostelworld.com and ⓦ hostelbookers.com, both of which require a small deposit.

**Checking in** Checking in involves filling in a form and paying a deposit; keep your receipt to ensure that you get this back when checking out. Remember to grab a few hotel business cards when you check in – vital for letting taxi drivers know where you're staying.

## FACILITIES

**Breakfast** Breakfast is usually included in the rate in mid- and upper-range hotels, where a choice of Western and

Chinese food is available. It is generally not included at hostels; exceptions have been noted in our reviews.

**Tour offices** All hotels and hostels have tour offices offering trips to the obvious sights: the Great Wall, acrobatics and Beijing opera shows. These are usually good value – show tickets generally cost no more than you'd pay at the door but give you free transport there, while the Great Wall and other out-of-town tours are by far the easiest way to reach said sights. Both hotels and hostels will also book train and plane tickets for you, for a small commission (¥30–50, usually slightly cheaper at hostels); for train tickets, you'll pay less if you go to a dedicated train ticket office (see p.24).

## HOTELS

### THE FORBIDDEN CITY AND TIAN'ANMEN SQUARE

**The Emperor** 皇家驿栈酒店 huángjiā yìzhàn jiǔdiàn 33 Qihelou Jie ☎ 010 65265566, ⓦ theemperor .com.cn; Tian'anmen East (line 1) or Dongsi subway (lines 5 & 6); map p.42. Boutique hotel that's, almost literally, a stone's throw from the Forbidden City, on a street that becomes wonderfully quiet when the tourists have toddled off to bed. The beds here are highly comfortable, set in quirkily designed rooms; like the common areas, there's a certain curvy space-age theme going on. They've also a great rooftop bar (see p.145). **¥980**

★ **Kapok** 木棉花酒店 mùmiánhuā jiǔdiàn 16 Donghuamen Dajie ☎ 010 65259988, ⓦ kapokhotel beijing.com; Tian'anmen East or Wangfujing subway (both line 1); map p.42. Swish boutique hotel a 10min walk from the Forbidden City, with clean lines, glass walls and a bamboo theme giving it a distinctive, modish look. There aren't too many luxury extras, but overall it's clean, chic and not too pricey, which makes it very popular – you'll have to book. **¥700**

### NORTH OF THE CENTRE

**Bamboo Garden** 竹园宾馆 zhúyuán bīnguǎn 24 Xiaoshiqiao Hutong, Jiugulou Dajie ☎ 010 58520088, ⓦ bbgh.com.cn; Guloudajie subway (lines 2 & 8); map pp.56–57. Old but not too musty thanks to a recent refurbishment, this hotel was converted from the residence of a Qing official, and today the courtyards and bamboo-filled gardens are by far its best features. The more expensive suites boast period furniture, but the standard rooms are fine and pretty good value, with garden views. It's tucked into an alley in an agreeable part of the city, near Houhai but still quiet. **¥680**

★ **Courtyard 7** 秦唐府客栈七号院 qíntángfǔ kèzhàn qīhàoyuàn 7 Qiangulouyuan Hutong ☎ 010 64060777, ⓦ courtyard7.com; Nanluoguxiang subway (line 6); map pp.56–57. Rooms in this courtyard hotel off Nanluogu Xiang might be on the small side, but it more

than makes up for it with a peaceful ambience and good location. It's single storey so all the rooms face the courtyard, and elegantly furnished throughout, with four-poster beds and colourful tiled bathrooms. Ask about discounts from the rack rate. **¥1200**

**Guxiang 20** 古巷20号商务会 gǔxiàng èrshí hào shāngwùhuì 20 Nanluogu Xiang ☎ 010 64005566, ⓦ bjgx20.com; Nanluoguxiang subway (line 6); map pp.56–57. Slick hotel well located right in the nightlife area of Nanluogu Xiang. It's done out in that discreet, orientalist style perennially popular in restaurants – dark, red and minimal. The best doubles have four-poster beds and there's a tennis court on the roof too. It seems aimed at young locals, and not much English is spoken. Doesn't maintain much presence on the street, bar the *Starbucks* in the foyer. **¥580**

★ **The Orchid** 65 Baochao Hutong ☎ 010 84044818, ⓦ theorchidbeijing.com; Nanluoguxiang subway (line 6); map pp.56–57. Located on newly trendy Baochao Hutong, this new boutique hotel is up there with the best value places to stay in the whole city. Its rooms, arranged around a delightful, bamboo-filled courtyard, are simply decorated but absolutely delightful, as is the breakfast on offer. The rooftop area offers superlative sunset views, and staff will encourage you to drink one of their delicious house cocktails up there. **¥700**

### EAST OF THE CENTRE
#### WANGFUJING

**Beijing** 北京饭店 běijīng fàndiàn 33 Dongchang'an Jie ☎ 010 65137766, ⓦ chinabeijinghotel.com.cn; Wangfujing subway (line 1); map pp.66–67. One of the most recognizable buildings in Beijing, this mansion block just east of Tian'anmen Square was built in 1900. The view over the Forbidden City from the top floors of the west wing is superb (after the addition of a new wing in 1974, an office block had to be constructed nearby so that top-floor guests couldn't see into Zhongnanhai). Unfortunately, the hotel rested on its laurels for decades, though recent

## COURTYARD HOTELS

Beijing has many small **courtyard hotels** in all budgets. Reminiscent of B&Bs, these intimate back-alley guesthouses are atmospheric and distinctively Chinese, with the central courtyard becoming a venue for guests to mingle. They're often surprisingly well located too, with the greatest concentration north of the centre. On the downside, the alleyways they are found on are often inaccessible to taxis, and can be a bit earthy. In addition, because of the age of the buildings, places at the lower end of the scale can be a little rough around the edges: rooms are sometimes a bit dark, and in winter you'll have to leave the heater on high. Basically, go courtyard if you want atmosphere and local colour, but be aware that facilities and comfort may not be comparable to a modern hotel at the same price. Here are our favourite courtyard hotels and hostels:

**Chinese Box Courtyard Hostel**
See p.132
**Cote Cour** See below
**Courtyard 7** See opposite
**Double Happiness Courtyard Hotel**
See below

**Fly By Knight Courtyard Hostel**
See p.131
**Kelly's Courtyard** See p.130
**Leo Hostel** See p.132
**The Orchid** See opposite

renovations to rooms and common areas have seen it catch up with the competition. **¥880**

**Cote Cour** 演东酒店 yǎndōng jiǔdiàn 70 Yanyue Hutong ☎010 65237981, ⓦhotelcotecourbj.com; Dongsi (lines 5 & 6) or Dengshikou subway (line 5); map pp.66–67. This fourteen-room courtyard-style boutique hotel is bang in the middle of the city but located in a quiet *hutong*. Skilfully decorated with oriental chic (though oddly it doesn't have the Chinese name you'd expect), it's a place to consider if style and character are more important to you than lavish facilities. There's no restaurant, but a free breakfast is served in the lounge. If you are coming by taxi, note that some drivers won't go down the alley, so you'll have to walk for 5min after being dropped off – best to call the hotel before you arrive and they'll arrange a taxi to pick you up. **¥1068**

**Crowne Plaza** 国际艺苑皇冠饭店 guójì yìyuàn huángguān fàndiàn 48 Wangfujing Dajie ☎010 65133388, ⓦcrowneplaza.com; Dengshikou subway (line 5); map pp.66–67. Well-established five-star chain hotel with arty pretensions (there's an on-site gallery) and a handy location for the shops and sights. The best of a number of pricey hotels in the area. **¥1280**

**Double Happiness Courtyard Hotel** 阅微庄四合院宾馆 yuèwēizhuāng sìhéyuàn bīnguǎn 37 Dongsi Sitiao ☎010 64007762, ⓦhotel37.com; Dongsi subway (lines 5 & 6); map pp.66–67. A courtyard hotel boasting larger rooms than most, with wooden floors and the usual traditional Chinese carved and lacquered decor. The courtyards are attractive, with red lanterns and plenty of foliage that provides the perfect environment for their weekly performances of traditional music. It's central, but 200m down a narrow alley that most taxis won't drive down – still, the subway station is only a couple of minutes' walk away. **¥550**

**Grand Hotel Beijing** 北京贵宾楼饭店 běijīng guìbīnlóu fàndiàn 35 Dongchang'an Jie ☎010

65137788, ⓦgrandhotelbeijing.com; Wangfujing subway (line 1); map pp.66–67. A central, if ageing, five-star palace with splendid views over the Forbidden City. Rooms feature period rosewood furniture, and there's plenty of elegant calligraphy around; facilities include a pool and gym. Service standards are high, making this a better bet than the *Beijing* next door. **¥950**

★ **Hilton Wangfujing** 王府井希尔顿酒店 wángfǔjǐng xī'ěrdùn jiǔdiàn 8 Wangfujing Dong Dajie ☎010 58128888, ⓦhilton.com.cn/BJSWFHI; Dengshikou subway (line 5); map pp.66–67. Newly refitted, luxurious and upscale, the *Hilton* is a safe international choice and there are some good discounts available. It's near the shopping district of Wangfujing, and some decent restaurants, and you can see the Forbidden City from the upper floors. Good on detail – there's judicious use of incense, rooms have iPod docks, and there's an impressive gym and pool. **¥2200**

**Peninsula Palace** 王府饭店 wángfǔ fàndiàn 8 Jinyu Hutong ☎010 85162888, ⓦpeninsula.com; Dengshikou subway (line 5); map pp.66–67. A discreet, upmarket place with a very good reputation, one up to the standard of its sister establishment in Hong Kong. It's well located, within walking distance of the Forbidden City, and rooms are decked out in pleasing earth tones. Nice touches include a nonsmoking floor, and fresh fruit left in the room daily. **¥1800**

### SANLITUN

★ **Hotel G** 极栈酒店 jízhàn jiǔdiàn A7 Gongren Tiyuchang Xilu ☎010 65523600, ⓦhotel-G.com; Dongsishitiao (line 2) or Chaoyangmen subway (lines 2 & 6); map pp.66–67. This slick, modern boutique hotel has a great gimmick – at night every window is lit up a different colour. If that seems a bit nightclubby, the

**8**

impression is only reinforced by the sharp lines and subdued lighting in the lobby; rooms though, are cosy, with big, soft beds, and service standards are very high. Aimed at a hip young crowd who like to party in nearby Sanlitun. Look at their site for special offers. **¥1100**

**Ibis** 宜必思酒店 yíbìsī jiǔdiàn 30 Nansanlitun Lu ☎010 65088100, ⒲accorhotels.com; Dongdaqiao (line 6) or Hujialou subway (lines 6 & 10); map pp.66–67. One of the only reliable cheap options in this expensive part of town. Rooms are surprisingly large and attractive for the price, and the bars and restaurants of Sanlitun are only 10min up the road. **¥420**

★**Opposite House** 瑜舍 yúshè 11 Sanlitun Lu ☎010 64176688, ⒲theoppositehouse.com; Tuanjiehu subway (line 10); map p.72. This trendy hotel is filled with modern Chinese art; if you think that you've walked into a gallery you'd be half right, since they've connections with UCCA in the 798 Art District (see p.103). Rooms offer minimalist chic with no stinting on comfort; bathrooms have oakwood tubs and waterfall showers. It's just around the corner from Sanlitun, so there's no shortage of restaurants and nightlife in the area. There's no sign on the outside – look for the green building next to the 3.3 mall. **¥2560**

**Yoyo** 优优客酒店 yōuyōu kèjiǔdiàn 10 Sanlitun Zhongjie ☎010 64173388, ⒲yoyohotel.cn; Tuanjiehu subway (line 10); map p.72. A little boutique-style hotel whose sleek, honey-coloured rooms are surprisingly attractive – they may be miniscule, but considering the location you won't do any better for the price. Do note that in some rooms the showering facilities are visible from the beds – check before you pay if this isn't your thing. It's located just a hop, skip and jump from Sanlitun on a quiet alley, due east of the 3.3 mall. **¥320**

### JIANGUOMEN DAJIE AND AROUND

**Jianguo** 建国饭店 jiànguó fàndiàn 5 Jianguomenwai Dajie ☎010 65002233, ⒲hoteljianguo .com; Yong'anli subway (line 1); map pp.66–67. Popular, thanks to its convenient (if hardly atmospheric) location

just down the road from the Silk Market (see p.160), this old stalwart has rooms of varying quality – ask to stay on the newly renovated executive floor or on a lower floor with a view of the garden. The restaurant, *Justine's*, has pretty good French food, and there are plenty of other drinking and dining options outside. Many walk-in rates only include breakfast for one; book online for the best deals. **¥1235**

★**Park Hyatt** 柏悦酒店 bóyuè jiǔdiàn 2 Jianguomenwai Dajie ☎010 85671234, ⒲beijing .park.hyatt.com; Guomao subway (lines 1 & 10); map pp.66–67. One of the most architecturally masterful hotels in the city, set on the 37th to 60th floors of an almost toy-like block that's illuminated rather beautifully at night. Rooms here offer all the pared-down luxury you'd expect of the chain, and there are stupendous views from all sides. There's a great bar and restaurant up top, an excellent gym (see p.164) and *Xiu* bar (see p.147) down below. **¥3600**

**St Regis** 国际俱乐部饭店 guójìjùlèbù fàndiàn 21 Jianguomenwai Dajie ☎010 64606668, ⒲starwood hotels.com; Jianguomen subway (lines 1 & 2); map pp.66–67. Up there with the plushest hotels in the city, this is the first choice of visiting dignitaries and celebs, from George Bush to Quentin Tarantino. It features real palm trees in the lobby, and there's butler service available for all guests. **¥2500**

### WEST OF THE CENTRE

**Kelly's Courtyard** 凯丽家 kǎilí jiā 25 Xiaoyuan Hutong, off Xidan Beidajie ☎010 66118515, ⒲kellys courtyard.com; Lingjing Hutong (line 4); map pp.86–87. A bit far away from things, though that's precisely why most guests are here – the tiny *hutong* it's on couldn't be any more old-style Beijing. The guesthouse itself is comfortable, with charmingly decorated rooms, though you get the sense that if you dropped a pin in your room, all of the other guests would know about it. **¥388**

**Templeside Deluxe House** 广济邻青年旅舍 guǎngjìlín qīngnián lǚshè 2 Baita Xiang, off Zhaodengyu Jie ☎010 66172571, ⒲templeside.com;

---

### BEIJING'S BEST

**Best for people-watching** Peking Youth Hostel (see opposite)
**Best for free kung fu lessons** Fly By Knight Courtyard Hostel (see opposite)
**Best for partying** Leo Hostel (see p.132)
**Best for sunset cocktails** The Orchid (see p.128)
**Best for night-time walks to the Forbidden City** Kapok (see p.128)
**Best for trendy vibes** Hotel G (see p.129)
**Best for celeb-spotting** St Regis (see above)
**Best for views** Park Hyatt (see above)
**Best for art** Opposite House (see above)
**Best for night-time visits to the Summer Palace** Aman@Summer Palace (see opposite)

Fuchengmen subway (line 2); map pp.86–87. This renovated courtyard house has really gone for a Chinese feel; everything, from the designs on the carpets to the latticework windows, is red, tassled or plastered with characters. Even the cisterns are decorated with Chinese motifs. But if you don't mind a bit of chintz, this is a pretty successful marriage of *hutong* house and comfy pad. The central courtyard has been turned into a sociable lounge by the addition of a glass roof, and it's cute and quiet with friendly staff; the only problem is that it's just a little out of the way, next to Baita Temple (see p.91). Rooms ¥290

### THE FAR NORTH

**Aman@Summer Palace** 安缦颐和 ānmàn yíhé 1 Gongmenqian Jie ☎010 59879057, ⓦamanresorts .com; Xiyuan subway (line 4); map p.98. This is about as close as you'll be able to stay to the Summer Palace

(see p.95), both in terms of location – it's just outside the east gate – and feel. Parts of the complex are centuries old, and there's even a secret gate into the palace, which can be opened at night for a crowd-free stroll. As with most *Aman* resorts, this is a place to get away from it all (for those who have the cash); the restaurants, pool and spa facilities are top-notch, though staff have a little to learn about what's expected of luxury service. ¥3880

**Grace** 格瑞斯酒店 géruìsī jiǔdiàn 798 Art District ☎010 64361818, ⓦgracebeijing.com; map pp.96–97. A great little hotel sitting pretty in the 798 Art District (see p.102). Sure, you're rather far away from central Beijing, but you're in one of the city's most characterful areas. Cheaper rooms are a tiny bit small for the price, but they're all suitably artistic, and there's a nice Italian restaurant downstairs. ¥880

## HOSTELS

### NORTH OF THE CENTRE

**Downtown Backpackers** 东堂青年旅舍 dōngtáng qīngnián lǚshè 85 Nanluogu Xiang ☎010 84002429, ⓦbackpackingchina.com; Nanluoguxiang subway (line 6); map pp.56–57. Long-time backpacker favourite, with an enviable location among the artsy boutiques of Beijing's trendiest *hutong*; you won't be short of eating and nightlife options. Graffiti all over the walls extol the virtues of the staff, though perhaps they've let it go to their heads. There are a few single and double rooms – priced according to whether they have windows and bathrooms – which get booked up rapidly. Small breakfast included. Dorms from ¥75, rooms ¥170

★ **Peking Youth Hostel** 北平国际青年旅舍 běipíng guójì qīngnián lǚshè 113-2 Nanluogu Xiang ☎010 84039098, ⓦpeking.hostel.com; Nanluoguxiang subway (line 6); map pp.56–57. Superb new hostel with immaculate rooms and a winning location on Nanluogu Xiang; there's some great people-watching to be done from the rooftop café, the downstairs component of which is extremely popular with passers-by. They've a far quieter annexe a 15min walk away. Dorms from ¥75, rooms ¥230

**Red Lantern House** 红灯笼宾馆 hóngdēnglóng bīnguǎn 5 Zhengjue Hutong, off Xinjiekou Nandajie ☎010 83285771, ⓦredlanternhouse.com; Xinjiekou subway (line 4); map pp.56–57. The main feature at this hostel, tucked into an appealingly earthy *hutong*, is an extraordinary courtyard overloaded with ornaments, including water features and a forest of red lanterns; it doubles as a café and bar of sorts. Hidden among the jungle of kitsch are a cat, a dog and a receptionist. The rooms themselves are comfy, and good value. They recently opened a highly appealing second venue; see website for details. Dorms from ¥85, rooms ¥220

**Sitting on the Walls Courtyard House** 城墙客栈 chéngqiáng kèzhàn 57 Nianzi Hutong ☎010 64027805, ⓦbeijingcitywalls.com; Nanluoguxiang subway (line 6); map pp.56–57. Tucked away in a quiet *hutong*, this is another converted courtyard house that offers an intimate atmosphere, a bit of character, friendly staff, pets, and dodgy plumbing. It's very central, just behind the Forbidden City, though a little tough to find first time; most taxi drivers won't know where it is. Wend your way through the alleyways, following the signs. Dorms ¥100, rooms ¥480

**Sleepy Inn Downtown Lakeside** 丽舍什刹海国际青年旅店 lìshè shíchàhǎi qīngnián jiǔdiàn 103 Deshengmennei Dajie ☎010 64069954; Jishuitan subway (line 2); map pp.56–57. This homely place has a great location, beside a canal just off Xihai Lake, and is probably the least backpackery of Beijing's hostels. A good terrace and pleasant staff make up for slightly overpriced rooms; the dorms are good value, though. Dorms ¥100, rooms ¥380

### EAST OF THE CENTRE

★ **Fly By Knight Courtyard Hostel** 夜奔北京四合院客栈 yèbēn běijīng sìhéyuàn kèzhàn 6 Dengcao Hutong ☎010 65597966, ⓦfacebook.com/hostel flybyknight; Dongsi subway (lines 5 & 6); map pp.66–67. Superb new courtyard hostel, tucked into an atmospheric *hutong* area east of the Forbidden City. It's a small, boutiquey place, and thus gets booked up early; those lucky enough to bag a room or bed will benefit from a relaxed atmosphere, one livened up with occasional martial arts lessons. Dorms from ¥130, rooms ¥500

**Sanlitun Youth Hostel** 三里屯青年旅舍 sānlǐtún qīngnián lǚshè Off Chunxiu Lu ☎010 51909288, ⓦitisbeijing.com; Dongsishitiao subway (line 2); map pp.66–67. Most notable for being the closest hostel to

**8**

Sanlitun, this is a friendly place that boasts a good bar of its own. The only problem for most backpackers is its distance from the nearest subway station. Dorms from ¥60, rooms ¥220

### SOUTH OF THE CENTRE

**365 Inn** 365 安怡之家宾馆 365 ānyí zhījiā bīnguǎn 55 Dazhalan Xijie ☎010 63085956, ⓦchina 365inn.com; Qianmen subway (line 2); map pp.78–79. Highly popular place on the bustling Dazhalan strip. Its rooms are cheery and relatively spacious, though guests tend to spend more time in the street-facing restaurant, which morphs into a busy bar come evening. Dorms from ¥50, rooms ¥250

★**Leo Hostel** 广聚园青年旅舍 guǎngjùyuán qīngnián lǚshè 52 Dazhalan Xijie ☎010 63031595, ⓦleohostel.com; Qianmen subway (line 2); map pp.78–79. Still the best hostel on Dazhalan, and particularly popular with younger backpackers on account of its cheap bar and fun vibe – like a reverse mullet, it's party at the front, business at the back. Leafy and attractive communal spaces make up for rooms that are a bit tatty round the edges; some of the dorms can be a bit cramped. It's easy to find, and an easy walk from Tian'anmen Square and the Forbidden City. Dorms from ¥50, rooms ¥240

### WEST OF THE CENTRE

★**Chinese Box Courtyard Hostel** 团圆四合院客栈 tuányuánsìhéyuàn kèzhàn 52 Xisi Beiertiao ☎010 66186768; Xisi subway (line 4); map pp.86–87. This charming little family-run courtyard hotel, hidden behind a sturdy red *hutong* door, only has a couple of rooms, so you'll certainly need to book ahead. The dorms are on the pricey side, but the rather incongruously luxurious double rooms are up there with the best in their price range; they feature huge beds, and imperial-style wallpaper and cushions. There are daily events such as musical performances, tea tastings and "dumpling parties". Small breakfast included. Dorms ¥120, rooms ¥450

**8**

# Eating

The Chinese are a nation of foodies: even pleasantries revolve around the subject. One way of asking "how are you?" – *nichīfàn le ma?* – translates literally as "have you eaten rice yet?", and they talk food like the British talk about the weather, as a social icebreaker. Meals are considered social events, and the Chinese like their restaurants to be *rènao* – hot and noisy. Given this obsession with food it follows, perhaps, that China boasts one of the world's most complex cuisines, with each region presenting a host of intricate varieties. The culinary wealth of Beijing is unique; it encompasses every style of Chinese food available, along with just about any Asian fare and most world cuisines. It's no surprise then that, for some visitors, eating becomes the highlight of their trip.

**9**

Every corner of Beijing is filled with restaurants, though their nature changes as you shift throughout the city. A few areas have become quite trendy, especially around **Sanlitun** and **Yonghe Gong** areas to the northeast of the centre and the **Drum Tower** in the north, which boast a cosmopolitan range of places to eat. **Wangfujing**, east of the Forbidden City, caters to the masses with its series of chain restaurants and night markets (see box, p.138), while south of the centre you'll find good duck south of **Qianmen** and Muslim food around **Niu Jie Mosque**; up near the university in the far north of the city, **Wudaokou** is a mini Koreatown.

## ESSENTIALS

### BEIJING SPECIALITIES

Beijing's most famous food – **Peking duck** – is actually not eaten that often by locals, but you should certainly give it a go while you're here; the same can be said for elaborate **imperial cuisine** (see box opposite). At the other end of the culinary spectrum, **hotpot** meals are among the most popular in the city, while Beijing's **street food** (see box, p.138) is not to be missed – not least at **breakfast** time (see box below).

**Peking duck** Succulent roast duck is Beijing's big culinary hitter, and deservedly so. Locals love to debate the merits of convection roasters over peach-wood ovens and the like, and every venerable restaurant has a different preparation technique. Once the duck has been brought to your table and carved, or vice versa, the routine is always the same; slather dark, tangy plum sauce onto pancakes, pop in a few scallions, add shreds of duck or duck fat (surprisingly delicious, if done correctly) with your chopsticks, roll it up and prepare for the local taste sensation. Nothing is wasted; the duck's entrails are usually made into a separate dish of their own, then served up alongside the meat and fat. Prices vary enormously depending on where you go, what grade you'd like (there are usually two "classes" to choose from), and what you'd like served alongside the duck (some places charge for the sauce and scallions).

These days it's tough to find a whole duck for under ¥100, while at the city's more famous duck restaurants you can expect to pay up to three times this price. Recommended places include: *Liqun* (see p.142), *Deyuan* (see p.142), *Quanjude* (see p.142) and *Dadong* (see p.137).

**Mongolian hotpot** Mongolian hotpot is Beijing's classic winter warmer, but makes for a fantastic communal meal at any time of year. The brass pot in the centre of the table has an outer rim around a chimney with a charcoal-burner underneath. Stock is boiled in the rim, and diners dip in slices of raw meat, vegetables, bean noodles, mushrooms and bean curd. Lamb is the traditional highlight, and it's sliced so finely that it takes only a few seconds to cook between your chopsticks. Shake to get rid of excess water, then dunk into the sesame-based dipping sauce, and it's ready to eat. There are hotpot restaurants all over town; just look for the steamed-up windows.

### OTHER CHINESE CUISINES

Beijing being the capital you can of course try every kind of Chinese cuisine here. A list of the principal dishes from each region is included in our menu reader (see p.193).

**Sichuan** Boisterous Sichuanese food, with its extravagant use of fiery chillies and pungent flavours, is a particular favourite among Beijingers and tourists alike. Try

---

### A REAL BEIJING BREAKFAST

Forget the trendy brunch spots in Sanlitun. Wherever you are at breakfast-time in Beijing, you're within easy walking distance of a place selling *jianbing* (煎饼, jiānbing), a sort of **savoury pancake**. These are usually sold from streetside windows, and the method of preparation is as entrancing as a lava lamp. First the hotplate will be greased up, then attacked with a scoop of batter. You'll be asked **là bu là?**: nod if you want spice, shake your head if not. Spice, if you want it, is flecked onto the rapidly frying mix, along with various bits of green veg; an egg is then cracked on top, to make a tasty, omelette-like layer. When it's nearly done, a rectangle of miscellaneous crispy substance is added, and in a flash the whole shebang will be folded and put in a plastic bag. The whole process takes well under a minute, even including your own input of ¥5 and a **xiè xiè**.

An alternative Beijing breakfast, and usually even cheaper, is sticks of **deep-fried dough** (油条, yóutiáo) served with warm **soy milk** (豆汁, dòu zhī); you may also care to look out for the telltale baskets indicating places selling **dumplings** (饺子, jiǎozi), which remain every old Beijinger's favourite form of morning sustenance. Lastly, be sure to hunt down some **Beijing yoghurt** (老北京酸奶, lǎobějīng suānnǎi) during your stay; sold in cute clay pots for ¥3–5 (including ¥1 deposit for the pot), it has a delicious, honey-like taste.

## IMPERIAL CUISINE

Pity the poor emperor. At mealtimes he wasn't allowed to take more than one mouthful of any one dish for fear that if he showed a preference a poisoner might take advantage. As a lowly citizen however, you are under no such compunction, and the city has some great places where you can indulge in the **imperial cuisine** that originated in the Qing dynasty kitchens. As well as meticulously prepared dishes created with extravagant ingredients such as **birds' nests** and **sharks' fins**, imperial cuisine is noted for fish that's so fresh it's still flapping (it's all about keeping the nerves intact) and fine **pastries** such as pea-flour cakes and kidney bean-flour rolls. Although you'll find dishes made with exotic meats such as **boar** and **camel**, these days you won't come across bear or wolf on the menu. Thankfully, one other ingredient is also no longer included: traditionally, imperial food always came with a strip of silver inside, as it was thought to turn black in the presence of poison.

*mapodoufu* (bean curd with pork), *gongbao jiding* (chicken and peanuts) and *suan cai yu* (fish soup with pickled greens) for a classic spicy meal.

**Cantonese** The joke that the Chinese will eat anything with four legs that isn't a table refers to Cantonese cuisine. Snake, dog and guinea pig are among the more unusual dishes, but more conventionally there are also plenty of lightly seasoned, fresh vegetables on offer. *Dim sum* (diǎnxīn in Mandarin), a meal of tiny buns, dumplings and pancakes, is a favourite for a long, leisurely lunch.

**Xinjiang** Food from the Turkic peoples of Xinjiang, in the far northwest, is perennially popular. It has a Central Asian flavour, with lamb kebabs, handmade noodles and some great mutton dishes on the menu. You'll often find Xinjiang food at street stalls (see box, p.138).

**Yunnanese** Among faddish foodies, Yunnan cuisine (from China's far south) has recently become popular; expats love to boast about finding the "new best place" to eat it. Among the tropical flavours that you might encounter are pineapple, seasoned pork and lots of mushrooms; dishes are often spicy, and some places serve them on banana leaves.

**Hunanese** If you think that Sichuanese food is spicy, just wait until you try some dishes from Hunan, a province south of Beijing. The Hunanese love their river fish, often served under a mountain of red-hot chilli peppers.

### INTERNATIONAL FOOD

**Elsewhere in Asia** Japanese, Thai and Korean food are widely available and well worth trying. You'll also find Indian, Russian and Middle Eastern cooking if you look hard enough.

**Western** There's ample opportunity to eat Western food in the city, and if you really want to clog your arteries up in a familiar fashion *KFC*, *McDonald's* and *Subway* are all well established here. Most large hotels offer some form of Western breakfast; alternatively, head to a bakery, to one of the many cafés which also offer Western brunch fare (see p.142), or have a crack at Beijing's own breakfast pancake (see box opposite).

### VEGETARIANS

The wide array of meat-free dishes on Chinese menus means that veggies should have no particular problems in Beijing, though dishes may be made on the same surfaces, or with the same implements, as used for meat. There are few dedicated vegetarian restaurants across the city; *The Veggie Table* (p.138) is a grand exception.

### PRACTICALITIES

**Opening hours** Note that the Chinese tend to eat early, sitting down to lunch at noon and dinner at six. Some places close for a couple of hours after the lunchtime rush, and in general places are open until fairly late. Opening hours are given for all establishments listed in this chapter.

**Costs** Prices are low in comparison with the West, and it's possible to eat well for less than ¥50 a head, although you can spend a lot more if you dine lavishly in palatial surroundings, and a lot less if you stick to noodle and rice dishes at local eateries. The sample prices of meals in our restaurant reviews are calculated on the basis of each person ordering a couple of dishes plus rice, or a main course and dessert.

**Booking** In Beijing you'll only ever really need to book at the very top places. In fact, at 99 percent of the city's restaurants, it isn't possible at all.

**Listings** You'll find good restaurant listings in the main expat magazines: *Time Out* (⊛timeoutbeijing.com), *The Beijinger* (⊛issuu.com/thebeijinger) and *City Weekend* (⊛cityweekend.com.cn).

**Tipping** Tipping isn't expected; if there is a service charge (usually at posher places), it will be on the bill.

**Chopsticks** Many restaurants in areas popular with tourists have knives (刀子, dāozi) and forks (叉子, chāzi), though most visitors are able to crack chopstick use within a few days. Tofu dishes should be eaten with a spoon (勺子, sháozi).

**Home delivery** Finally, you could even forego the whole tedious business of leaving your room to eat by contacting Beijing Goodies (⊛beijinggoodies.com) or the brilliantly named Sherpa (⊛sherpa.com.cn) who, for a small service

9

## BEIJING'S BEST

**Best hotpot** Hai Di Lao (see box below)
**Best Yunnanese** Lost Heaven (see below)
**Best Korean** Saveurs de Coree (see opposite)
**Best Xinjiang** Crescent Moon (see p.138)
**Best vegan** The Veggie Table (see p.138)

**Best dumplings** Din Tai Fung (see p.140)
**Best Manchu** Najia Xiaoguan (see p.141)
**Best for weirdness** Unban Bulgogi (see p.141)
**Best falafel** Biteapitta (see p.140)
**Best Peking duck** Deyuan (see p.142)

charge, deliver from many of the city's popular restaurants. Your food will likely be a little lukewarm after delivery, but after a night out in Sanlitun it'll taste like manna from the gods.

**Supermarkets** Supermarkets are covered under "Shopping" (see p.155).

## RESTAURANTS

### THE FORBIDDEN CITY AND TIAN'ANMEN SQUARE

★ **Lost Heaven** 花马天堂 huāmǎ tiāntáng 23 Qianmen Dongdajie ☎010 85162698, ⓦlostheaven. com.cn; Qianmen subway (line 2); map p.42. This Yunnanese restaurant is more than a little strange. Set in the fashionable, newly renovated 23 Ch'ienmen complex (see p.54), it's spellbindingly beautiful and surprisingly cheap (around ¥100 per head), while the food is up there with the best of Beijing's many Yunnanese restaurants. The mystery? It's hardly ever full. Daily noon–2pm & 5pm–1am.

**Maison Boulud** 布鲁宫 bùlǔ gōng 23 Qianmen Dongdajie ☎010 65599200, ⓦmaisonboulud.com; Qianmen subway (line 2); map p.42. In the mood for something fancy near the Forbidden City? Look no further than this splendid restaurant, whose high ceilings, giant mirrors and chequered flooring simply ooze class. The menu is largely French, with a few

interesting local twists, and varies by the month. Come for dinner and you'll pay a fortune, but weekday lunch specials are great value at ¥198 for three courses; alternatively, you're free to come by for cocktails (from ¥75). Daily noon–3pm & 5–10pm.

**Renhe** 仁和酒家 rénhé jiǔjiā 19 Donghuamen Dajie ☎010 65241955; Tian'anmen East subway (line 1); map p.42. A short walk from the Forbidden City's East Gate, and owned by a chap who's the living spit of Ai Weiwei, this is a cut above the area's other (mostly horrendous) restaurants. Here you're far less likely to be ripped off or served yesterday's rice; in fact, the food is rather good, especially their tasty tofu dishes (from ¥22). Its outdoor seats are also a good place for evening beers. Daily 6am–1am.

### NORTH OF THE CENTRE

**18 Garden** 十八茶院 shíbā cháyuàn 18 Banchang Hutong ☎010 64060918; Nanluoguxiang subway

## CHAIN RESTAURANTS: FAST FOOD, ASIAN STYLE

While branches of *KFC*, *McDonald's* and *Subway* are ubiquitous, there are a number of local and Asian food chains worth trying; they're all over the city, but easiest to find in shopping malls or complexes and outside the train stations. Opening hours vary. It's also worth knowing that every shopping centre, mall and plaza also holds a **food court** – generally in the basement, or on the top floor – which offers inexpensive meals from a cluster of outlets.

**Ajisen** 味千拉面 wèiqiān lāmiàn ⓦajisen .com.cn. Superior fast food from this Japanese chain offering ramen, noodles, miso and basic curries.

**Bellagio** 鹿港小镇 lùgǎng xiǎozhèn ⓦbellagio cafe.com.cn. A Taiwanese chain, despite the name, selling specialities such as *migao* (steamed glutinous rice flavoured with shrimp and mushroom) and *caipu dan* (a turnip omelette). The best one is in the Tai Koo Li complex, Sanlitun.

**Hai Di Lao** 海底捞 hǎidǐlāo ⓦhaidilao.com. Reasonably priced Sichuan hotpot chain, with a good choice of broths and a make-your-own-dipping-sauce

counter. There's a 24hr one on the top floor of the Intime Lotte mall, Wangfujing.

**Kungfu Catering** 真功夫 zhēn gōngfū ⓦzkungfu.com. Simple, cheap steamed Chinese food; they'll surely get into trouble eventually for their Bruce Lee rip-off logo. Try the fragrant sauce ribs.

**Yonghe King** 永和大王 yǒnghé dàwáng ⓦyonghe.com.cn. Fast-food chain known for its *youxtiao* (fried dough sticks) and cheap, noodle dishes.

**Yoshinoya** 吉野家 jíyějiā ⓦyoshinoya.com. A Japanese chain offering bowls of rice topped with slices of meat – cheap, tasty and relatively healthy.

(line 6); map pp.56–57. Within easy walking distance of Nanluogu Xiang, this is an understated but truly beautiful courtyard venue, with mint-coloured bead curtains hanging from every ledge. The food is a seemingly unwieldy fusion of Italian and Japanese cuisine (¥50–80), though it's all done very well indeed. They also serve a large range of tea and Japanese alcohol. Daily 11am–7pm.

**Café Sambal** 桑芭 sāngbā 43 Doufuchi Hutong ☎010 64004875, ⓦcafesambal.com; Guloudajie subway (lines 2 & 8); map pp.56–57. Authentic Malay food in a laidback courtyard restaurant, tucked away inside a *hutong* and actually quite easy to miss. There are a variety of places to sit, from the bar-like room by the entrance to the floor-cushions abutting the courtyard; dishes start at ¥45, with the house chicken and tofu particularly recommended. Daily 10am–11pm.

**Dali Courtyard** 大理院子 dàlǐ yuànzi 67 Xiaojingchang Hutong ☎010 84041430; Beixinqiao subway (line 5); map pp.56–57. A charming courtyard restaurant tucked down a *hutong*. It has no menu – you simply turn up, pay the fixed price (¥128, or ¥200 for a few extra dishes), then the chef gives you whatever Yunnanese food he feels like cooking; dishes are generally rice-based, and all sets will have a fish dish. Call to reserve. Daily noon–2.30pm & 6–10.30pm.

**Drum and Gong** 锣鼓洞天 luógǔ dòngtiān 104 Nanluogu Xiang ☎010 84024729; Nanluoguxiang subway (line 6); map pp.56–57. One of the more reliable options on Nanluogu Xiang, this busy place serves big portions of cheap Sichuan and home-style food. Most dishes are in the ¥20–45 range. Daily 10am–midnight.

**Hutong Pizza** 胡同批萨 hútóng pīsà 9 Yindingqiao Hutong ☎010 83228916; Beihai North subway (line 6); map pp.56–57. A charming little courtyard restaurant serving up delicious pizzas, though at over ¥100 each they're a bit pricey. It's hidden away in an alley; follow the signs from the bridge over the lakes. Daily 11am–11pm.

**Kaorouji** 烤肉季 kǎoròujì 14 Qianhai Dongyuan ☎010 64045921; Beihai North or Nanluoguxiang subway (both line 6); map pp.56–57. This lakeside Muslim restaurant, run by the same family for 150 years, takes advantage of its location with big windows and, in summer, balcony tables. The beef and barbecued lamb dishes are recommended. You'll spend around ¥100 a head. Daily 11am–2pm & 5–11pm.

**Nuage** 庆云楼 qìngyún lóu 22 Qianhai Dongzhao ☎010 64019581, ⓦnuage.com.cn; Beihai North or Nanluoguxiang subway (both line 6); map pp.56–57. Decent Vietnamese food served in a smart upstairs bar-restaurant. Try the steamed garlic prawns and battered squid, and finish with super-strong Vietnamese coffee if you don't intend to sleep in the near future. You'll spend upwards of ¥100 per head. Don't miss the extraordinary tropical fantasy toilets. Daily 11am–2pm &

5.30–10.30pm.

**Private Kitchen 44** 细管胡同44号 xìguǎnhútóng sìshísìhào 70 Deshengmennei Dajie ☎010 64001280; Jishuitan subway (line 2); map pp.56–57. Cosy restaurant serving home-style Guilin food, which is strong on pickles and tart flavours. Stick to the set meal (¥68), and wash it down with rice osmanthus wine. Daily 11am–2pm & 4.30–10pm.

**Saveurs de Coree** 韩香馆 hánxiāng guǎn 20 Ju'er Hutong ☎010 54715753, ⓦsaveursdecoree.com.cn; Nanluoguxiang subway (line 6); map pp.56–57. Trendy Korean bistro which prides itself on MSG-free dishes. If you're new to Korea's spicy cuisine, go for the ¥59 bibimbap (mixed rice, vegetables, egg and beef); if you fancy something more adventurous, try the barbecued *galbi* (marinated beef or pork). Ginseng-flavoured *baekseju* wine goes well with either. Daily 11am–10pm.

**The Source** 都江源 dūjiāng yuán 14 Banchang Hutong ☎010 64003736; Nanluoguxiang subway (line 6); map pp.56–57. A world away from the Nanluogu Xiang hubbub, though actually quite close to it, this artfully decorated courtyard restaurant serves set meals of the kind once favoured by Sichuanese aristocracy (they'll go easy on the spices if you ask). Starts at ¥188 per person, with the price and variety of sets increasing with each added person. Daily 10.30am–2pm & 5–10pm.

## EAST OF THE CENTRE
### WANGFUJING AND AROUND

**Dadong** 大董烤鸭店 dàdǒng kǎoyādiàn 88 Jinbao Jie ☎010 85221234, ⓦdadongdadong.com; Dengshikou subway (line 5); map pp.66–67. A bright, modish place that's garnered a good reputation for its crispy-skinned, succulent Beijing duck (from ¥228). Don't restrict yourself to these signature dishes though – the rest of the Chinese food is fine too. Daily 11am–10pm.

**Lei Garden** 利苑酒家 lìyuàn jiǔjiā 3F Jinbao Tower, 89 Jinbao Jie ☎010 85221212, ⓦleigarden.hk; Dengshikou subway (line 5); map pp.66–67. This well-established, upmarket Cantonese restaurant really comes into its own at lunchtime, thanks to its big selection of tasty *dim sum*. Speciality dishes include crab with egg yolk; think at least ¥200 per head. Daily 11am–2.30pm & 5.30–10.30pm.

★ **Made in China** Grand Hyatt, 1 Dongchang'an Jie ☎010 65109608, ⓦbeijing.grand.hyatt.com; Wangfujing subway (line 1); map pp.66–67. An element of drama is added to this dim, traditionally styled restaurant by the spectacle of chefs toiling over the giant woks and ovens in the open kitchen. It's one of the swankiest places in town, and the food is reliably excellent; their signature menu goes for ¥398 per person (minimum two), but à la carte items go from around ¥100. Daily 11.30am–2.30pm & 5.30–10.30pm.

9

## STREET FOOD

Any backpacker worth their salt will be itching to have a crack at Beijing's wonderfully weird street food, but even if you're not on a budget the city's street stalls can be up there with its most atmospheric places to eat. The best place to try street food is at one of the designated **night markets**, which are at their busiest and best in the summer. The Noah's Ark-like fare on offer would make a vegetarian heave: chicken hearts, sparrows, crickets, silkworm pupae, scorpions (still alive, until fried), sheep testicles (and willies)… the list goes on. Generally, though, what's on offer is hygienic, and you can feel confident of food cooked in front of you.

At more regular street stands, which you'll find in every single part of the city, most popular are the **skewers** (串, chuàn, though pronounced *chuar* in Beijing's pirate-like accent) of heavily spiced, barbecued meat, often served up by Uyghurs from Xinjiang, China's far west; lamb skewers (羊肉串, yángròu chuàn) are top dog, though there are usually various cuts of chicken to choose from too. If you want the most authentic possible experience, head to the streets just north of Niujie Mosque (see p.82). Not far behind in the popularity stakes are places serving *malatang* (麻辣烫, málà tàng), various skewered comestibles boiled in a spicy broth, and often served with a peanut paste.

### NIGHT MARKETS

**Dong'anmen Night Market** 东安门夜市, dōngānmén yèshì Dong'anmen Dajie; Wangfujing (line 1) or Dengshikou subway (line 5); map pp.66–67. Set up along the north side of this main road are red-canopied stalls offering all sorts of weird and wonderful goodies, generally of a higher quality and lower price than you'd get in Xiaochi Jie. Sadly, it shuts rather early for a "night" market. Daily 4–10pm.

**Xiaochi Jie Night Market** 小吃街 xiǎochī jiē Xiaochi Jie; Wangfujing subway (line 1); map pp.66–67. This pedestrianized alley is lined with stalls selling *xiao chī* – literally, "little eats" – from all over China. Though vendors are pushier than those at Dong'anmen, it's more atmospheric, and has the added bonus of tables at which you can actually sit down – perhaps with an ice-cold glass of beer. Daily 10am–midnight.

**Qin Tang Fu** 秦唐府 qíntángfǔ 69 Chaoyangmen Nanxiaojie ☎010 65598135; Dongsi subway (lines 5 & 6); map pp.66–67. A short walk from *Fly By Knight* hostel (see p.131), this is the best place in town for a famous Xi'an dish known as *paomo* (泡沫), a spicy, broth-like dish made with beef or lamb, and a disc of ripped-up bread. It's far, far more delicious than it may sound, and backpacker-friendly at just ¥28. Daily 11am–11pm.

### YONGHE GONG AND AROUND

**Crescent Moon** 弯弯月亮 wānwānyuèliàng 16 Dongsi Liutiao ☎010 64005281; Dongsi subway (lines 5 & 6); map pp.66–67. You can't really go wrong at a decent Xinjiang restaurant as long as you eat meat. Stick with classics such as roast leg of mutton, hand-pulled noodles and kebabs and you won't be disappointed. Daily 11am–11pm.

**Huajia Yiyuan** 华家怡园 huājiā yíyuán Beixinqiao Toutiao ☎010 64058440; Beixinqiao subway (line 5); map pp.66–67. This secluded courtyard restaurant, with songbirds and pleasant outdoor seating, is an excellent place to sample Beijing duck – a bargain at ¥108. It's one *hutong* north of Ghost Street, where there's a second branch (see box, p.142). Daily 10.30am–4am.

★ **Jin Ding Xuan** 金鼎轩 jīndǐng xuān 77 Hepingli Xijie ☎010 85968887, ⓦjindingxuan.com.cn; Yonghegong Lama Temple subway (lines 2 & 5); map pp.66–67. A stone's throw from Ditan Park, this four-storey place is amazingly cheap considering the lavish-looking exterior. Choices include shrimp and pork dumplings (¥19), Sichuan noodles (¥12), wonton soup (¥16) and breakfast-style dough sticks (¥5; see box, p.134); you'll need a few things to fill up, but it shouldn't cost too much. Leave room for the mango pudding (¥8). Daily 24hr.

**Red Capital Club** 新红资俱乐部 xīnhóngzī jùlèbù 66 Dongsijiu Tiao ☎010 84018886, ⓦred capitalclub.com.cn; Zhangzizhonglu subway (line 5); map pp.66–67. Imperial cuisine in an environment of pure communist kitsch – an old state guesthouse decorated with Mao memorabilia; there's even a red-flag limo parked out front. The dishes are all the favourites of Chinese modern and historical leaders; don't miss the roast beef favoured by Genghis Khan. All this irony and decadence will set you back about ¥350 a head. Daily 6–11pm.

**The Veggie Table** 吃素的 chīsù de 19 Wudaoying Hutong ☎010 64462073; Yonghegong Lama Temple subway (lines 2 & 5); map pp.66–67. Organic vegan food makes this place absolute heaven for a certain chunk of

**9**

Beijing travellers and expats, though even for carnivores it's pretty darn tasty. Couscous, curries and meze (including superb hummus) are on the menu, though pride of place goes to their famed mushroom burger (¥62). Mon–Fri 11.30am–3.30pm & 5.30–10.30pm, Sat & Sun 11.30am–11.30pm.

### SANLITUN

**Biteapitta** 吧嗒饼 bāda bing 2F Tongli Studio ☎010 64672961; Jintaixizhao subway (line 10); map p.72. Israeli-run snack restaurant whose falafel pitta wraps (¥25) are by far the best in the city – not that you'll notice, or care, after a few beers in the nearby bars. The other offerings are great too, with a special shout out for their six varieties of hummus. Lastly, say the restaurant's Chinese name aloud, and you'll be inadvertently impersonating Sonny Corleone from The Godfather. Daily 11am–11pm.

★ **Ding Ding Xiang** 鼎鼎香 dǐngdǐngxiāng 8 Dongdaqiao ☎010 64179289; Dongdaqiao subway (line 2); map pp.66–67. The gig at this upmarket hotpot chain is that everyone gets their own pot, which is handy if one of your party can't take spice or meat. Choose from a wide variety of broths – chicken is recommended – then pick the raw ingredients to cook up. For a hotpot place, the ambience here is a little rarefied (the white tablecloths are a surprise, considering how messy a hotpot dinner always gets) but it shouldn't set you back more than ¥250 per head. Daily 11am–midnight.

**Element Fresh** 新元素餐厅 xīnyuánsù cāntīng 3F Tai Koo Li South ☎010 64171318, ⓦwww.element fresh.com; Tuanjiehu subway (line 10); map p.72. All right, it's not very Chinese, but if you're craving a salad and a smoothie, head for this trendy Shanghainese health-food chain; the Asian sets such as pepper chicken salad are the best value for money. Mon–Fri 10am–10pm, Sat & Sun 8am–10pm.

**Hatsune** 隐泉日本料理 yǐnquán rìběnliàolǐ 3F Tai Koo Li South ☎010 64153939; Tuanjiehu subway (line 10); map p.72. Hip, young, American-styled Japanese restaurant with a reputation for good sashimi, which will cost you around ¥200 per head. Daily 11.30am–2pm & 5.30–10pm.

**Karaiya Spice House** 拉屋 làwū 3F Tai Koo Li South ☎010 64153535; Tuanjiehu subway (line 10); map p.72. Spicy Hunanese fine dining from the owner of Hatsune (see above). Specialities at this expat favourite are the hot and sour pork ribs and steamed Mandarin fish – a meal will set you back about ¥150 per person. Watch out for the trick front door. Daily 10.30am–2pm & 5.30–10pm.

**Middle 8th** 中8楼 zhōngbālóu 8 Dongsanlitun Lu ☎010 64130629; Tuanjiehu subway (line 10); map p.72. This classy Yunnanese restaurant is not as pricey as its frosty modernist decor might have you believe; you can fill up for

less than ¥150. Specialities are the mushroom dishes, but the goat's cheese and wild herb salad are also very good. Wash it down with rice wine. There is even a selection of fried insects for the adventurous. There's another branch in the Tai Koo Li complex. Daily 11am–11pm.

**One Thousand and One Nights** 一千零一夜 yīqiān língyīyè 21 Gongti Beilu ☎010 65324050; Tuanjiehu subway (line 10); map pp.66–67. Beijing's oldest Middle Eastern restaurant is still popular both with Western bigwigs who come here to fill up on kebabs before or after hitting the bars, while homesick diplomats puff on hookahs on the pavement outside. There's music and belly dancing nightly, too. Try the hummus as a starter and the baked chicken for a main course, and leave enough room for some baklava. About ¥100 per head. Daily 11am–11pm.

**Serve the People** 为人民服务 wèi rénmín fúwù 1 Sanlitun Xiwujie ☎010 64153242; Agricultural Exhibition Center subway (line 10); map p.72. Trendy Thai restaurant serving staples such as green curry, pork satay with peanut sauce and tom yum, all of which are worth trying, and you can ask them to tone down the spices. The stylish T-shirts worn by the staff are available to buy. About ¥80 per person. Daily 10.30am–10.30pm.

**Sureño** 榆舍地中海餐厅 yúshè dìzhōnghǎi cāntīng B1 Opposite House, 11 Sanlitun Lu ☎010 64105240, ⓦsurenorestaurant.com; Tuanjiehu subway (line 10); map p.72. This expat favourite, featuring an open kitchen and a wood-fired oven, is the city's best venue for Mediterranean-style fine dining. A meal will set you back about ¥400 per person. Mon–Fri noon–10.30pm, Sat 6–10.30pm, Sun noon–10.30pm.

**Three Guizhou Men** 三个贵州人 sāngè guìzhōurén 8 Gongti Xilu ☎010 65518517; Dongsishitiao subway (line 2); map pp.66–67. This artsy joint has carved itself a niche by offering hearty Guizhou cuisine in a stylish environment. Try house specialities such as rice tofu and vermicelli with pork, and leave some room for the steamed ribs too. It's open around the clock, and makes a good place to sate post-drink peckishness. A meal should come to around ¥150 a head. Daily 24hr.

### JIANGUOMEN DAJIE AND AROUND

**Din Tai Fung** 鼎泰丰 dǐngtàifēng 6F Shin Kong Place, 87 Jianguo Lu ☎010 65331536, ⓦwww.dintaifung .com.tw; Dawanglu subway (line 1); map pp.66–67. Slick, upscale Taiwanese restaurant still riding a wave of popularity generated from a decades-old magazine review in which it was ranked among the world's top ten restaurants. Hyperbole aside, its famous dumplings are really rather good, weighing in at ¥30–50 per batch. Make sure to leave space for the delectable red bean paste buns for dessert. Daily 11.30am–10pm.

**The Elephant** 大笨像 dàbènxiàng Off Ritan Beilu ☎010 85614073; Dongdaqiao subway (line 6); map

## LUNCHTIME AT NALI PATIO

Just off Sanlitun's main road, and snuggled into the gap between Tai Koo Li's north and south malls, is **Nali Patio** (map p.72), Beijing's current lunch venue of choice for expats and more affluent locals. This building's various levels are full of interesting choices, with most restaurants putting on good-value **lunch sets** from noon to 3pm; at the time of writing, tapas was the taste *du jour*, though this is the fastest-moving place in Beijing – by the time you visit, everything could have changed.

**Agua** 4F ☎010 52086188. Classy Spanish place with some outdoor seating. ¥88, plus ¥11 for dessert. Daily noon–2pm & 6–10pm.

**Jubang** 2F ☎010 52086071. Korean food that's moderately priced through the day; no lunch specials. Daily 11am–2am.

**Let's Seafood** GF ☎010 52086038. No dedicated lunch sets, though their ¥98 mussels make a good meal at this time of day. Daily 11.30am–2am.

★ **Migas** 6F ☎010 52086061, ⓦmigasbj.com. Probably the best of the bunch (and also a great place to drink; see p.147), with an artfully decorated interior

and tapas-like dishes from various Spanish regions. ¥85 for three courses. Daily noon–3.30pm & 6–10pm.

**Mosto** 3F ☎010 52086030, ⓦmostobj.com. Yet another Spanish place, and a very good one too. They often liven up their lunch options with good Central American dishes; keep your fingers crossed that their famed *ceviche* is on the menu. ¥95, plus ¥15 for dessert. Daily noon–2.30pm & 6–10pm.

**Mughal's** 3F ☎010 52086082. Decent Indian/Pakistani restaurant offering a 35 percent lunchtime discount. Mon–Fri 11am–3pm & 6–11pm, Sat & Sun 11am–11pm.

pp.66–67. A popular, reasonably priced restaurant that keeps the area's sizeable Russian population happy. Decor and service are ordinary but there's nothing wrong with staples such as borscht (¥25), beetroot and walnut salad (¥25) and *shashlik* (¥50). The outdoor area is great for evening drinks, though the interior is surprisingly attractive. Daily 9am–1am.

**Justine's** Jianguo Hotel, 5 Jianguomenwai Dajie ☎010 65002233, ⓦhoteljianguo.com; Yong'anli subway (line 1); map pp.66–67. Beijing's oldest French restaurant still has the best wine list in the capital, and is suitably fancy – think super-plush carpets, giant mirrors, golden chandeliers and stained glass. The menu switches around with pleasing regularity; try the lobster soup or grilled lamb. Service is attentive. Around ¥250 per person. Daily 6.30am–10.30am, noon–2pm & 6–10pm.

**Lime** 青柠 qīngníng Building 15, Central Park ☎010 65970887; Jintaixizhao subway (line 10); map pp.66–67. A friendly Thai venue serving fairly authentic food for ¥30–60 per dish; the *tom yum* and green curries are particularly recommended. Their outdoor seats are the best place from which to gaze over Central Park, a cosmopolitan area that's one of Beijing's most impressive examples of urban rebuilding. Daily 11am–10pm.

**Makye Ame** 玛吉阿米 mǎjí āmǐ 2F A11 Xiushui Nanjie ☎010 65069616; Jianguomen (lines 1 & 2) or Yong'anli subway (line 1); map pp.66–67. Hearty Tibetan food in a cosy atmosphere, rather more upscale than anywhere in Tibet. Try the *tashi delek* (yak meat lasagne; ¥68) and wash it down with butter tea. Tibetan singing and dancing on Wed & Fri nights. Daily 10am–2am.

**Nadaman** 滩万 tānwàn 3F China World Trade Centre Annexe ☎010 65052266; Guomao subway (lines 1 & 10); map pp.66–67. Discreet, minimalist and seriously expensive Japanese restaurant with a set meal of lots of small dishes priced at ¥260–450 per person. Most of the ingredients are flown in from Japan. Take someone you want to impress. Daily 11.30am–2pm & 5.30–9.30pm.

★ **Najia Xiaoguan** 那家小馆 nàjiā xiǎoguǎn 10 Yong'an Xili ☎010 65686553; Yong'anli subway (line 1); map pp.66–67. In the shadow of the LG Twin Towers, and therefore packed to the gills come lunchtime, this is a superb little place to eat with friendly service, cheap prices and an attractive, tearoom-like interior. Served on faux-dynasty plates, their food is of the Manchu variety, with most dishes in the ¥50–70 range; go for one of the venison meals, or something more interesting like sweet potato and taro with cheese (¥36). Daily 11am–11pm.

**Steak and Eggs** 喜来中 xǐláizhōng 5 Xiushui Nanjie ☎010 65928088; Jianguomen (lines 1 & 2) or Yong'anli subway (line 1); map pp.66–67. Good-value American diner food has made this rough-and-ready place an expat favourite, especially for Sunday brunch. Their eponymous dish, served with toast, costs ¥95; it's half that for eggs Benedict. Daily 7.30am–midnight.

★ **Unban Bulgogi** 车轮烧烤 chēlún shāokǎo Fancaodibei Hutong ☎010 85633191; Dongdaqiao subway (line 6); map pp.66–67. Restaurant serving decent Korean food, including barbecued meat from ¥32 per portion and excellent *naengmyeon* (cold buckwheat noodles) for ¥24. Still not convinced? How about this: all of the waitresses are North Korean, and here with the blessings of the government in Pyongyang, whose

9

## GHOST STREET

Nicknamed "Ghost Street" (簋街, *guǐ jiē*), a 1km-long stretch of **Dongzhimennei Dajie** is lined with hundreds of restaurants, all festooned with red lanterns and neon – a colourful and boisterous scene, particularly on weekends. Note that staff in these restaurants will probably speak little or no English, and few places will have an English menu though plenty have a picture menu. It's an atmospheric place, for sure, though when the crowds arrive in the evening the whole street can resemble a car park.

embassy is just around the corner. Most of the customers are, in fact, North Korean diplomats – look for anyone wearing a Kim Il-sung badge. Daily noon–3pm & 5–10pm.

### SOUTH OF THE CENTRE

★ **Deyuan** 德缘 déyuán 57 Dazhalan Xijie ☎010 63085371; Qianmen subway (line 2); map pp.78–79. Miraculously, this is a decent restaurant on tourist-heavy Dazhalan. And, miracle of miracles, prices are at a level that could suit the area's many backpackers; it's just ¥128 for a duck, including all the trimmings (enough to feed two or three), and the quality would put many more expensive places to shame. Daily 10am–2pm & 5–9pm.

**Goubuli** 狗不理 gǒubùlǐ 31 Dazhalan Dajie ☎010 63533338; Qianmen subway (line 2); map pp.78–79. Delicious steamed buns with various fillings (try the pork, shrimp and sea cucumber combo) for ¥48 and up per batch. You can eat them here or take away, while there's also good duck (¥88 for half) and other regular Chinese dishes on the menu. Daily 7.30am–9pm.

**Liqun** 利群烤鸭店 lìqún kǎoyādiàn 11 Beixiangfeng Hutong ☎010 67025681; Qianmen subway (line 2); map pp.78–79. A well-kept secret for years, though no longer – the entrance to this duck restaurant is now covered with photos of famous guests such as Chow Yun Fat and Jet Li. Prices have correspondingly shot up – it's now ¥198 per duck, without the trimmings – and you'll likely have to queue even after you've made a reservation (essential, in any case). Quality remains high, however, and the earthy, courtyard-house atmosphere is just the same. Daily 11.30am–10pm.

**Quanjude** 全聚德 quánjùdé 30 Qianmen Dajie ☎010 67011379, ⓦ quanjude.com; Qianmen subway (line 2); map pp.78–79. Beijing's most famous duck restaurant by far – reservations are not essential, but advised if you don't want to spend ages in the queue. Though too popular for its own good, the duck remains up there with the city's best; with the trimmings, a whole one is ¥296. Other duck delicacies are available, including seared duck hearts in liquor, and fried duck mince in bird's nest. Daily 11am–1.30pm & 4.30–8pm.

### THE FAR NORTH

**Lush** 2F 1 Huaqing Jiayuan ☎010 82863566, ⓦ lushbeijing.com; Wudaokou subway (line 13); map pp.96–97. Super-popular student venue serving all sorts of good Western food; most plump for the burgers, sandwiches or fried breakfasts, all of which cost around ¥30. Come evening, it's one of the area's busiest bars (see p.147) – it never, in fact, closes at all. Daily 24hr.

**Shido Noodles** 食竞拉面馆 shídù lāmiànguǎn 798 Art District; map pp.96–97. The 798 district's restaurants are well overpriced, but the area's single cheapie is where many gallery staff come to eat. It's nothing special, but you'll get a huge, filling bowl of good noodles for under ¥25. Daily 11am–6pm.

**Tantan Dalu** 坦坦大炉 tǎntǎn dàlú 4F 35 Chengfu Lu ☎010 62560471; Wudaokou subway (line 13); map pp.96–97. The best of the Wudaokou area's many Korean restaurants; there are, indeed, several in this building alone. Try *bibimbap* (mixed rice, veggies and spice) or *naengmyeon* (cold buckwheat noodles) for around ¥25; a little more will buy you a portion of barbecued meat. Daily 10am–11pm.

## CAFÉS

**Coffee** culture has exploded in Beijing, though prices are as high as in any Western country – they're for foreigners and well-to-do locals only. As well as those places listed below, note that some bars are also great spots to linger over a cappuccino, notably *Pass By Bar* (see p.146) and *Drum and Bell* (see p.146). Conversely, some of the places below also do great **food**, most commonly of the Western variety. All have **free wi-fi**.

**@ Café** 798 Art District; map pp.96–97. The best café in the 798 district, with good coffee (surprisingly cheap for the area at ¥20–30) and a nice range of meals. Try the pasta dishes (from ¥40), some of which use fresh, hand-made spaghetti. Daily 11am–6pm.

**Bookworm** 书虫 shūchóng 4 Nansanlitun Lu ☎010 65869507, ⓦ chinabookworm.com; Tuanjiehu subway (line 10); map p.72. Despite god-awful coffee, and staff who often seem hellbent on redefining the word "apathy", this remains hugely popular with Beijing's expat crowd, largely on account of its excellent book selection (see p.157) and regular literary events and lectures. Check the website for details. Daily 9am–2am.

**Café Zarah** 飒哈 sàhā 42 Gulou Dongdajie ☎010 84039807, ⓦ cafezarah.com; Beixinqiao (line 5) or Nanluoguxiang subway (line 6); map pp.56–57. This is Beijing's prime spot for expats updating their blog/writing a book/thinking of making a film about life in China. Not much talking goes on: it's a sea of Apple logos. They're here for a reason, though: a cosy, attractively converted courtyard house, serving good continental breakfasts (from ¥45) and plenty of snacks, including tasty home-made ice cream and a few cakes plonked, rather unfairly, on the counter. Daily except Tues 10am–midnight.

**Confucius Café** 秀冠 xiùguān 25 Guozijian Lu ☎010 64052047; Yonghegong Lama Temple subway (line 5); map pp.66–67. Just down the road from the Confucius Temple, this café has employed similar themes in its design – a bold move, but it works. Good coffee, too. Daily 9am–8pm.

★ **Dareen's** 达林咖啡 dálín kāfēi Sanlitun Lu ☎010 64150557; Agricultural Exhibition Center subway (line 10); map p.72. The Sanlitun area is full of cafés, and though this Palestinian-run one has one of the least attractive interiors, from springtime to autumn its outdoor area is hugely popular – tuck into some great Arabic coffee (¥20), made with cardamom seeds, under an umbrella-like canopy of trees. Daily 11am–6pm.

**Starbucks** 星巴克 xīngbākè 1 Qianmen Dajie ☎010 63010108; Qianmen subway (line 2) ⓦ starbucks.com.cn; map pp.78–79. Branches of *Starbucks* are all over the city – you know exactly what to expect – but their Qianmen branch stands out. As with the rest of the street, it's been decorated in a mock-dynastic style, and views from the upper levels are very pleasant indeed. Daily 9am–10pm.

★ **Vineyard Café** 葡萄院儿 pútáoyuàn'er 31 Wudaoying Hutong ☎010 64027961, ⓦ vineyardcafe .cn; Yonghegong Lama Temple subway (lines 2 & 5); map pp.66–67. Good Western wine and food, including pizza, makes this bright, cheery place popular with the local expats. Serves good brunches too (from ¥75), making it a good target before or after a trip to Yonghe Gong. Tues–Sun 11.30am–midnight.

**Wen Yu** 文宇奶酪店 wényǔ nǎilàodiàn 49 Nanluogu Xiang; Nanluoguxiang subway (line 6); map pp.56–57. Take a walk down Nanluogu Xiang, and before long you'll spy people bearing blue-and-white plastic pots. They've all been to *Wen Yu*, a yoghurt café so popular that they've long thrown away the tables – better to accommodate a queue that regularly spills way out into the road. ¥10–15 per pot; cold coffee ¥5. Daily noon–6pm.

**Xiaoxin's** 小新的店 xiǎoxīn de diàn 103 Nanluogu Xiang ☎010 64036956; Nanluoguxiang subway (line 6); map pp.56–57. This cosy courtyard hideaway is one of the better Nanluogu Xiang cafés, though the staff could be a little more alert. Limited menu; try their smoothies and cheesecakes. Daily 9am–2am.

VICS

# Drinking and nightlife

In 1995, Sanlitun Lu in the east of the city had just one bar, and it was losing money. A new manager bought it, believing the place had potential but that the *feng shui* was wrong – the toilet was opposite the door and all the wealth was going down it. He changed the name, moved the loo and – so the story goes – the city's bar scene took off from there. Now the area is choked with drinking holes, and new bars open all the time. Many mimic their popular neighbours; if one does well, a couple more will open around it, and before you know it, the original will have closed down. These days Beijing also boasts slick, international-style clubs (many with imported DJs), while the city's live music scene continues to improve.

You'll have to choose where to drink carefully, since each city quarter has its own distinct vibe. The main bar area, **Sanlitun**, remains as popular as ever; branching off its neon-soaked main strip are a fascinating array of diverse venues, from cheap and cheerful pick-up joints to exclusive jazz bars. South of here, there is a clutch of smarter bars on **Jianguomen Dajie**, and the business district to its north. In the north of the city, there's a fun scene alongside **Houhai**, with plenty of chilled-out venues sunk in the *hutongs* all around, though bars here are much of a muchness and resemble the boring Sanlitun beer-plus-band places of yore; nearby, the **Drum Tower** and **Nanluogu Xiang** areas attract an artsier crowd. For something a bit edgier – and the heart of the rock scene – head to **Wudaokou**; the student clientele means that bars here tend to be cheaper and grungier.

As for dancing, most of the classier **clubbing** venues are northeast of the centre, in two clusters – around distant **Chaoyang Park** and Sanlitun. There's a dense concentration of clubs around the west side of the **Workers' Stadium**, and on Saturday night the car park here is full of white Mercedes dropping off the *dakuans* (big moneys) and their *xiaomis* (little honeys). African guys work the crowds, selling the shaky head drug (ecstasy): welcome to the new China. Live music venues are dotted around town, though most common in the studenty **Wudaokou** area.

## BARS

**Opening hours** are flexible – a bar tends to close only when its last barfly has lurched off – though everywhere will be open until at least midnight (and well into the early hours at weekends). There's usually a cover charge to get in (around ¥30) when a band is playing. Though Chinese **beer** can be cheaper than bottled water if bought in a shop, a 350ml bottle of Tsingtao or the local Yanjing at a bar will usually cost ¥20–40. Many bars also sell Western draught beers such as Guinness and Boddingtons, which cost at least ¥40; wine and cocktails cost this at the cheapest places, but double that price in fancier bars. For the most up-to-date information on all the comings and goings, check the bar **listings** in Beijing's main expat magazines: *Time Out* (ⓦ timeoutbeijing.com), *The Beijinger* (ⓦ issuu.com/thebeijinger) and *City Weekend* (ⓦ cityweekend.com.cn).

### THE FORBIDDEN CITY AND TIAN'ANMEN SQUARE

★ **What? Bar** 什么酒吧 shénme jiǔba 72 Beichang Jie ❶ 133 41122757; Tian'anmen West subway (line 1); map p.42. Though primarily a live music bar (see p.148), this tiny venue is a great place for a drink on any evening – especially their tasty Beer Lao (part pun, since the bar's nickname, *lao wo*, sounds like the Chinese word for Laos). They've table football, and outdoor chairs on the super-quiet-at-night street running alongside the Forbidden City; after you're done here, you could even grab a beer and go for a drink by the canal. Hours vary; usually open 6pm–late.

★ **Yin** 饮酒把 yǐnjiǔbǎ The Emperor Hotel, 33 Qihelou Jie ❶ 010 65265566, ⓦ theemperor.com.cn; Tian'anmen East (line 1) or Dongsi subway (lines 5 & 6); map p.42. Sat pretty atop *The Emperor*, this bar has one major draw card – its wonderful views of the Forbidden City, best enjoyed over sunset, cocktail in hand. Okay, the hot tub counts as an incentive too. Daily noon–2am.

### NORTH OF THE CENTRE

**Bed Bar** 床 chuáng 17 Zhangwang Hutong ❶ 010 84001554; Guloudajie subway (lines 2 & 8); map pp.56–57. A simple courtyard nightspot, rather hidden

### BEIJING'S BEST

**Best for Forbidden City views** Yin (see above)
**Best for Drum and Bell tower views** Drum and Bell (see p.146)
**Best for imported beer selection** El Nido (see p.146)
**Best microbrewery** Great Leap (see p.146)
**Best for distance above the ground** Atmosphere (see p.147)
**Best whisky selection** Ichikura (see p.147)
**Best cocktails** Apothecary (see p.148)
**Best gay club** Destination (see p.149)
**Best for big-screen sports** Paddy O'Shea's (see p.147)
**Best meat market** Propaganda (see p.148)

**10**

away from the action and all the better for it. Lined with rugs and traditional beds, it is aimed at the horizontally inclined, so perhaps better for a second date than a first. They also serve good tapas. Daily 2pm–2am.

★ **Drum and Bell** 鼓钟咖啡馆 gǔzhōng kāfēiguǎn 41 Zhonglouwan Hutong ☎010 84033600; Guloudajie subway (lines 2 & 8); map pp.56–57. With welcoming staff and a great location between the Drum and Bell towers, this little place is always crowded. The rooftop patio is an added bonus in summer, and they serve decent thin-crust pizzas. Daily noon–2am.

**East Shore Live Jazz Café** 东岸咖啡 dōng'àn kāfēi 2F 2 Qianhai Nanyan ☎010 84032131; Beihai North subway (line 6); map pp.56–57. Dark, mellow jazz bar, set on the second floor with a view of the lake and occasional live shows (see p.149). Daily 3pm–2am.

★ **Huxleys** 德比酒吧 débǐ jiǔbā 16 Yandai Xiejie ☎010 64027825; Beihai North or Nanluoguxiang subway (both line 6); map pp.56–57. Cheap booze, no attitude and approachable staff – a total contrast to the places lining nearby Houhai. It's a real winner with young locals and expats alike. Daily 5pm–late.

**Pass By Bar** 过客酒吧 guòkè jiǔbā 108 Nanluogu Xiang ☎010 84038004; Nanluoguxiang subway (line 6); map pp.56–57. A renovated courtyard house turned comfortable bar/restaurant, popular with backpackers and students. There are lots of books and pictures of China's far-flung places to peruse, and well-travelled staff

to chat to – if you can get their attention. Daily 9am–4am.

**Sex and da City** 欲望都市 yùwàng dūshì Lotus Lane ☎010 59056358; Beihai North subway (line 6); map pp.56–57. A pick-up joint with bar-top dancing; Carrie might not approve, but Samantha probably would. Daily 5pm–late.

★ **Siif** 如果 rúguǒ 67 Beiluogu Xiang ☎010 64069496, ⓦsiif.cn; Andingmen subway (line 2); map pp.56–57. Nobody, even the staff, seems quite sure exactly what this place is called. It matters not, however, since it's a highly friendly place with quirkily designed tables and chairs; head on downstairs for table football, or clamber up to the roof terrace for a drink. Daily 1pm–2am.

### EAST OF THE CENTRE
#### YONGHE GONG AND AROUND

**El Nido** 方家小酒馆 fāngjiā xiǎojiǔguǎn 59 59 Fangjia Hutong ☎010 84029495; Beixinqiao subway (line 5); map pp.66–67. Tiny bar that somehow manages to squeeze in over a hundred different varieties of imported beer, plus plenty of wines and stronger stuff – what else do you need to know? Daily 6am–late.

#### SANLITUN

★ **Apothecary** 酒术 jiǔshù 3F Nali Patio ☎010 52086040; Tuanjiehu subway (line 10); map p.72. Probably the best cocktails in town (from ¥80), served in a

---

## BEIJING'S MICROBREWERIES

Microbrewed beer is the latest Beijing drinking fad, though such is the aplomb with which hop addicts have embraced the nectar, it looks like this one may be here to stay. At all of the venues below, it's ¥25–50 for a pint (well, half-litre) of the good stuff.

**The Big Smoke** 京 jīng A 57 Xingfucun Zhonglu ☎010 64165195, ⓦcapitalbrew.com; Dongsishitiao subway (line 2); map pp.66–67. This is the home base of the Capital Brewing Company, also known as "Jing Ah". As well as a selection of seasonal brews, they've four beers on tap year-round: a pale ale, an IPA and the more interesting Smoke on the Beach (a brown ale) and Mandarin Summer Wheat. Mon–Thurs & Sun 11.30am–midnight, Fri & Sat 11.30am–late.

★ **Great Leap** 悠航鲜啤 yōuhàng xiānpì 6 Doujiao Hutong ⓦslowboatbrewery.com; Zhangzizhonglu subway (line 5); map pp.56–57. Hard to find the first time around, and perhaps even harder to leave if you end up having too many of their great ales, best imbibed in the bustling outdoor courtyard. You've got to love their Socialist Realist logo, too. Tues–Thurs 5–10.30pm, Fri 5–11pm, Sat 2–11pm, Sun 2–10pm.

**Malty Dog** 51 Beiluogu Xiang ☎010 84083763; Andingmen subway (line 2); map pp.56–57. Sitting pretty on Beiluogu Xiang – the calmer, trendier northern equivalent to Nanluogu Xiang – this small place was still finding its feet at the time of writing, but its ales hold much promise. Try six of them at once from their taster set. Tues–Fri 6pm–2am, Sat & Sun 2pm–2am.

**Slow Boat Taproom** 悠航鲜啤 yōuháng xiānpí 56-2 Dongsi Batiao ⓦslowboatbrewery.com; Zhangzizhonglu subway (line 5); map pp.66–67. This brewery's Monkey's Fist, an IPA, became an instant hit with Beijing's hop cognoscenti; Slow Boat do, indeed, seem to specialize in IPA, but there are always plenty of other options available. They sell cheap pitchers on Thurs, and two-for-one on Tues. Tues & Wed 5pm–midnight, Thurs 5pm–1am, Fri & Sat 5pm–late, Sun 2–10pm.

trendily minimalist setting. If you're not a mixologist like the guys behind the bar, check out the informative menu, which will tell you all you need to know about what you're drinking. The food's good, too. Tues–Sun 7pm–late.

**Jazz Ya** 爵士屋 juéshì wū Nali Patio ☎010 64151227, ⓦjazzya.com.cn; Tuanjiehu subway (line 10); map p.72. Just off the main road, this mellow Japanese place, full of rough-hewn wooden tables, has a better drinks menu than most of its neighbours. Occasional live music (see p.149). Daily noon–2am.

**Mesh** Opposite House, 11 Sanlitun Lu ☎010 64105220; Tuanjiehu subway (line 10); map p.72. Cosy, classy lounge bar in the basement of a chic hotel (see p.130), attracting a trendy, international crowd. Dress up, order a cocktail (from ¥80), and try to look sophisticated. Daily 5pm–2am.

★ **Migas** 米家思 mǐjiāsī Nali Patio ☎010 52086061, ⓦmigasbj.com; Tuanjiehu subway (line 10); map p.72. The bar sitting atop this excellent Spanish restaurant (see p.141) was Beijing's "it" place at the time of writing: views from here are simply superb, and there's barely room to wiggle your butt during the weekend DJ sets. Weekdays are a different story, with lounge music pulsing over a nattering crowd, all sat on funky furniture. Daily 7pm–late.

**Paddy O'Shea's** 爱尔兰酒吧 àiěrlán jiǔbā 28 Dongzhimenwai Dajie ☎010 64156389; Dongzhimen subway (lines 2 & 13); map pp.66–67. This Irish bar is the place to come if you need your fill of EPL, NBA, NFL or any other three-letter sports-related acronym. They also, of course, sell Guinness. Daily 10am–late.

**Q Bar** Q吧 Q bā 6F Eastern Hotel, Sanlitun Nanlu ☎010 65959239, ⓦqbarbeijing.com; Hujialou subway (lines 6 & 10); map pp.66–67. Sleek and well-run lounge bar with good cocktails; it is at its best in summer when drinkers spill out onto the terrace. Daily 6pm–late.

**Tree** 树酒吧 shù jiǔbā Behind 3.3 mall ☎010 64151954, ⓦtreebeijing.com.cn; Tuanjiehu subway (line 10); map p.72. Relaxed and unassuming little bar, with a selection of Belgian white beers and decent pizza; if you'd like to mix things up a bit, they've a great sister bar within stumbling distance. Daily noon–late.

### JIANGUOMEN DAJIE AND AROUND

**Atmosphere** 云酷酒吧 yúnkù jiǔbā 80F China World Summit Wing ☎010 85716459, ⓦshangri-la.com; Guomao subway (lines 1 & 10); map pp.66–67. Eighty

floors up, this is Beijing's loftiest bar – for now, at least – and sells costly cocktails (from ¥90). Though the building is brand-new, the bar's decoration seems a little dated; no matter, just persuade your date/colleague to look outside instead. Book ahead to get a window seat; use the lifts facing the building's east entrance. Daily noon–2am.

**Centro** 炫酷酒廊 xuànkù jiǔláng 1F Kerry Centre Hotel, 1 Guanghua Lu ☎010 65618833, ⓦshangri-la .com/beijing/kerry; Jintaixizhao subway (line 10); map pp.66–67. Slinky lounge bar whose lavish cocktails will cost the best part of a red bill. Dress up. Daily 24hr.

**Ichikura** 一藏酒吧 yīcáng jiǔbā Chaoyang Theatre, 36 Dongsanhuan Beilu ☎010 65071107; Hujialou subway (lines 6 & 10); map pp.66–67. This two-storey Japanese whisky bar is as tasteful and understated as the acrobatic shows next door are glitzy and vulgar. A great range of single malts – including superb Japanese varieties – and fine attention to detail (check out the round ice cubes) make this dark, cosy venue a hidden gem. Daily 7pm–2am.

★ **Xiu** 秀 xiù 6F Park Hyatt, 2 Jianguomenwai Dajie ☎010 85671107, ⓦxiubeijing.com; Guomao subway (lines 1 & 10); map pp.66–67. With some of the most wonderful views of any Beijing bar from its outdoor terrace, *Xiu* has been up there with the most popular in the city for several years, serving up good cocktails amid a stylish, yet raucous, atmosphere. There's a dancefloor inside, though be warned that it's a notorious hunting ground for local prostitutes. Daily 6pm–late.

### SOUTH OF THE CENTRE

**365 Inn** 365 安怡之家宾馆 365 ānyí zhījiā bīnguǎn 55 Dazhalan Xijie ☎010 63085956, ⓦchina365inn.com; Qianmen subway (line 2); map pp.78–79. The bar fronting this hostel (see p.132) is just about the best place to drink in the backpacker-heavy Dazhalan area; *Leo Hostel* across the road has a great bar too, but this one has the added benefit of being able to people-watch on one of Beijing's most intriguing streets (see p.77). Daily 7am–late.

### THE FAR NORTH

★ **Lush** 1 Huaqing Jiayuan ⓦlushbeijing.com; Wudaokou subway (line 13); map pp.96–97. A café/restaurant by day (see p.142), beer bottles start to pop as soon as the sun dares to approach the horizon. Prices are cheap, in keeping with the area's student population. Daily 24hr.

## CLUBS

Gone are the days when everything stopped at 10pm for a raffle; Chinese clubs are pretty slick these days, with hip-hop and house music proving enduringly popular. All places listed here have a **cover charge**, quoted in our reviews, which generally increases at weekends. If you just want to dance, and aren't too prissy about the latest music, check our bar reviews (see above) for venues with their own dancefloor. There are several venues around **Chaoyang Park**, and though a few bus routes head this way, everyone heads here by taxi – it's around ¥25 from Sanlitun.

**10**

### EAST OF THE CENTRE

**Bling** Solana 5–1, 6 Chaoyang Park Lu ☎010 59056999, ⓦall-starclub.com; map pp.66–67. Aimed, as the name might suggest, at those captivated by shiny things, heavy bass and exposed flesh, Beijing's newest hip-hop venue wows its beautiful, vapid clientele with features such as a DJ booth made out of a Rolls-Royce. ¥50 cover charge. Wed–Sat 9pm–3am.

**GT Banana** 赛特饭店 sàitè fàndiàn Scitech Hotel, 22 Jianguomenwai Dajie ☎010 65283636; Jianguomen subway (lines 1 & 2); map pp.66–67. Huge, gaudy and in-your-face, this megaclub has three sections – techno, funk and chill-out – and features go-go girls, karaoke rooms and an enthusiastic, young crowd. Cover charge ¥30 weekdays, ¥50 weekends, and more when a big-name DJ is playing. Daily 9pm–4.30am.

★**Haze** Guanghualu Soho, Guanghua Lu ⓦhazebeijing.com; Yong'anli subway (line 1); map pp.66–67. This was one of Beijing's most popular clubs at the time of writing – whatever that's worth in this hectic city. House, nu-disco and techno pulse from two floors' worth of speakers, and the atmosphere is relaxed, rather than manic. Cover charge ¥50. Fri & Sat 8pm–late; occasionally Thurs too.

**Vics** 威克斯 wēikèsī North Gate, Workers' Stadium ☎010 52930333, ⓦvics.com.cn; Dongsishitiao subway (line 2); map pp.66–67. Long-running hip-hop club, with a sweaty dancefloor filled with enthusiastic booty grinders. The low cover charge and cheapish drinks (bottled beer ¥20) make it popular with students and embassy brats. On Wednesdays, women get in free and receive free drinks until midnight. Thursday is ragga/reggae night, with hip-hop, R&B and techno all weekend. ¥50 on weekends, free Mon–Thurs. Daily 9.30pm–2am.

**World of Suzie Wong** 苏西黄酒吧 sūxīhuáng jiǔbā Outside the west gate of Chaoyang Park ☎010 65003377, ⓦclubsuziewong.com; map pp.66–67. Not as fashionable as it was, but still a stalwart with its striking neo-Oriental decor – think lacquer and rose petals. Dancing downstairs and a cocktail bar above. ¥50 cover charge. Daily 8pm–3am.

### THE FAR NORTH

**Propaganda** Huaqing Jiayuan ☎010 82863991; Wudaokou subway (line 13); map pp.66–67. "Oh god, *that* place…" is the stock reaction when mentioning this bar to someone who's been in Beijing for a while. Both the most famous, and the most infamous, of Wudaokou's student clubs, it's a shameless meat market whose ¥50 all-you-can-drink nights (every Wed) are crazily popular. The spirits are dodgy for sure, though; stick to the beer. Daily 8pm–late.

## LIVE MUSIC VENUES

Mainstream **Chinese pop** – mostly slushy ballads sung by Hong Kong or Taiwanese heartthrobs – is hard to avoid; it pumps out of shops on every street and can be heard live at the Workers' Stadium (see opposite). There's also a thriving **underground** scene, and a few **jazz** bars. There will generally be a cover of around ¥30–80 at the following venues. In addition to the regular city magazines (see p.27), good event and venue listings are available online at ⓦ beijinggigguide .com. Chinese and Western classical music are covered in the "Entertainment and the arts" chapter (see p.150).

### INDIE

★**2 Kolegas** 两个好朋友 liǎnggè hǎopéngyǒu 21 Liangmaqiao ☎010 81964820, ⓦ2kolegas.com; map pp.66–67. Best accessed by cab, this dive bar in the far northeast of the city is great for checking out the indie rockers and their fans, though it's a fair way out. In summer the crowd spills out onto the lawn. Daily 8pm–late.

**Mao Livehouse** 毛现场 mào xiànchǎng 111 Gulou Dongdajie ☎010 64025080, ⓦmaolive.com; Andingmen (line 2) or Nanluoguxiang subway (line 6); map pp.56–57. Managed by Japanese music label Bad News, who know their stuff, this great, decent-sized venue hosts all the best local rock and punk bands. There may be no frills – not even a cloakroom – but it has the best sound system around, and drinks are refreshingly cheap (¥10).

**School** 53 Wudaoying Hutong ☎010 64028881; Yonghegong Lama Temple subway (lines 2 & 5); map pp.66–67. It's mainly rock and punk at this intimate, youthful venue, which has pleasingly regular shows from up-and-coming local bands – a bit hit and miss, but you never know. It's well located on trendy Wudaoying Hutong.

★**What? Bar** 什么酒吧 shénme jiǔbā 72 Beichang Jie ☎133 41122757; Tian'anmen West subway (line 1); map p.42. Oddly, this rock and punk gig venue is within spitting distance of the Forbidden City. It's so small you'll probably get spattered with the guitarist's sweat. A good introduction to the local rock scene, and a great bar outside performance time too (see p.145). Hours vary; usually open 6pm–late.

**Yugong Yishan** 寓公移山 yúgōngyíshān 3–2 Zhangzigong Lu ☎010 64042711, ⓦyugongyishan .com; Zhangzizhonglu subway (line 5); map pp.66–67. With a big dancefloor, an up-for-it crowd and an eclectic mix of live acts, this has to be the best all-round venue in town. The sounds on offer here are mostly rock and electro, though there's a pleasing genre mix across each month. Daily 5pm–midnight.

## THE MIDI FESTIVAL

Periodically banned and with foreign acts occasionally refused permission to play, the **Midi Rock Music** festival (ⓦmidifestival.com) – held at the beginning of May in Haidian Park, just west of Beijing University campus – has always been controversial. Still, plenty of local talent is on display, and the audience is enthusiastic. You can even camp, for the full-on "Chinese Glastonbury" experience. Tickets ¥280 for all three days, or ¥120 per day.

10

### JAZZ

**East Shore Live Jazz Café** 东岸咖啡 dōng'àn kāfēi 2F 2 Qianhai Nanyanlu ☎010 84032131; Beihai North or Nanluoguxiang subway (both line 6); map pp.56–57. A fine bar outside performance time (see p.146), this has live shows Thurs to Sun. Daily 3pm–2am.

**Jazz Ya** 爵士屋 juéshì wū 18 Sanlitun Beilu ☎010 64151227, ⓦjazzya.com.cn; Tuanjiehu subway (line 10); map p.72. Another great bar (see p.147) hosting occasional live jazz. Daily noon–2am.

### MAINSTREAM

**Workers' Stadium** 工人体育场 gōngrén tǐyùchǎng Off Gongti Beilu ☎010 65016655, ⓦgongti.com.cn; Dongsishitiao (line 2) or Dongdaqiao subway (line 6); map pp.66–67. This is where giant gigs are staged, mostly featuring Chinese pop stars, though the likes of Björk have also played here (though, given her views on Tibet, that'll never happen again).

## GAY BEIJING

Official attitudes towards homosexuality have softened in China – it's been removed from the official list of psychiatric disorders and is no longer a national crime – and in cosmopolitan Beijing, pink power has a big influence on fashion and the media. Bars for the *tongzhi* (literally, comrades) are no longer required to hand out pamphlets urging clients to go home to their wives but there are still few dedicated gay or lesbian venues; some "regular" places do, however, have dedicated gay nights. As well as the places listed below, the classy lounge bar *Mesh* (see p.147) hosts gay nights every Thursday.

**Alfa** Opposite North Gate of Workers' Stadium ☎010 64130086; Dongsishitiao subway (line 2); map pp.66–67. Not gay but certainly gay-friendly, especially on their irregular gay and lesbian nights; keep an eye on the city listings magazines (see p.135) for details. It's free to get into the bar area (which makes surprisingly good food); for the dancefloor you'll have to cough up an extra ¥30. Daily 8pm–late.

★ **Destination 7** Gongti Xilu ☎010 65528180, ⓦbjdestination.com; Dongsishitiao subway (line 2); map pp.66–67. Beijing's biggest and most popular gay club by far, with two floors full of half-naked men (mainly local), as well as women who'd rather avoid non-gay fellas for the night. Entry ¥60. Daily 8pm–late.

**Vinyl Café** 206 Gulou Dongdajie ☎010 64001679; Nanluoguxiang subway (line 6); map pp.56–57. This cafe's walls are lined with framed LP covers, and the artists in question (who on earth were *Spanky and Our Gang*?) betray the intended clientele even more than the rainbow flag out front. It's a relaxed place for coffee by day and beers of an evening. Daily 24hr.

ACROBATIC SHOW, CHAOYANG THEATRE

# Entertainment and the arts

Most visitors to Beijing make a trip to see Beijing opera – whether in a
dedicated opera venue or in a traditional teahouse – and the superb Chinese
acrobatics displays, both of which remain timeless arts. Fewer investigate the
equally worthwhile contemporary side of the city's entertainment scene
– the indie music (see p.183), classical music, theatre and dance events. There
are also a number of cinemas where you can check out the provocative
movies emerging from new, underground film-makers. Some of the venues
are a little inconveniently located; many, in particular, lie in a wide stretch
south of Tian'anmen Square but it's worth remembering that many "tours" to
the most popular shows often cost the same as the regular ticket price, yet
throw transport in for free.

## ESSENTIALS

**Listings** For mainstream cultural events – visiting ballet troupes, large-scale concerts and so forth – check the listings in the *China Daily* (available at most hotels). For a more in-depth view and comprehensive listings, including gigs and art happenings and the like, check the expat magazines: *Time Out* (ⓦ timeoutbeijing.com), *The Beijinger* (ⓦ issuu.com/thebeijinger) and *City Weekend* (ⓦ cityweekend.com.cn).

**Tickets** Tickets for all big shows are available at the venue box offices, or from China Ticket Online (ⓣ 400 6103721, ⓦ en.damai.cn). It's amazing how many of them cost exactly ¥180. However, for opera, martial arts and acrobatic performances, it's usually better to book directly through your hotel or hostel since transport to and from the venue in question are sometimes thrown in for free. The only problem with this is that it'll be their choice of venue rather than yours.

## TRADITIONAL OPERA

A trip to see Beijing's famous **opera** (see box below) is one of the most popular diversions for international travellers. Apart from checking out the dedicated venues below, most of which are in the south of the city, you could also visit a **teahouse** for your opera fix. Teahouse performances are short and aimed at foreigners: you can also slurp tea or munch on snacks – often Beijing duck as well – while being entertained.

### OPERA VENUES

★ **Chang'an Grand Theatre** 长安大戏院 cháng'ān dàxìyuàn 7 Jianguomennei Dajie ⓣ 010 65072421; Jianguomen subway (lines 1 & 2). A modern, central theatre putting on a wide range of performances throughout the day – it's probably the most popular place in town for Beijing opera. From ¥180.

**Huguang Guild Hall** 湖广会馆 húguǎng huìguǎn 3 Hufang Lu ⓣ 010 63518284; Caishikou subway (line 4). As well as a fine performance hall, this reconstructed theatre also has a small opera museum on site, with costumes and pictures of famous performers though no English captions. Nightly performances at 7.15pm. From ¥180.

**Liyuan Theatre** 梨园剧场 líyuán jùchǎng 1F Jianguo Qianmen Hotel, 175 Yong'an Lu ⓣ 010 63016688, ⓦ qianmenhotel.com; Caishikou subway (line 4). Pricey but perhaps the best place to see opera, with an emphasis on accessibility: as you go in you pass the actors putting on their make-up – a great photo op. The opera itself is a visitor-friendly bastardization, lasting an hour and jazzed up with some martial arts and slapstick. A display board at the side of the stage gives an English translation of the few lines of dialogue. Nightly performances at 7.30pm; tickets can be bought from the office in the front courtyard of the hotel (daily 9–11am, noon–4.45pm & 5.30–8pm; ¥70–180). The more expensive seats are at tables at the front, where you can sip tea and nibble pastries during the performance.

**National Centre for the Performing Arts** 国家大剧院 guójiā dàjùyuàn 2 Xichang'an Jie ⓣ 010 66550000, ⓦ chncpa.org; Tian'anmen West subway (line 1). This is one venue you can't miss – it's that giant egg west of Tian'anmen Square (see p.85). The opera hall seats over 2000, with fantastic acoustics and lighting to capture every nuance of the performance. There's an English subtitle screen too. You'll probably be in elevated company: former premier Wen Jiabao is a big fan. There is a performance every night at 7.30pm. The box office is open daily from 9.30am or you can ring to reserve. Ticket prices vary, but cost at least ¥180.

**Zhengyici Theatre** 正义祠剧场 zhèngyìcí jùchǎng 220 Qianmen Xiheyanjie ⓣ 010 63189454; Hepingmen subway (line 2). The genuine article, performed in the only surviving wooden Beijing opera theatre and worth a visit just to check out the architecture. Tickets from ¥380.

### TEAHOUSE THEATRES

**Lao She Teahouse** 老舍茶馆 lǎoshě cháguǎn 3F Dawancha Building, 3 Qianmen Xidajie ⓣ 010 63036830;

**11**

---

### BEIJING OPERA

**Beijing opera** (京戏, jīng xì) is the most celebrated of China's 350 or so regional operatic styles – a unique combination of song, dance, acrobatics and mime. Performances are highly stylized, and to the outsider the can often seem obscure and wearying as they are punctuated by a succession of crashing gongs and piercing, discordant songs. But it's worth seeing once, especially if you can acquaint yourself with the story beforehand. Most of the **plots** are based on historical or mythological themes – two of the most famous sagas, which any Chinese will explain to you, are *The White Snake* and *The Water Margin* – and full of moral lessons. Offering an interesting, if controversial, variation on the traditions are those operas that deal with contemporary themes, such as the struggle of women to marry as they choose. The **colours** used on stage, from the costumes to the make-up on the players' faces, are highly symbolic: red signifies loyalty; yellow, fierceness; blue, cruelty; and white, evil.

**11**

Qianmen subway (line 2). At this long-running venue, you can watch the 90min-long "Old Beijing Variety Show"; popular with tour groups, it gives a gaudy taste of traditional Chinese culture. Daily 7.40pm; ¥180–380.

**Tianqiaole Teahouse Theatre** 天桥乐茶园 tiānqiáolè cháyuán 113 Tianqiao Nandajie ☎010 51655060; Qianmen subway (line 2), then taxi. The organizers here have tried hard to create an authentic atmosphere, from the mock-traditional building right down to the Qing costumes worn by the staff. "Crosstalk" performances begin at 7pm and last 3hr, and mostly comprise segments of traditional opera with a little acrobatics in between. Buying tickets in advance is advised, as the place is sometimes booked out with tour groups. ¥180 including tea and snacks; ¥330 including a duck dinner as well.

## DRAMA AND DANCE

Most evenings you can catch Chinese song and dance simply by turning on the TV, though there's plenty of opportunity to see it live. Some venues, such as the Beijing Exhibition Theatre, occasionally stage performances in the original language of imported **musicals** like *The Sound of Music*, which, with tickets at ¥50–100, are a lot cheaper to watch here than at home. **Dance** is popular in Beijing, generally more so at the traditional end of the spectrum, though you can see more contemporary forms at a few small venues. There are also a number of places in which to see **theatre**, both traditional and imported; in addition to the venues listed below, check the Poly Theatre (see opposite) for its programme of theatre and dance.

**Beijing Exhibition Theatre** 北京展览馆剧场 běijīng zhǎnlǎnguǎn jùchǎng 135 Xizhimenwai Dajie ☎010 68354455, ⊛bjexpo.com; Beijing Zoo subway (line 4). This giant hall, containing nearly 3000 seats, stages classical ballet, folk dance and large-scale song-and-dance revues.

**Capital Theatre** 首都剧场 shǒudū jùchǎng 22 Wangfujing Dajie ☎010 65121598, ⊛bjry.com; Dongsi subway (lines 5 & 6). Look out for the People's Art Theatre company here (see box below) – their photo archive, documenting their history, is displayed in the lobby. Most performances are in Chinese. Tickets generally start at ¥80.

**China Puppet Theatre** 中央木偶剧院 zhōngyāng mùòu jùyuàn Corner of Anhua Xili & Third Ring Road ☎010 64254798, ⊛puppetchina.com; Anhuaqiao subway (line 8). Once as important for commoners as opera was for the elite, Chinese puppetry usually involves hand puppets and marionettes. Occasionally, shadow puppets made of thin translucent leather and supported by rods are used. Beijing opera, short stories and Western fairy tales are put on, aimed at kids. 5 shows daily 10am–3pm; from ¥100.

**Penghao Theatre** 蓬蒿剧场 pénghāo jùchǎng 35 Dongmianhua Hutong ☎010 64006452, ⊛penghao theatre.com; Nanluoguxiang subway (line 6). Intimate, privately run theatre set in a beautifully converted courtyard house in a *hutong* just behind the Central Academy of Drama. In addition to fascinating performances that range from Shakespeare to modern dance, they also have a rather nice rooftop bar.

## ACROBATICS AND MARTIAL ARTS

Certainly the most accessible and exciting of the traditional Chinese entertainments, **acrobatics** covers anything from gymnastics through to magic tricks and juggling. The tradition of professional acrobatics has existed in China for two thousand years and continues today at the country's main training school, Wu Qiao in Hebei Province, where students begin training at the age of 5. The style may be vaudeville, but performances are spectacular, with truly awe-inspiring feats of dexterity – sixteen people stacked atop a bicycle and the like. Just as impressive are martial arts displays, which usually involve a few mock fights and feats of strength, such as breaking concrete slabs with one blow.

### THE BIRTH, DEATH AND RESURRECTION OF CHINESE DRAMA

Spoken **drama** was only introduced into Chinese theatres in the twentieth century. The **People's Art Theatre** in Beijing became the best-known company and staged Chinese-language translations of European plays – Ibsen and Chekhov were among the favourite playwrights. But with the onset of the Cultural Revolution in 1968, Jiang Qing, Mao's third wife, declared that "drama is dead". The company, along with most of China's cinemas and theatres, was almost completely out of action for nearly a decade afterwards, with a corpus of just eight plays (deemed socially improving) continuing to be performed. Many of the principal actors, directors and writers were banished, generally to rural hard labour. In 1979, the People's Art Theatre reformed and quickly re-established its reputation.

**Beijing Workers' Club** 北京工人俱乐部 běijīng gōngrén jùlèbù 7 Hufang Lu ☎010 63528910; Caishikou subway (line 4). Popular for its "Legend of Jinsha" show, which adds a few interesting quirks to the old acrobatic routines – silk-rope dancing, water cannon and some zany motorbike stunts. Daily 5.30pm & 7.30pm; from ¥180.

★ **Chaoyang Theatre** 朝阳剧场 cháoyáng jùchǎng 36 Dongsanhuan Beilu ☎010 65072421, ⓦchaoyangtheatre.com; Hujialou subway (lines 6 & 10). If you want to see acrobatics, come to one of the spectacular, colourful shows at this long-running venue, where the stage size allows for the use of some impressive props – bicycles, swings, barrels and the like. There are plenty of souvenir stalls in the lobby (make your purchases after the show rather than during the interval, as prices drop at the end), and consider dropping into the on-site bar, *Ichikura* (see p.147). Daily 7.15–8.30pm; from ¥180.

**Red Theatre** 红剧场 hóng jùchǎng 44 Xingfu Dajie ☎010 67142473, ⓦredtheatre.cn; Tiantandongmen subway (line 5). A lively kung fu routine featuring smoke, fancy lighting and some incredible stunts. Daily 7.30–8.50pm; from ¥180.

## CLASSICAL MUSIC VENUES

**Traditional Han Chinese music** is usually played on the *erhu* (a kind of fiddle) and *qin* (a seven-stringed zither). Contemporary compositions tend to be in a pseudo-romantic, Western-influenced style – easy on the ear, they can be heard live in upmarket hotels and restaurants. To hear traditional pieces, however, visit the concert halls. **Western classical music** is popular – the best place to catch it is the Beijing Concert Hall – as is jazz, which you can hear at a few venues, notably *Jazz Ya* (see p.147).

**11**

**Beijing Concert Hall** 北京音乐厅 běijīng yīnyuètīng 1 Beixinhua Jie ☎010 66057006, ⓦbjconcerthall.cn; Tian'anmen West (line 1) or Xidan subway (lines 1 & 4). This hall seats a thousand people and hosts regular concerts of Western classical and Chinese traditional music by Beijing's resident orchestra and visiting orchestras from the rest of China and overseas. Tickets from ¥80.

**Century Theatre** 世纪剧院 shìjì jùyuàn Sino-Japanese Youth Centre, 40 Liangmaqiao Lu, 2km east of the Kempinski Hotel ☎010 64663311, ⓦwww .centurytheatre.net; Liangmaqiao subway (line 10). An intimate venue for soloists and small ensembles, mostly Chinese modern and traditional classical compositions. Evening performances. ¥120–150.

**Forbidden City Concert Hall** 北京中山公园音乐堂 běijīng zhōngshāngōngyuán yīnyuètáng Zhongshan Park, Xichang'an Jie ☎010 65598285, ⓦfcchbj.com; Tian'anmen West subway (line 1). A stylish hall, with regular performances of Western and Chinese classical music and occasionally jazz too. Tickets from ¥80.

★ **National Centre for the Performing Arts** 国家 大剧院 guójiā dàjùyuàn 2 Xichang'an Jie ☎010 66550000, ⓦchncpa.org; Tian'anmen West subway (line 1). The giant egg-shaped structure just west of Tian'anmen Square (see p.85) hosts the best international performances in its huge concert hall. Note that you can't bring a camera.

**Poly Theatre** 保利大厦国际剧场 bǎolìdàshà guójì jùchǎng Poly Plaza, 14 Dongzhimen Nandajie ☎010 65001188; Donsishitiao subway (line 2). A gleaming hall that presents diverse performances of jazz, ballet, classical music, opera and modern dance for the edification of Beijing's cultural elite. Daily 7.30, from ¥180.

## CINEMAS

There are plenty of **cinemas** showing Chinese and dubbed Western films, usually action movies. The government picks just twenty Western films for release every year, and when they're too popular, they get pulled: *Avatar* disappeared from Chinese screens to give home-grown borefest *Confucius* a chance, for example. Despite such restrictions, these days most Beijingers have an impressive knowledge of world cinema, thanks both to the prevalence of cheap, pirated DVDs and, of course, the internet. Beijing's biggest cinemas tend to show both mainstream Chinese and foreign films with **tickets** around ¥80. There are usually two showings of foreign movies, one dubbed into Chinese, the other subtitled; ring to check.

### MAINSTREAM CINEMAS

**East Gate Cinema** 东环影城 dōnghuán yīngchéng B1 Building B, East Gate Plaza, 9 Dongzhong Jie ☎010 64185930; Dongsishitiao (line 2) or Dongzhimen subway (lines 2 & 13). Small and a little ragged, which makes this a good choice if you don't fancy the whole mulitplex experience.

★ **Megabox** 美嘉欢乐影城 měijiāhuānlè yīng chéng Tai Koo Li ☎010 64176118, ⓦimegabox.com; Tuanjiehu subway (line 10). Beijing's most reliable option for international, non-dubbed films.

**Star City** 新世纪影城 xīnshìjì yīngchéng B1 Oriental Plaza Mall, 1 Dongchang'an Jie ☎010 85186778; Wangfujing subway (line 1). Another biggie, located in the highly presentable Oriental Plaza Mall.

**Wanda Cineplex** 万达电影 wàndá diànyīng 3F Building 8, Wanda Plaza, 93 Jianguo Lu ☎010 59603399,

ⓦwandafilm.com; Guomao subway (lines 1 & 10). Big, comfortable cinema that usually has at least one international film going.

## ART-HOUSE CINEMAS

★ **Broadway Cinematheque** 当代MOMA 百老汇电影 dāngdài MOMA bǎilǎohuì diànyǐng F3 Building 4, MOMA North, 1 Xiangheyuan Lu ☎010 84388258, ⓦb-cinema.cn; Dongzhimen subway (lines 2 & 13). Cinema running regular themed events, often international in nature.

**Space for Imagination** 盒子咖啡馆 hézi kāfēiguǎn 5 Xiwangzhuang Xiaoqu, Haidian ☎010 62791280; Wudaokou subway (line 13). A charming cineastes' bar opposite the east gate of Qinghua University, showing avant-garde films every Saturday at 7pm.

# Shopping

Appropriately for the capital of a major commercial power, Beijing has some first-class shopping. Much of it is concentrated in three main shopping districts: Wangfujing has mostly mid-market shops and malls selling famous Chinese brands; Xidan hosts giant department stores; and Qianmen has been reinvented as an open-air mall. Elsewhere, Liulichang, a street of imitation Ming buildings aimed especially at visitors, is a good spot to furnish yourself with souvenirs; shops here are much of a muchness, though there are some better places on nearby Dazhalan Lu. Jianguomenwai Dajie is the place to head for clothes, and Guomao is where you'll find the really high-end stuff. Shopping is more exciting, and cheaper, in the city's many markets, even though they offer no guarantee of quality; you can – and should – bargain.

## ON THE SOUVENIR HUNT

Good, widely available, inexpensive **souvenirs** include kites, art materials, papercuts (images cut into thin card), knotwork, tea sets, jade bracelets, mah jong sets and ornamental chopsticks (try any department store). Seals are another popular choice, with your name put into a soapstone "chop" in either Chinese characters or Roman letters; prices start at around ¥50, and if you want to see ancient traditions meeting modern technology, go round the back and watch them laser-cut it. For something a little unusual, you could get some Cultural Revolution kitsch – porcelain Mao figurines, the *Little Red Book*, Red Guard alarm clocks – from an antique store.

## ESSENTIALS

**Opening hours** Shops generally stay open from Monday to Saturday from 9am to 6 or 7pm, closing earlier on Sunday; the large shopping centres are open every day until around 9pm. Outdoor markets don't have official opening times, but tend to trade from about 7am to 6pm.

We have listed opening times throughout.

**Addresses** Phone numbers are given for shops contactable in this way; if you're stuck for directions, head there in a taxi and ask the driver to call.

## ANTIQUES, CURIOS AND SOUVENIRS

There's no shortage of **antique stores** and **markets** in the capital, offering opium pipes, jade statues, mah jong sets, Fu Manchu glasses, and all manner of bric-a-brac – pretty much all of it fake. The jade is actually soapstone, inset jewels are glass, and that venerable painting is a print stained with tea. There are very few real antiques for sale in Beijing, and no bargains. However, there are some great places to shop for items that at least *look* old. **Liulichang**, south of Hepingmen subway stop, has the densest concentration of curio stores in town, with a huge selection of wares, particularly of art materials, porcelain, musical instruments and snuffboxes; prices can be steep. For contemporary curios, try **Yandaixie Jie**, a *hutong* full of little stores selling souvenir notebooks, matchboxes and the like, at the north end of Qianhai lake.

**12**

## SHOPS

**+86 Design Store** 245 Gulou Dongdajie ☎010 57623086; Andingmen subway (line 2); map pp.56–57. Terrific little shop selling all sorts of arty paraphernalia: cute backpacks, laptop cases, mugs, pens, pencils, T-shirts, small items of furniture... the list goes on. There's another branch in the 798 Art District. Daily 10am–7pm.

**Mansudae Art Studio** 万寿台创作社美术馆 wànshòutái chuàngzuòshè měishùguǎn 798 Art District ☎010 59789317, ⓦ myinweb.com/mansudae; map pp.96–97. This studio (see box, p.103) specializes in North Korean art, and also has a range of North Korean goodies on sale – buy a Kim Il-sung pin-badge, some English-language propaganda magazines or (if you've got a big wad of cash) an authentic painting from Pyongyang. Tues–Sun 10am–6pm.

★ **The One** 69 Yandaixie Jie; Nanluoguxiang subway (line 6); map pp.56–57. The only real standout shop remaining on Yandaixie Jie (referred to as "tat alley" by some visitors), this is a quality place selling quirky, if slightly pricey, items – all sorts from pictures to cutlery and cups to cuddly monk dolls. Daily 9am–8pm.

**PMT** 75 Nanluogu Xiang ☎010 64008520; Nanluoguxiang subway (line 6); map pp.56–57. This shop (despite its slightly unfortunate name) prides itself on Chinese photography – there are all sorts of prints available, large and small. However, it's just as notable for its tremendous selection of fans; again, there's something

for everyone, from cheap designs to expensive carved sandalwood. Daily 9.30am–6.30pm.

★ **Three Stone** 三石斋风筝坊 sānshízhāi fēngzhēngfǎng 25 Di'anmen Xidajie ☎010 84044505; Nanluoguxiang subway (line 6); map pp.56–57. A specialist kite shop with a rich history – the ancestors of the current owner once made kites for the Qing royals. Though there are plenty of fancy designs here, they also sell a fair few cheapies. Daily 9am–8pm.

**View Pottery** 视界 1 Mao'er Hutong ☎010 64023529; Nanluoguxiang subway (line 6); map pp.56–57. Despite its location on kitschy Nanluogu Xiang, this is a quality place, selling pretty tea sets and other fired ware for decent prices. Daily 9.30am–6.30pm.

## MARKETS

**Beijing Curio City** 北京古玩城 běijīng gǔwánchéng Huawei Nanlu; Panjiayuan subway (line 10); map pp.78–79. A giant arcade of more than 400 stalls, best visited on a Sunday, when other antique traders come and set up in the surrounding streets. Daily 9.30am–6.30pm.

**Liangma Antique Market** 亮马收藏品市场 liàngmǎ shōucángpǐn shìchǎng 27 Liangmaqiao Lu; Liangmaqiao subway (line 10); map pp.66–67. This market is small but also less picked over than others, with good carpet and furniture sections. One for the serious collector with time to root around; you might even find the odd real antique. Daily 9am–7pm.

## BEIJING'S BEST

**Best for tea** Ten Fu (see p.162) and Zhang Yiyuan (see p.162)
**Best for riot-cop key-fobs** Police Museum (see p.65)
**Best for goat-penis aphrodisiac** Tongrentang pharmacy (see box, p.34), Silk Market (see p.160)
**Best for drily witty t-shirts** Plastered (see p.160)
**Best for antiques** Panjiayuan Market (see below)
**Best for local music** C Rock (see p.158)
**Best for artsy local fashion** Shanghai Tang (see p.160)
**Best for genuine North Korean badges** Mansudae Art Studio (see opposite)
**Best for tea sets** View Pottery (see opposite)
**Best for fans** PMT (see opposite)

★ **Panjiayuan Market** 潘家园市场 pānjiāyuán shìchǎng Panjiayuan Lu; Panjiayuan subway (line 10); map pp.78–79. Also called the "Dirt Market", this is Beijing's biggest antiques market, with a huge range of souvenirs and secondhand goods on sale (sometimes in advanced states of decay), including many from Tibetan traders. It's at its biggest and best at weekends between 6am and 3pm, when the surrounding streets are packed with stalls – worth a visit even if you're not buying. The initial asking prices for souvenirs are more reasonable than anywhere else. Mon–Fri 8am–6.30pm, with earlier opening at weekends.

## BOOKS

There are plenty of English-language books on Chinese culture on sale in Beijing, including many hard to find in the West, ranging from giant coffee-table tomes celebrating new freeways in China to comic-book versions of Chinese classics. Even if you're not buying, Beijing's **bookshops** are pleasant environments in which to browse; some have cafés and art galleries attached.

★ **Bookworm** 书虫 shūchóng Sanlitun Nanjie ☎010 65689507, ⓦchinabookworm.com; Tuanjiehu subway (line 10); map pp.66–67. Popular café (see p.142) with a good English-language selection, which also hosts regular literary events and lectures. Check the website for details. Daily 9am–2am.

**Charterhouse** B1 The Place, 9 Guanghua Lu ☎010 65871325; Dongdaqiao subway (line 6); map pp.66–67. A good selection of imported books and magazines. Daily 10am–10pm.

**Foreign Language Bookstore** 外文书店 wàiwén shūdiàn 235 Wangfujing Dajie ☎010 65126911, ⓦbpiec.com.cn; Wangfujing (line 1) or Dengshikou subway (line 5); map pp.66–67. This store has the biggest selection of foreign-language books in mainland China. The English books on offer downstairs include fiction, textbooks on Chinese medicine and translations of Chinese classics. The upper floors, too, have more fiction in English, magazines, wall hangings, and Japanese *manga*. Sometimes, the same book is cheaper upstairs than downstairs. Daily 8am–5pm.

★ **Page One** 叶壹堂 xiéyītáng Tai Koo Li (south mall), Sanlitun Lu ☎010 64176626; Tuanjiehu subway (line 10); map p.72.Wonderful new bookstore, with a wide selection of English-language books, including travel guides, novels and artsy stuff. Daily 10am–10pm.

## CARPETS

Created mainly in Xinjiang, Tibet and Tianjin, the beautiful handmade **carpets** on sale in Beijing aren't cheap, but are nevertheless pretty good value. Tibetan carpets are yellow and orange and usually have figurative mythological or religious motifs; rugs from Xinjiang in the northwest are red and pink with abstract patterns, while weaves from Tianjin are multicoloured. Check the colour for consistency at both ends – sometimes, large carpets are hung up near a hot lamp, which causes fading. As well as the places reviewed below, you can get carpets at the Friendship Store (see p.161; bargain hard here), Yuanlong Silk Corporation (see p.161) and on Liulichang.

**Khawachen Tibetan Rugs** 客瓦坚西藏手工地毯 kèwǎjiān xīzàng shǒugōng dìtǎn 3–2FA, Solana Shopping Park, Chaoyang Park ☎010 59056311; Liangmaqiao subway (line 10); map pp.66–67. Handmade Tibetan rugs from about ¥2000, plus custom designs produced to order. Daily 10am–10pm.

**Qianmen Carpet Company** 前门地毯厂 qiánmén dìtǎnchǎng 59 Xingfu Jie, just north of the Tiantan hotel ☎010 67151687; Tiantandongmen subway (line 5); map pp.78–79. A converted air-raid shelter selling carpets mostly from Xinjiang and Tibet; the silk carpets from Henan in central China are very popular. A typical 2m by 3m carpet can cost

**12**

around ¥50,000, though the cheapest rugs start at around ¥2000. Mon–Fri 8.30am–5pm.

**Zhaojia Chaowai Market** 兆佳朝外市场 zhàojiā cháowài shìchǎng Off 3rd East Ring Road; north of

Panjiayuan subway (line 10); map pp.78–79. Some carpets and enormous quantities of reproduction traditional Chinese furniture in all sizes and styles – for those whose lives lack lacquer. Daily 10am–5.30pm.

## CDS AND DVDS

**Pirated CDs and DVDs** are sold by chancers who approach foreigners around the Silk Market (see p.160), on Dazhalan and in bars in Houhai and Sanlitun. The discs generally work, though sometimes the last few minutes are garbled. You can get DVDs for as little as ¥8, CDs for ¥5, though the asking price starts out at ¥15. Note that with DVDs of newly released films, you're likely to get a version shot illicitly in a cinema, with heads bobbing around at the bottom of the screen. Otherwise, music shops selling **legitimate CDs** can be found throughout the city; a couple of the best are reviewed below.

**Beijing Huashiweiye** 北京花市伟业 běijīng huāshìwěiyè West side of Yashow Market; Tuanjiehu subway (line 10); map p.72. Forget the name of this place, since even the proprietors aren't sure; it's marked from the outside as "CD DVD SHOP", and that's what they sell. Thanks to a wide selection of films, they've a regular base of expat customers. Daily 8am–5pm.

**C Rock** 99 Gulou Dongdajie ☎010 64072530; Andingmen

subway (line 2); map pp.56–57. One of the best places in the city to go hunting for CDs by local bands. The friendly owner will be pleased to make recommendations and give you a listen to a few choice tracks. Hours vary; generally 11am–5pm.

**Hongyun** 宏运音像中心 hóngyùn yīnxiàng zhōngxīn 62 Xinjiekou Beidajie; Xinjiekou subway (line 4); map pp.56–57. A huge collection of legitimate CDs, Western imports, Mando-pop and local rock. Daily 8am–5pm.

## CLOTHES AND FABRICS

**Clothes** are a bargain in Beijing but be sure to check the quality carefully. Head for **Jianguomen Dajie**, where the Silk Market (see p.160), the Friendship Store (see p.161) and the plazas (see p.161) offer something for every budget. If you're particularly tall or have especially large feet you'll generally have difficulty finding clothes and shoes to fit you, though there's a reasonable chance of finding clothes in your size at the Silk Market. One big Asian trend that seems unlikely to catch on in the West is the phenomenon of matching T-shirts for couples – if you want to check out the "his and hers" T-shirts that are all the rage among the kids, take a look at the clothes shops near the universities. Far more traditional are figure-hugging dresses known as *qipao*; these can be made to order from **tailors** or bought off the peg from stores around the city: in addition to the tailors reviewed below, check out the Silk Market and, in particular, Yashow Market.

### TAILORS

**Hongdu Tailor** 28 Dongjiaomin Xiang ☎010 63519282; Qianmen subway (line 2); map pp.78–79. This tailor, just west of the *Capital Hotel*, once made suits for Chairman Mao himself; he may not have been much of a fashion icon but the offering here is of very high quality. A full suit will set you back about ¥10,000, and take a month to make. Mon–Sat 9am–5pm.

**Lisa Tailor** 5F, 3.3 Mall, 33 Sanlitun Beilu ☎139 10798183, ⦿beijingtailor.com; Tuanjiehu subway (line 10); map p.72. A reliably good bet for bargain tailoring, with English-speaking staff; suits start at around ¥1000, and ladies' *qipao* at around the same price.

Next-day service is available for a little more. Mon–Sat 9am–6pm.

### SHOPS

**A You** 阿尤 āyóu 108 Xinjiekou Beidajie ☎010 65242400; Xinjiekou subway (line 4); map pp.56–57. Trendy, ethnic-style designer clothes from an established local design brand. Prices start at around ¥200 for striking summer dresses. Mon–Sat 9am–5pm.

**Beijing Silk Store** 北京谦祥益丝绸商店 běijīng qiānxiángyì sīchóu shāngdiàn 50 Dazhalan Jie ☎010 63016658; Qianmen subway (line 2); map pp.78–79. This is an excellent place to buy quality silk

---

## FAKING IT

China has a massive industry in **fakes** – nothing escapes the counterfeiters. You'll no doubt hear assurances to the contrary, but you can assume that all antiques and collectable stamps, coins and posters are replicas, that paintings are prints and that Rolex watches will stop working as soon as you turn the corner. If you don't mind robbing artists of their livelihood, pirated CDs and DVDs are very cheap, while even more of a bargain are the widely available fake designer-label clothes and accessories.

clothes in Chinese styles, with a wider selection and keener prices than any of the tourist stores. The ground floor sells silk fabrics, while clothes can be bought upstairs. Daily 8am–5pm.

**Dong Liang Studio** 栋梁 dòngliáng 26 Wudaoying Hutong ☎010 84047648; Yonghegong Lama Temple subway (lines 2 & 5); map pp.66–67. Chic, elegant and affordable clothes by local designers; look out for beautiful dresses by JJ, Ye Qian and Shen Ye. Mon–Sat 9am–5pm.

**Five Colours Earth** 五色土 Wǔsètǔ 1505, Building 5, Jianwai SOHO ☎010 58692923, ⓦfivecoloursearth.cn; Guomao subway (lines 1 & 10); map pp.66–67. Interesting and unusual collections by a talented local designer, often incorporating fragments of old embroidery. Not too expensive either: you can pick up a coat for ¥600. Daily 9.30am–7pm.

**Neiliansheng Shoes** 内联升布鞋 nèiliánshēng bùxié 34 Dazhalan Lu ☎010 63013041, ⓦnls1853.com; Qianmen subway (line 2); map pp.78–79. Look out for the giant shoe in the window. All manner of handmade flat, slip-on shoes and slippers in traditional designs, starting from ¥200 or so – they make great gifts. Daily 9am–8pm.

**NLGX Design** NLGX 设计 NLGX shèjì 33 Nanluogu Xiang ☎010 64048088, ⓦnlgxdesign.com; Nanluoguxiang subway (line 6); map pp.56–57. Hipster streetwear from local designers, with much made from recycled materials. Designs are generally grouped around a theme, which changes regularly. There's another branch in Terminal 2 of the airport. Daily 10am–11pm.

★ **Plastered T-Shirts** 创可贴T恤 chuàngkětiē tīxù 61 Nanluogu Xiang ☎134 88848855, ⓦplasteredtshirts.com; Nanluoguxiang subway (line 6); map pp.56–57. Hipster T-shirts and sweatshirts whose witty designs reference everyday Beijing life – subway tickets, thermoses and so on. It's a standard ¥180 per T-shirt. Daily 9am–7pm.

**Ruifuxiang Store** 瑞蚨祥丝绸店 ruìfúxiáng sīchóudiàn 5 Dazhalan Lu, off Qianmen Dajie ☎010 63035313, ⓦruifuxiang.com; Qianmen subway (line 2); map pp.78–79. Silk and cotton fabrics and a good selection of shirts and dresses, with a tailor specializing in made-to-measure qipaos. You should aim to barter a little off the quoted price. Daily 9.30am–8.30pm.

**Shanghai Tang** 上海滩 shànghǎi tān B1 Grand Hyatt Hotel, 1 Dongchang'an Jie ☎010 85187228, ⓦshanghaitang.com; Wangfujing subway (line 1); map pp.66–67. This renowned Chinese designer label offers brightly coloured luxury chinoiserie. Nice bags and cufflinks, as well as cushions, purses, robes and neo-Mao jackets, though it's all a bit pricey. It's straight down the steps from the Hyatt lobby. Daily 10am–9.30pm.

**Sheng Xifu Hat Store** 盛锡福帽店 shèngxīfú màodiàn 196 Wangfujing Dajie ☎010 65130620; Wangfujing subway (line 1); map pp.66–67. China's most famous hat brand, with a display in the store of headwear worn by luminaries. A cap of cotton is ¥128, rabbit fur ¥680. Daily 8am–6pm.

★ **Ullens Center for Contemporary Art** 尤伦斯当代艺术中心 yóulúnsī dāngdài yìshùzhōngxīn 798 Art District ☎010 64386675, ⓦucca.org.cn; map pp.96–97. The shop connected to this excellent gallery (see p.103) sells limited-edition fashions by local designers for around ¥1000 and handwoven bags for ¥300. Tues–Sun 10am–7pm.

## MARKETS

**Aliens Street Market** 老番街 lǎofān jiē Yabao Lu, north of Ritan Park; Chaoyangmen subway (lines 2 & 6); map pp.66–67. This bustling warren of stalls is where the Russian expats come en masse, though there's a refreshing lack of hassle from the vendors. A vast range of (cheap) goods are on offer, but it's particularly worth picking over for clothes and accessories; take a close look at the stitching before you hand over your cash. Daily 9.30am–7pm.

**Beijing Zoo Market** 动物园服装批发市场 dòngwùyuán fúzhuāng pīfā shìchǎng Xizhimenwai Nanlu; Beijing Zoo subway (line 4); map pp.86–87. This giant, hectic indoor market is full of stalls selling very cheap non-branded clothes, shoes and accessories to locals in the know. Almost everything has a price tag so you won't have to bargain. Note that there won't be anything in large sizes. Daily 8am–5pm.

**Silk Market** 秀水市场 xìushuǐ shìchǎng Off Jianguomenwai Dajie ⓦxiushui.com.cn; Yong'anli subway (line 1); map pp.66–67. This huge six-storey mall for tourists has electronics, jewellery and souvenirs, but its main purpose is to profit through flouting international copyright laws, with hundreds of stalls selling fake designer labels. You'll need to haggle hard. There are also a few tailors – pick out your material, then bargain, and you can get a suit made in 24hr for ¥800 or so. It's incredibly busy, attracting over 50,000 visitors a day on weekends, and vendors are tiresomely pushy. There is a huge toy market on the third floor, a branch of the Tongrentang Pharmacy (see p.34) on the fourth floor, and a Quanjude roast duck restaurant (see p.142) on the sixth. Daily 9.30am–9pm.

**Yansha Outlets Mall** 燕莎奥特莱斯购物中心 yànshā àotèláisī gòuwù zhōngxīn 9 Dongsihuannan Jie ☎010 67395678, ⓦyansha.com.cn; Jinsong subway (line 10), then a taxi (¥15); map pp.78–79. At the southern end of the eastern section of the Fourth Ring Road, this is a huge outlet for genuine designer clothes and bags, all old lines, at discounts of 30–50 percent. Very popular with expats. Daily 10am–10pm.

★ **Yashow Clothing Market** 雅秀服装市场 yǎxìu fúzhuāng shìchǎng 58 Gongrentiyuchang Beilu; Tuanjiehu subway (line 10); map p.72. A four-storey mall of stalls selling designer fakes, very like the Silk Market but a little less busy. The third floor is filled with tailors (try Alice My Tailor or Tailor Ma), and shop assistants speak basic

English. Turn up with any design, or even just a picture from a fashion magazine, and they'll gamely give it a go. A suit should cost around ¥800 and tailored shirts around ¥150; they will take about a week to make, three days at the least. If you want to be certain of getting exactly what you want, make sure in advance that they'll sort out any issues when you pick up your clothes., both on the third floor. Also here is Sally Tailor, who are great for women's clothing; it'll cost

¥1000–1600 for something in vaguely Chinese style, or upwards of ¥3000 for a real *qipao*. Daily 9.30am–8pm.
**Yuanlong Silk Corporation** 元隆顾绣绸缎商场 yuánlóng gùxiù chóuduàn shāngchǎng 55 Tiantan Lu ☎010 67052451; Ciqikou subway (line 5); map pp.78–79. A good selection of silk clothes, blankets and bedding at this large, mall-like building, located just opposite the Tiantan Park wall. Mon–Sat 9am–6.30pm.

## COMPUTER EQUIPMENT

You can pick up memory sticks, an MP3 player, webcams, laptops, phones, tablets and more for less than at home if you go for unglamorous Chinese brands such as Acer and Lenovo, but be aware that there is little after-sales support. **Pirated software**, though a steal in more ways than one, should be given a wide berth. The main area for electronic goodies is **Zhongguancun** in northwest Beijing, nicknamed "Silicon Alley" for its plethora of computer shops and hightech businesses.

**Buy Now Mall** 百脑汇 bǎinǎohuì 10 Chaoyangmenwai Dajie, opposite the Dongyue Temple; Dongdaqiao subway (line 6); map pp.66–67. Convenient and orderly four-storey mall of stores, and a good place to load up on cheap laptops, phones or tablets. You can barter, but this isn't the Silk Market – you might get at most a quarter off. Daily 9am–8pm.

**Hailong Electronics Market** 海龙大厦 hǎilóng dàshà 1 Zhongguancun Dajie; Zhongguancun subway (line 4); map pp.96–97. The biggest in the area, with six storeys, this is a veritable bazaar, piled high with all manner of gadgetry. There is a little leeway for bargaining. Mon–Sat 9am–6pm.

## DEPARTMENT STORES AND MALLS

12

For general goods, and an idea of current Chinese taste, check out the city's **department stores** and **malls**. Maybe it's the air of exclusivity and sophistication, or just a reaction to Beijing's bad weather, but the appetite for vast and sterile shopping warrens seems insatiable. The new giant malls sell goods (clothes mostly) that cost as much as they do in the West, and also have supermarkets, coffee shops, restaurants, chemists and food courts, and sometimes cinemas and bowling alleys.

**APM** 北京 APM běijīng APM 138 Wangfujing Jie ☺beijingapm.cn; Wangfujing subway (line 1); map pp.66–67. Large, bright mall that's probably the cheeriest in the city. All your favourite Western high-street names are here, and the top two levels have some good places to eat. Daily 9am–10pm.

**Friendship Store** 北京友谊商店 běijīng yǒuyì shāngdiàn Jianguomenwai Dajie ☎010 65003311, ☺bjyysd.com.cn; Jianguomen (lines 1 & 2) or Yong'anli subway (line 1); map pp.66–67. Built in the late 1970s as the first modern department store in China, this was for a time the only place in the city selling imported goods; Chinese shoppers, barred from entering, would bribe foreigners to buy things for them. The store has since failed to reinvent itself, and is known for high prices and insouciant staff. Daily 9.30am–8.30pm.

**Galaxy Soho** 银河SOHO yínhé SOHO Nanshuiguan Hutong ☺galaxysoho.sohochina.com; Chaoyangmen subway (lines 2 & 6); map pp.66–67. Newly opened at the time of writing, this latest addition to the Galaxy empire is another architectural delight, a range of interconnected, cocoon-like structures with a distinctive horizontal slatting effect. Its shops are worth a poke around, though it's mostly office space. Daily 10am–8pm.

**Intime Lotte** 乐天银泰百货 lètiān yíntài bǎihuò 88 Wangfujing Jie; Wangfujing subway (line 1) ☎010

59785114, ☺intimelotte.com; map pp.66–67. You can't miss this mall, housed in a distinctive building fronted by ripple-like waves of glass. Inside it's actually more like a department store; head on up to the top level for some great hotpot at *Hai Di Lao* (see p.136). Daily 10am–9pm.

**Oriental Plaza** 东方广场 dōngfāng guǎngchǎng 1 Dongchang'an Jie ☺www.orientalplaza.com; Wangfujing subway (line 1); map pp.66–67. Extremely long mall featuring a number of excellent boutiques (including Shanghai Tang; see p.160), an array of international brand names, and a good food court on the lower level. Daily 9.30am–10pm.

**The Place** 世贸天阶 shìmào tiānjiē 9 Guanghua Lu ☺theplace.cn; Dongdaqiao (line 6), Jintaixizhao (line 10) or Yong'anli subway (line 1); map pp.66–67. Fancy mall with some upscale shopping opportunities in two long wings. Many, however, come for the giant LED screen (see p.73), which makes the open-air path running beneath it a great place for a stroll. Daily 10am–10pm.

**Sanlitun Soho** 三里屯SOHO sānlǐtún SOHO Gongren Tiychang Beilu ☺sanlitunsoho.sohochina.com; Tuanjiehu subway (line 10); map p.72. You probably won't be coming here for the shops, but this mix of office space and shops constitutes some of the most adventurous architecture in the city, its black-and-white striped towers rising up like giant barcodes. Daily 10am–8pm.

**Tai Koo Li** 太古里 tàigǔlǐ Off Sanlitun Lu ⓦwww .taikoolisanlitun.com; Tuanjiehu subway (line 10); map p.72. Some of Beijing's malls are beautiful constructions, and others are merely excellent places to shop. These twin malls, however, are the most successful effort so far, with their best-of-both-worlds mix of elegant dining and high-end consumerism. The north mall is a little bit snobby, but its southern counterpart is a favourite strolling and dating spot with young Beijingers. Mall open 24hr; shop times vary.

## JEWELLERY AND ACCESSORIES

**Jewellery** is a good buy in Beijing, and often much cheaper than at home. Handmade pieces by minorities such as the Miao and Tibetans are perennially popular with foreigners, and are currently trendy with the Chinese.

**D-SATA** Unit A116, Nali Patio 81 Sanlitun Beilu ☎010 64156802, ⓦd-sata.com; Tuanjiehu subway (line 10); map p.72. Stylish, quirky fashion bags and jewellery made from recycled materials (such as snakeskin that's been discarded from restaurants). Daily 1–9pm.

**Dragon House** 龙家 lóngjiā East side of Yashow Market ☎010 64132929; Tuanjiehu subway (line 10); map p.72. Lovely silver and gold jewellery in Chinese and Western styles. Daily 2–10pm.

**Hongqiao Department Store** 红桥百货中心 hóngqiáo bǎihuò zhōngxīn 52 Tiantan Donglu; Tiantandongmen subway (line 5); map pp.78–79. This giant mall remains hugely popular with foreigners owing to its location by the east gate of the Temple of Heaven, though it's not terribly interesting. The top floors function as a pearl and jewellery market. Daily 9am–8pm.

## SUPERMARKETS

Beijing is well stocked with supermarkets, especially useful if you want to get a picnic, or have **self-catering** facilities. All sell plenty of Western food alongside all the Chinese, though few have a decent range of dairy products. Most new malls also have supermarkets in their basements.

**12**

**Carrefour** Guangqumen Neidajie ⓦcarrefour.com.cn; Ciqikou subway (line 5); map pp.78–79. The most conveniently located Beijing outpost of the French hypermarket empire; like the others, it's a decent hunting ground for bicycles, wines, cheese, nappies and much more. Daily 8am–10pm.

**City Shop** B1 The Place, 9 Guanghua Lu ⓦcityshop .com.cn; Dongdaqiao (line 6), Jintaixizhao (line 10) or Yong'anli subway (line 1); map pp.66–67. A particularly well-stocked supermarket, and conveniently located right in the centre of Beijing's prime business district. Daily 9am–9pm.

★ **Jenny Lou** 6 Sanlitun Beilu ⓦwww.jennyshop .com.cn; Agricultural Exhibition Center subway (line 10); map p.72. A chain of small, almost deli-like supermarkets with branches all over the east of the city. All sorts of goodies line their crowded shelves, making this the place to head if you want exotic goodies like olives, cheese (often incredibly cheap), or international cereals. Daily 8am–11pm.

## TEA

There are tea shops all over the city, and many offer free samples; some also double as places in which to buy **tea sets**, though these will be cheaper in dedicated pottery or souvenir shops.

**Maliandao Lu** 马连道茶叶街, mǎliándào cháyèjiē. Behind Beijing West train station; Beijing West subway (line 9); map pp.86–87. If you're in the mood for something truly special, check out this street, which hosts hundreds of tea shops along a 1.5km-long stretch. They all offer free tastings, but remember that you're expected to bargain for the actual product. You're spoilt for choice, of course, but check out four-storey Tea City, about halfway down. There's plenty of tea paraphernalia around, too, much of which makes good gifts – look for porous Yixing ware teapots.

**Ten Fu** 天福茶 tiānfú chá 53 Qianmen Dajie ⓦtenfu .com; Qianmen subway (line 2); map pp.78–79. Huge chain with stores across the city; one of their best is on pedestrianized Qianmen Dajie. Some staff speak English, and there's very little pressure to buy – so many people shop here each day that they don't need to hassle for custom. All sorts of tea available, from the extremely cheap to the extraordinarily expensive. Daily 8am–9pm.

**Zhang Yiyuan** 张一元茶 zhāngyīyuán chá 86 Qianmen Dajie ⓦzhangyiyuan.net; Qianmen subway (line 2); map pp.78–79. Fantastic tearoom with a great location on pretty Qianmen Dajie; as well as a wide range of teas and tea sets, in summer months they serve delectable green-tea ice cream from a shopfront window. Other branches across the city. Daily 8am–9pm.

BEIJING DUCKS

# Sports and fitness

During the 2008 Olympics, a passion for athletic activity became a patriotic duty. Now the dust has settled, the legacy of the Games includes a range of good sports facilities across the capital, from the outdoor workout machines placed in every neighbourhood to the showpiece stadiums themselves. However, the most visible kinds of exercise need no fancy equipment; head to any park in the morning and you'll see citizens going through all sorts of martial arts routines, as well as performing popular exercises deemed good for the *qì* (气, life force), such as walking backwards, chest slapping, and tree hugging. In addition, plenty of people cycle (see p.25), play table tennis (often with a line of bricks as a net) and street badminton (with no net at all), while in the evening many public spaces – parks in particular – become the venue for mass ballroom-dancing.

**13**

## GYMS

Gyms are becoming as popular as they are in the West. There are a growing number of private gyms, while most large hotels have at least some gym equipment. In the more expensive places, non-guests will be able to use the facilities for a charge (from ¥100).

**China World Hotel** China World Trade Centre, Jianguomenwai Dajie ☎010 65052266, 🅦shangri-la .com/beijing/chinaworld; Guomao subway (lines 1 & 10). A pricey place filled with a range of excellent equipment (even if those using it occasionally seem more interested in showing off than working out).

**Evolution Fitness** Blue Castle Centre, 3 Xidawang Lu ☎010 85997650; Dawanglu subway (line 1). Beijing's best private gym, whose branches charge ¥100 for one visit, and ¥2000 for three months' membership.

★ **Park Hyatt** ☎010 85671234, 🅦beijing.park .hyatt.com; Guomao subway (lines 1 & 10). Surely the most attractive gym in the city, based on the 59th floor of the fancy *Park Hyatt* hotel (see p.130). The views over the CBD are fantastic, especially from the nearby lap-pool. The only problem is the price, which for non-guests will start at a princely ¥500 per day, or ¥25,000 per year. Ouch.

## HIKING AND JOGGING

If you thought that Beijing's crowded streets and polluted air put paid to any thoughts of physical exertion… you'd be right. If you *do* fancy **jogging**, one interesting option is the road running between the Forbidden City's east and west gates; this is near empty at night, and incredibly atmospheric.

**Beijing Hikers** ☎010 64322786, 🅦beijinghikers.com. Expat-run group organizing frequent, imaginative hikes in the city's environs to dilapidated sections of the Great Wall, caves and the like. Reservations are required. Meet every Saturday at the *Starbucks* in the *Lido Holiday Inn*.

## ICE SKATING

In winter, try Qianhai, the Summer Palace (see box, p.99) or the Shicha Lakes for **ice skating**. Otherwise, there are a couple of indoor venues around town. However, you may not fancy visiting any of these places as a novice, as Chinese skaters are very good and expect a certain degree of confidence.

**Le Cool** B2 China World Trade Centre; Guomao subway (lines 1 & 10). The city's most accessible indoor rink: small, but still a lot of fun, and family-friendly. From ¥30 for 90min. Mon–Sat 10am–10pm, Sun 10am–8pm.

## MARTIAL ARTS

Beijing has some good places to study Chinese **martial arts** such as *tai ji*, Shaolin kung fu and *bagua*. However, if you're visiting China for this reason, it may be better to arrange things though your own school or national association beforehand. For **kick boxing** and other non-Chinese martial arts, try Evolution Fitness (see above). Note that both of the following places have facilities for English-language instruction.

**Beijing Language and Culture Institute** 15 Xueyuan Lu, Haidian ☎010 66629493, 🅦www.new.blcu.edu. cn; Wudaokou subway (line 13). Classes begin at 5pm and cost ¥50.

**Beijing Milun Kung Fu School** 33 Xitangzi Hutong, off Wangfujing ☎138 1170 6568, 🅦kungfuinchina .com; Dengshikou subway (line 5). Renowned school with a wonderful *hutong* location, though they decamp to Ritan Park during the summer months. Rates start at ¥100 a session.

---

### ATHLETIC EVENTS AROUND BEIJING

Some intriguing events take place around Beijing. Most interesting is the **Genghis Khan Extreme Grasslands Marathon** (🅦genghiskhanmtbadventure.com), which sees runners pound a standard-length marathon course through some of China's most enchantingly beautiful scenery. This usually takes place in early July, and is immediately followed by the **Genghis Khan Mountain Bike Adventure**, a three-day, 206km race organized by the same team. Do them back to back and live to tell the tale, and you'll have had the ideal preparation for September's **Beijing International Triathlon** (🅦beijinginternationaltriathlon.com), an event resuscitated in 2013.

**13**

## MASSAGE AND SPA

Beijing is full of dodgy **massage** joints, but reliable venues do exist – plenty of them, too. Prices are rising, but are still less than you'd pay in most Western countries. **Spa** services are even easier to track down – most upper-end hotels offer such treatments.

**Aibosen** 11 Liufang Beilu ☎010 64652044; Liufang subway (line 13). The blind staff at this clinic are trained in Chinese medical massages. Most popular with foreigners are the 1hr deep-tissue massages (¥118). If you like them and are sticking around for a while, you can pick up discount cards for ten (¥790) or twenty (¥1380) massages. Daily 10am–1.30am.

**Bodhi** 17 Gongti Beilu, opposite Workers' Stadium ☎010 64130226, ⓦbodhi.com.cn; Dongsishitiao subway (line 2). Ayurvedic and Thai massages are among the many options available at this Southeast Asian-styled clinic. Ayurvedic massage ¥288 for 1hr. Daily 11am–12.30pm.

**Chi** Shangri-La Hotel, 29 Zizhuyuan Lu ☎010 68412211, ⓦshangri-la.com/beijing/shangrila; Chedaogou subway (line 10). Therapies at this luxurious New Age spa claim to use the five Chinese elements – metal, fire, wood, water and earth – to balance your *yin* and *yang*. It might look like a Tibetan temple, but there can't be many real Tibetans who could afford to darken its

doors. A Chi Balance massage costs ¥1430, a Himalayan Healing Stone Massage ¥1700 (and there's a 15 percent service charge). Daily 10am–midnight.

**Dragonfly** 1F Eastern Inn, Sanlitun Nanlu ☎010 65936066, Hujialou subway (lines 6 & 10); 60 Donghuamen Dajie, just outside the East Gate of the Forbidden City ☎010 65279368, Tian'anmen East subway (line 1); ⓦdragonfly.net.cn. This well-reputed Shanghai chain has opened a couple of conveniently located centres in the capital. Their two-hour hangover release special (¥288) is always popular, as are the foot massages. Daily 10am–11pm.

**St Regis Spa Centre** St Regis Hotel, 21 Jianguomenwai Dajie ☎010 64606688, ⓦstarwoodhotels.com/stregis; Jianguomen subway (lines 1 & 2). Traditional Chinese massage, aromatherapy and facials are among the treatments on offer at this very upscale hotel (see p.130). Prices start at ¥350 for a head and shoulders massage. Daily 10am–10pm.

## ROCK-CLIMBING

**Dianshi Club** Ritan Park ☎138 0105 2361; Dongdaqiao subway (line 6). This outfit has a popular climbing wall at Ritan Park, charging ¥50 per session, with discounts for

regular participants. They also arrange climbing trips to areas outside Beijing (from ¥40/day), which can be an awful lot of fun.

## SKIING

**Nanshan** 60km northeast of the city ☎010 89091909, ⓦnanshanski.com; bus #980 from Dongzhimen bus station to Miyun Xidaqiao (¥14), then taxi (about ¥20), or direct shuttle bus (¥40) daily 8.30am from Wudaokou subway (line 13). The best of Beijing's ski resorts, with thirteen 1500m-long runs. For snowboarders there are two kickers, a mini pipe and more than a dozen boxes and rails, and there's also sledging and cable gliding.

Entrance ¥20, 2hr skiing session ¥120 Mon–Fri, ¥180 Sat & Sun; gear rental will come to just under ¥100.

**Qiaobo Mellow Park** 6 Shun'an Lu, Sunyi ☎010 84972568, ⓦwww.mellowparks.cn; bus #915 from Dongzhimen bus station. The city's best indoor snowboard slope. A 2hr session costs ¥210 Mon–Fri, ¥250 at weekends, and a little less at night; equipment rental is ¥100 for the set.

## SNOOKER AND POOL

**Pool** and **snooker** are very popular in China, and increasingly so thanks to the exploits of local stars such as Ding Junhui, who won the China Open (see p.27) in 2005 – an event watched on television by an estimated 110m across the land. A great many want to follow in his footsteps, and some locals are expert cue-wielders; you can take them on at any number of places around town (some say there are over 2000), so just ask at your accommodation for the nearest. It'll be around ¥20 per hour for a table, and even at swankier venues, beer is usually available.

## SWIMMING

Avoid **swimming pools** at the weekends, when they're full of teenagers doing just about everything but swimming. Bear in mind that some **hotels** open their lavish pools and gym facilities to non-guests; we've listed the most impressive of them below.

### HOTEL POOLS

**CITIC Hotel** 9 Xiaotianzhi Nanlu ☎010 64565588, ⓦcitichotelbeijing.com. For family pool fun, this hotel (formerly the *Sino-Swiss*) up by the airport has hot springs

and the capital's only indoor-outdoor pool. ¥130/day.

**Doubletree by Hilton** 168 Guang'anmen Waidajie ☎010 63381888, ⓦdoubletree3.hilton.com; Beijing West subway (line 9). ¥150/day.

**13**

## SPECTATOR SPORTS

The Chinese now have more leisure time than ever before, and many spectator sports have seen large gains in attendance figures. **Basketball** is king here, though fans of Beijing Guo'an **football** team may beg to differ. In addition, the Chinese excel at "small ball" games such as **squash**, **badminton**, **snooker** and **table tennis**; tournaments – like snooker's China Open (see p.27) – take place all the time, but it's perhaps more interesting to see the champions of the future being coached at outdoor tables in places such as Ritan Park.

### BASKETBALL

The **Beijing Ducks** are the capital's main basketball team; they compete in the CBA (Chinese Basketball Academy) and won their first national title in 2011–12. They play at the MasterCard Center (Wukesong subway, way out west on line 1), which also hosted basketball games in the 2008 Olympics. In theory, it's possible to buy tickets online at ⓦ en.damai.cn, though these tend to sell out in a matter of minutes, usually ending up in the hands of scalpers; you'll have to haggle them down to a good price (try ¥50) outside the stadium.

### FOOTBALL

European football leagues have a surprisingly strong following, and English, Spanish and German games are shown on CCTV5 and BTV. The domestic **Chinese Super League** is improving, and decent wages have attracted a fair few foreign players and coaches, though it continues to be rocked by match-fixing scandals.

   In season (mid-March to mid-Oct), **Beijing Guo'an** football team is one of its hitters; they play most of their games in the 66,000-capacity Workers' Stadium (Dongsishitiao subway, line 2). Though this rarely fills up, poorly regulated ticket sales mean that it can be hard to buy one yourself – many regulars, even those who go along every couple of weeks, routinely buy their tickets just before kick-off from scalpers outside the stadium. ¥50 is a fair price, though you may have to wait until the game has actually started to get it down to this level. Games with local rivals Tianjin Teda and title challengers Shanghai Shenhua are the liveliest, but even at these, the atmosphere is relaxed, and there's no trouble; no one sees the need to segregate fans, for example. Glamorous foreign teams often include Beijing on their pre season warm-up tours, usually playing at the National Stadium (aka Bird's Nest; see p.102).

**Ritz-Carlton** 1 Jinchengfang Dongjie ☎010 66016666, ⓦ ritzcarlton.com; Fuchengmen subway (line 2). ¥220/day.
**Westin Chaoyang** 1 Xinyuan Nanlu ☎010 59228888, ⓦ starwoodhotels.com; Liangmaqiao subway (line 10). ¥250 for a weekend pass.

### PUBLIC POOLS

**Ditan Swimming Pool** 地坛游泳馆 dìtán yóuyǒngguǎn 8 Hepingli Zhong Jie ☎010 64264483; Andingmen subway (line 2). If you just want a cheap swim, try this place, open year-round (¥30). In the summer, there are outdoor pools open for the same price at nearby

Qingnian Lake. Daily 7am–10pm.
**National Aquatics Centre** 国家游泳中心 guójiā yóuyǒng zhōngxīn Olympic Green ☎010 84370112, ⓦ water-cube.com; Olympic Green subway (line 8). Since the games, the famous Water Cube (see p.102) has reopened as a water theme park, featuring spas, slides and a wave pool. ¥200. Daily 10am–9.30pm.
**Sino–Japanese Youth Centre** 中日青年交流中心 zhōngrì qīngnián jiāoliú zhōngxīn 40 Lianmaqiao Lu, by the Century Theatre ☎010 64683311; Lincuiqiao subway (line 8). Serious swimmers should check out this Olympic-size pool. Entry ¥88. Daily 9am–9pm.

### TEAM SPORTS

#### FOOTBALL
**Club Football** ⓦ clubfootball.com.cn. Year-round five-a-side competitions for men, women and kids alike.
**International Friendship Football Club** ⓦ iffc1994 .com. A bit more serious, this club controls two leagues' worth of teams. The standard is pretty high.

#### HANDBALL
**Handball in China** ⓦ handballinchina.org. Group that

meets every Thurs evening for some handball fun. Free for first timers and a good mix of skills.

#### RUGBY
**Beijing Devils** ⓦ beijingdevils.com. Extremely cosmopolitan rugby club, whose men's, women's and touch teams meet for training at least once per week.

# Contexts

# History

Zip through Beijing in a taxi, and you'd be hard-pressed to guess that this relentlessly forward-marching city has been a centre of power for nearly a thousand years. While the overwhelming majority of the city you'll see today has shot up since the formation of the People's Republic in 1949, look behind the right walls and you'll find plenty of sights dating back to the Qing (1644–1911) and Ming (1368–1644) dynasties; during these times, and going back even further to the Yuan (1271–1368), Beijing functioned, at almost all points, as capital of China. At times, it was also arguably the centre of the civilized world – a title that it clearly wants back.

## Beginnings

**Peking man** (*Homo erectus pekinensis*) walked the Beijing area from 750,000–250,000 BC, as evidenced by a number of fossils unearthed in caves between 1921 and 1937 near the village of Zhoukoudian, a site around 60km southwest of what is today the city centre. *Homo sapiens* inhabited the same area at a later date (c.30,000 BC); tools and bone fragments from this time have also been discovered in Wangfujing, right in the middle of the modern city. The first actual settlements in and around Beijing go back almost as far, to the end of the **Paleolithic era**; evidence of dozens of **Neolithic** settlements, including burial sites, has also been discovered across the city and its environs.

While the city's pre-imperial history is shrouded in myth and legend, the first recorded event occurred in the eleventh century BC, when the **Zhou dynasty** conquered the Shang, and went on to use Beijing as a regional capital. Evidence suggests that this base city-state, named Ji after one particular Zhou leader, was near Guang'anmen, not too far at all from the centre of modern Beijing. Around 690 BC, during what is now known as the **Spring and Autumn Period**, Ji was absorbed by the competing Yan state (eleventh century to 222 BC), based just to the south, and it was during the last decades of Yan's existence that the city received its first protective walls. Far greater fortifications, though still earthen in nature, were built during the **Qin dynasty** (221–207 BC); Beijing was at this time a mere regional base, with the imperial capital way out west in Xi'an. It remained relatively unimportant for half a millennium until the Former Yan, one of the **Sixteen Kingdoms** which jostled for power during – and after – the latter part of the **Jin dynasty** (265–420 AD), moved their capital here in 352; this only lasted for five years, but the Northern Wei restored Beijing as capital four decades later. This on-off arrangement became a pattern – increasing in importance after being connected to Shanghai by the **Grand Canal** during the Sui dynasty (581–618), Beijing served as an occasional regional capital during the Tang (618–907), Five dynasties (907–960) and Liao (907–1125) periods.

| 11th century BC | 690 BC | Late 2nd century BC | 250 AD |
|---|---|---|---|
| Zhou dynasty conquers Shang; Beijing becomes a regional capital for the first time | Beijing absorbed by Yan state | First protective walls built | First extensive irrigation systems installed, increasing agricultural productivity |

**HISTORICAL CHRONOLOGY**

| | |
|---|---|
| **21st–16th centuries BC** Xia dynasty | **581–618** Sui dynasty – China united for the first time since Han dynasty |
| **16th–11th centuries BC** Shang dynasty | |
| **11th century to 771 BC** Zhou dynasty | **618–907** Tang dynasty |
| **770–476 BC** Spring and Autumn Period – China fragments into city states and small kingdoms | **907–1125** Liao dynasty |
| | **1125–1234** Jin (Jurchen) dynasty |
| | **1271–1368** Yuan dynasty |
| **457–221 BC** Warring States – China's fragmentation continues | **1368–1644** Ming dynasty |
| | **1644–1911** Qing dynasty |
| **221–207 BC** Qin dynasty | **1911–45** Republic founded, its fall followed by civil war between Nationalists and Communists, and Japanese occupation |
| **206 BC–220 AD** Han dynasty | |
| **222–280** Three Kingdoms Period: China is divided into three competing territories, the Wei, Shu Han and Wu | |
| **265–420** Jin dynasty | **1945–49** Further period of civil conflict between Guomindang and the Communist People's Liberation Army |
| **420–581** Southern dynasties and Northern dynasties – rapid succession of short-lived dynasties | **1949** Communists take power over mainland China; establishment of People's Republic |

The **Liao dynasty** saw the Khitan, a nomadic barbarian tribe from the northern grasslands, erect another major series of city walls, and make full use of the Grand Canal as a means of trade. The city walls could not prevent the Khitan being overthrown by the Southern Song, who razed Beijing but failed to fully defeat the Liao. This was eventually accomplished with the aid of the Jurchen, another nomadic group, who made Beijing capital of the Jurchen or (second) **Jin dynasty** (1125–1234) in 1153. The city's walls were then expanded as the population swelled to half a million, and it became one of the first places in the world in which paper currency was used.

## The Yuan dynasty

Beijing's true pre-eminence dates back to the latter half of the thirteenth century, and the formation of Mongol China under **Genghis Khan** (1162–1227), and subsequently **Kublai Khan** (1215–94). It was Genghis who took control of the city in 1215, his Mongol army breaking through the walls and demolishing Beijing. It was not until 1264 that Kublai set about its reconstruction; the **Yuan dynasty** was proclaimed seven years later with Beijing as capital, replacing the earlier power centres of Luoyang and Xi'an.

**Marco Polo** visited Kublai here and was impressed with the city's sophistication: "So great a number of houses and of people, no man could tell the number…", he wrote. "I believe there is no place in the world to which so many merchants come, and dearer things, and of greater value and more strange, come into this town from all sides than to any city in the world…" The wealth he depicted stemmed from Beijing's position at the start of the **Silk Road**, the trading route that stretched all the way to Central Asia: Marco Polo described "over a thousand carts loaded with silk" arriving in the city

| Early 7th century | 1122 | 1125 | 1214 |
|---|---|---|---|
| Grand Canal fully connected, linking Beijing to Shanghai | City captured by Jurchen tribe, given to Song | Jurchens retake Beijing | City under siege from Mongol army, led by Genghis Khan; surrender follows the next year, and the city is sacked |

almost every day. It allowed the Khans, who later proclaimed themselves emperors, to aspire to new heights of grandeur, with Kublai building himself a palace of astonishing proportions, walled on all sides and approached by great marble stairways; sadly, nothing remains of it now, though its name, "Xanadu", lives on.

## The Ming dynasty

With the accession of the **Ming dynasty**, who defeated the Mongols in 1368, the capital shifted temporarily to Nanjing. However, the second Ming emperor, **Yongle**, returned to Beijing, building around him prototypes of the city's two great monuments, the Forbidden City and the Temple of Heaven. It was during Yongle's reign, too, that the city's basic layout took shape, rigidly symmetrical, extending in squares and rectangles from the palace and inner-city grid to the suburbs, much as it is today. It's estimated that over 250,000 prisoners of war were used as slaves during these epic waves of construction, numbers which – along with arrivals (sometimes forced) from the previous capital of Nanjing – swelled the city's population to over one million. The city almost certainly became the first place on earth to reach that figure.

### The Great Wall

Though the Yuan dynasty had been brought to a close, the threat from the north remained. Beijing found itself under regular attack from Mongol horsemen, who occasionally reached the very gates of the city; they also hampered communications with the rest of the empire, with the situation coming to a head in the early fifteenth century. The solution was simple but incredibly ambitious: it was at this time that construction of the famed **Great Wall** got going in earnest. Unlike previous walls, this was no mere barrier of rammed earth, but a sinuous snake of brick and stone – several of them, in fact. Mighty as the wall may have been, it was only as strong as its weakest link – the fact that guards will always be conducive to bribery meant that it became a grandiose but ultimately futile attempt to stem the incursions of northern Manchu tribes into China.

## The Qing dynasty

Beijing's subsequent history is dominated by the rise and eventual collapse of the **Manchu** who, as the **Qing dynasty**, ruled China from the city from 1644 to the beginning of the twentieth century. Three outstanding Qing emperors brought an infusion of new blood and vigour to government early on. **Kangxi**, who began his 61-year reign in 1654 at the age of 6, was a great patron of the arts, as borne out by the numerous scrolls and paintings blotted with his seals, indicating that he had viewed them – you'll see plenty in the Forbidden City. His fourth son, the Emperor **Yongzheng** (1678–1735), ruled over what is considered one of the most efficient administrations ever enjoyed by China; as well as cracking down on the corruption that had plagued the rules of previous emperors, he formed the Grand Council, a high-level body whose policies went on to shape much of Qing society. He was succeeded by **Qianlong** (1711–99), whose reign saw China's frontiers greatly extended and the economy stimulated by peace and prosperity. In 1750, the capital was perhaps at its

| 1266 | 1271 | 1272 | 1302 | 1403 | 1420 |
|------|------|------|------|------|------|
| Marco Polo pops by for a visit | Kublai Khan declares new Yuan dynasty with Beijing as capital | Drum Tower erected | Confucius Temple constructed | The city is named Beijing for the first time | Forbidden City completed; Beijing likely the largest city in the world at this time |

---

### HISTORY TODAY: THE MING AND QING

**Ancient Observatory** An underrated sight, this old observatory boasts a clutch of breathtakingly beautiful Ming-dynasty astrological instruments. See p.74

**Chengde** A wonderful small city in Hebei Province, featuring Bishu Shanzhuang, an old imperial retreat, and a series of stunning temples. See p.117

**Drum Tower** Looming over the Shicha Lakes, just north of the Forbidden City, this tower can be climbed for great views. The neighbouring Bell Tower is also Ming, but has since been rebuilt. See p.62

**The Forbidden City** One of China's biggest tourist draws, this old imperial stomping ground goes back to the Mongol era, but its present structure is essentially Ming. Also of note here are a series of splendid exhibition halls – one of them houses one of the world's finest collections of Ming vases. See p.48

**The Great Wall** Another world-famous sight, the wall also pre-dates the Ming, but it's work from this period that's most visible. See p.105

**The Ming Tombs** The resting place of several Ming-dynasty emperors. See p.111

**The Temple of Heaven** Justly regarded as the epitome of Ming design, and a real Beijing must-see. See p.80

**Yonghe Gong** This Tibetan Lama temple is one of the most visually arresting in the land. See p.68

---

zenith, the centre of one of the strongest, wealthiest and most powerful countries in the world. It was at this time that the extraordinary **Summer Palace** was constructed. With two hundred pavilions, temples and palaces, and immense artificial lakes and hills, it was the world's most remarkable royal garden, and, along with the Forbidden City, a magnificent symbol of Chinese wealth and power.

### European expansionism and the First Opium War

In the late eighteenth century expansionist European nations were sniffing around Asia, looking for financial opportunities. China's rulers, immensely rich and powerful and convinced of their own superiority, had no wish for direct dealings with foreigners. When a British envoy, **Lord Macartney**, arrived in Chengde in 1793 to propose a political and commercial alliance between King George III and the emperor, his mission was unsuccessful. This was partly because he refused to kowtow to the emperor, but also because the emperor totally rejected any idea of allying with one whom he felt was a subordinate. Macartney was impressed by the vast wealth and power of the Chinese court, but later wrote perceptively that the empire was "like an old crazy first-rate man-of-war which its officers have contrived to keep afloat to terrify by its appearance and bulk".

Foiled in their attempts at official negotiations with the Qing court, the British decided to take matters into their own hands and create a clandestine market in China for Western goods. Instead of silver, they began to pay for tea and silk with **opium**, cheaply imported from India. As the number of addicts escalated during the early nineteenth century, China's trade surplus became a deficit as silver drained out of the country to pay for the drug. The emperor suspended the traffic in 1840 by ordering the destruction of more than twenty thousand chests of opium, an act that led to the outbreak of the **First Opium War**. This brought British and French troops to the walls of

| 1643 | 1644 | 1669 | 1750s |
|---|---|---|---|
| Plagues hit, claiming over 200,000 lives | Beijing taken in peasant rebellion, then taken back by Manchu; Qing dynasty begins | Tongrentang pharmacy (see p.34) opens its doors for the first time | Summer Palace constructed |

---

## HISTORICAL NAMES OF BEIJING

**Ji** (11th century BC–607 AD), the first recorded name of Beijing, employed from the Zhou to the Northern Dynasties periods; "Yan" was also used at times, and referred to a separate settlement to the south.

**Zhuojun** (607–616) Used for a short time during the Sui dynasty.

**Youzhou** (616–938) During the Tang and Five dynasties periods; "Fanyang" and "Yanjing" were also used at times.

**Nanjing** (938–1125) During the Liao dynasty; the name "Yanjing" was also employed.

**Yanjing** (1125–1271) In addition to its earlier use, this became the city's official name in the Jin dynasty, as well as the early Yuan; it remains a nickname for the city, best evidenced as the brand name of its best-selling beer.

**Dadu** (1271–1368) The name given to Beijing when it was chosen to serve as the Yuan dynasty capital.

**Beiping** (1368–1403) The name chosen following the Ming conquest; it was also used at points after the proclamation of the Republic.

**Beijing** (1403–present) "North Capital" was first chosen as a name under the Ming, used as a sole name under the Qing, occasionally eschewed by the Republic in favour of Beiping (see above), then brought back in 1949 by the People's Republic.

**Peking** Never an official name in Mandarin, though used as a transliteration by the Western world until the dawn of *pinyin* in 1958. Though "Beijing" has been the official romanized spelling since then, the erroneous name still lives on in the form of Peking duck and Peking man, and in various European languages.

---

the capital, and the Summer Palace was first looted then burned, more or less to the ground, by the British.

### Cixi and the Second Opium War

While the imperial court lived apart, within the gilded cage of the **Forbidden City**, conditions in the capital's suburbs for the civilian population were starkly different. Kang Youwei, a Cantonese visiting in 1895, described this dual world: "No matter where you look, the place is covered with beggars. The homeless and the old, the crippled and the sick, with no one to care for them, fall dead on the roads. This happens every day. And the coaches of the great officials rumble past them continuously."

The indifference spread from the top down. China was now run by the autocratic, out-of-touch **Cixi** (see box, p.69), who could hardly have been less concerned with the fate of her people. She squandered money meant for the modernization of the navy on building a new Summer Palace of her own, a project which became the last grand gesture of imperial architecture and patronage – like its predecessor, it was badly burned by foreign troops, in another outbreak of the Opium Wars. By this time, in the face of successive waves of occupation by foreign troops, the empire and the city were near collapse.

### The Boxer Rebellion and Xinhai revolution

Towards the end of the nineteenth century, a rebel peasant movement now known as the **Boxers** attempted to stymie the Western advance; though initially suppressed by the

| 1860 | 1864 | 1900 | 1911 | 1915 |
|------|------|------|------|------|
| French and British armies victorious in Second Opium War; both loot Summer Palace | *Quanjude* restaurant introduces new kind of oven, heralding birth of what is now known as Peking duck | Legation quarter besieged during Boxer Rebellion | Qing dynasty overthrown; Republic of China founded | Empire of China declared |

Qing court, Cixi soon allowed them greater leeway. In 1900, they laid siege to Beijing's legations quarter for almost two months, before being beaten by an eight-nation alliance of over 20,000 troops. These forces proceeded to loot the city (a substantial amount of treasure remains abroad to this day), occupy much of northern China and impose crippling indemnities on the ailing Qing government.

A full-scale **revolution** took place in 1911 after trouble bubbled up in the south of China; **Yuan Shikai** (1859–1916) led an army sent to suppress the rebellion, but ended up negotiating with them instead. Newly returned from exile, the idealistic revolutionary **Sun Yatsen** (1866–1925) declared the **Republic of China** at the very dawn of 1912, offering Yuan Shikai its stewardship on the condition that he compel the Qing court to abdicate. They duly did so a month later – the end of two millennia of imperial rule, though **Puyi** (1906–67), the last emperor, was kept on as a powerless figurehead.

# The republic

The short-lived republic was in trouble from the outset, with its first months marked by infighting, factionalism and the not insignificant matter of where to base the national capital. One of Sun's preconditions for transferring power to Yuan was that **Nanjing** should become capital; the Senate, ignoring this, voted for Beijing instead. Sun insisted on a second vote, with Beijing not one of the options, and this saw Nanjing emerge victorious; not to be stopped, Yuan engineered reasons to stay put in Beijing, with forces loyal to him setting off a wave of rioting and destruction down south in Nanjing.

In 1913, Sun Yatsen's second attempt at a revolution failed and he was forced into exile once again, while the senate was cleared of any Nationalist members who may have supported his return. Yuan went a step further the next year, dissolving parliament and a constitution whose ink was still wet; in 1915 he went further still, declaring himself emperor of the new **Empire of China**. Rebellion inevitably bubbled up once more in the south, and Yuan resumed the mantle of president in March 1916; he died a few months later. China fell under the control of warlords, with eight presidents in the twelve years following Yuan's death, together with a twelve-day resuscitation of Manchu rule. Amazingly, the city managed to grow and modernize itself during this period of chaos, with streets widened, city gates smartened up, and a new tram system inaugurated.

## The Guomindang

In 1928, Beijing came under the military dictatorship of the Nationalist **Guomindang** party, led by **Chiang Kaishek** (1887–1975), losing its mantle as capital to Nanjing, and nine years later was taken by Japanese forces during the second Sino–Japanese War (often referred to as World War II in China). The war known as such by most of the rest of the world began immediately afterwards, and at its close Beijing was controlled by an alliance of Guomindang troops and American marines.

World war was followed by **civil war** – the Nationalists and Chinese Communists had been allies during the fight against Japan, but following a hastily arranged, oft-broken truce they entered a full state of war as soon as 1947. The **Communist People's Liberation Army (PLA)** took Beijing in early 1949, and advanced south; despite appeals from Nanjing for a truce, they crossed the Yangtze soon afterwards, and took southern China from the Nationalists too.

| 1921 | 1928 | 1937 | 1945 |
|---|---|---|---|
| Bones of Peking man unearthed; tram lines introduced | Beijing falls under Nationalist control; replaced as capital of nation, then as capital of Hebei Province | Empire of Japan takes over Beijing, makes the city capital once more | Nationalists retake control following Japanese defeat in World War II |

## The Communist era

On October 1, 1949, **Mao Zedong** (see box, p.51), Chairman of the Communist Party, proclaimed the inauguration of the **People's Republic of China** from Tian'anmen gate, in the process making Beijing the nation's capital once more. The city that Mao inherited for the Chinese people was in most ways primitive. Imperial laws had banned the construction of houses higher than the official buildings and palaces, so virtually nothing was more than one storey high. The roads, although straight and uniform, were narrow and congested, and there was scarcely any industry.

The rebuilding of the capital, and the erasing of symbols of the previous regimes, was an early priority for the Communists. They wanted to retain the city's sense of ordered planning, with **Tian'anmen Square**, laid out in the 1950s, as its new heart. Initially their inspiration was Soviet, with an emphasis on heavy industry and a series of poor-quality high-rise housing programmes. Most of the traditional courtyard houses, which were seen to encourage individualism, were destroyed. In their place anonymous concrete buildings were thrown up, often with inadequate sanitation and little running water. Much of the new social planning was misguided; after the destruction of all the capital's dogs – for reasons of hygiene – in 1950, it was the turn of **sparrows** in 1956. This was a measure designed to preserve grain, but it only resulted in an increase in the insect population. To combat this, all the grass was pulled up, which in turn led to dust storms in the windy winter months.

### The Great Leap Forward and the Cultural Revolution

Dogs, sparrows and grass were one thing, but the regime had loftier aims. Mao announced the so-called **Great Leap Forward** in 1957, with the intention of dramatically reorganizing the nation along Communist lines. In theory, farms were to be collectivized in order to improve agricultural output, with the resultant extra food taken to cities to feed the workers in communal mess halls, leading to greater industrial output. What it actually resulted in was, of course, poverty and mass malnutrition; even when the mess halls were phased out, people had nothing left to cook with, since they'd all been required to have their pots and pans melted down for communal use. In addition, in the zeal to be free of the past and create a modern "people's capital", much of Beijing was destroyed or co-opted. In the 1940s, there were eight thousand temples and monuments in the city; by the mid-1960s, there were only around 150. Even the city walls and gates, relics mostly of the Ming era, were pulled down, their place taken by ring roads and avenues.

More destruction was to follow during the **Great Proletarian Cultural Revolution** – to give it its full title – that began in 1966. Under Mao's guidance, Beijing's students organized themselves into a political militia, the **Red Guards**, who were sent out to destroy the Four Olds: old ideas, old culture, old customs and old habits. The students attacked anything redolent of capitalism, the West or the Soviet Union. Few of the capital's remaining ancient buildings escaped destruction.

### The end of Mao

Mao's hold on power finally slipped in the 1970s, when his health began to decline. A new attitude of pragmatic reform prevailed, deriving from the moderate wing of the

| 1949 | 1958 | 1966 | 1971 |
|------|------|------|------|
| Communist army marches into Beijing; Mao Zedong declares People's Republic of China from Tian'anmen | Great Leap Forward begins | Cultural Revolution begins | Nixon visits |

Communist Party, headed by Premier **Zhou Enlai** (1898–1976) and his protégé, **Deng Xiaoping** (1904–1997).

In July 1976, a catastrophic earthquake in the northeast of the country killed half a million people. The Chinese hold that natural disasters always foreshadow great events, and no one was too surprised when Mao himself died on September 9. Deprived of their figurehead, and with memories of the Cultural Revolution clear in everyone's mind, Mao's supporters in the Party quickly lost ground to the right, and Deng was left running the country.

## Capitalism with Chinese characteristics

The subsequent move away from Mao's policies was rapid: in 1978, anti-Maoist dissidents were allowed to display wall posters in Beijing, some of which actually criticized Mao by name. Though such public airing of political grievances was later forbidden, by 1980 Deng and the moderates were secure enough to officially sanction a cautious questioning of Mao's actions. In the capital, his once-ubiquitous portraits and statues began to come down. However, criticism of Mao was one thing – criticism of the Party was viewed quite differently. When demonstrators assembled in **Tian'anmen Square** in 1989, protesting at corruption and demanding more freedom, the regime dealt with them brutally, sending tanks and soldiers to fire on them (see box, p.50).

Deng's "open door" policies of economic liberalization and welcoming foreign influences brought about new social (though not political) freedoms, massive Westernization, and the creation of a consumer culture. Western fast food, clothes and music and Japanese motorbikes became – and remain – all the rage.

Deng stepped down in the early 1990s and was succeeded by **Hu Jintao** (1942–) and **Wen Jiabao** (1942–), pragmatic technocrats under whose stewardship the Chinese economy grew at a sustained rate of around ten percent a year. Urban Chinese became much better off: in the 1970s, the "three big buys" – consumer goods that families could realistically aspire to – were a bicycle, a watch and a radio; in the 1980s, they were a washing machine, a TV and a refrigerator. Now, like their counterparts in South Korea and Japan, the middle classes own cars and computers.

# Beijing today

The glitz and pomp of the **2008 Olympic games** (see box, p.101), in which China topped the medals table, served to mark the city's arrival on the world stage. Before the games, Beijing benefited from massive investment in infrastructure, including new subway lines and freeways – as recently as 2007, Beijing only had three subway lines, but by 2013 it had broken the world record for daily ridership. And the city's restless **reinvention** continues. A ramshackle charm has been lost in its wholesale redevelopment, but on the whole Beijing has improved. It will never perhaps be memorable for attractiveness, but it's undeniably dynamic, inventive and exciting.

The **embrace of capitalism** has, however, brought with it new problems. Short-term gain has become the overriding factor in planning, with the result that the future is mortgaged for present wealth, and Beijing's cultural heritage has vanished as *hutongs* are pulled down to clear space for badly made skyscrapers.

| 1976 | 1987 | 1989 | 1995 | 1997 |
|---|---|---|---|---|
| Death of Chairman Mao | *The Last Emperor* released | Tian'anmen protests halted by massacre | Artists first start to trickle into 798 factory district | Midi Music Festival first held |

Xi Jinping (1953–) became the People's Republic's seventh president in 2013, with Li Keqiang (1955–) as his premier. One senses that by the end of their tenure, Beijing as a city, and China as a whole, will have had to jump a fair few hurdles.

## The economy

First of all, there's the question of the **economy**. Even before Xi's accession, measures were being taken to put the brakes on to avoid a burst financial bubble, and after two decades of double-digit growth, it's now down to a far more manageable 7–8 percent, with many suspecting that even these figures are most likely exaggerated.

Then, of course, there are China's mammoth **income disparities**. Peasants, attracted by the big city's prospects, now flood to Beijing en masse – you'll see plenty outside Beijing station, many of them finding the capital as novel as any foreigner does. The lucky ones end up working on building sites, though even they, far from home and non-unionized, are often exploited. Though the majority are family men who send the little money that they earn home, they are treated with suspicion by most city-dwellers – indicative of China's current class divisions. Steps are being taken to combat this, including a minimum wage of 40 percent of urban salaries.

A reform of Beijing's restrictive **hukou** policies has also been on the agenda for some time. These residence permits were introduced as a means of keeping the population in check and in place during the Great Leap Forward, and while restrictions on work and movement were gradually lifted from the 1980s on, those heading to work in big cities remain unable to benefit fully from healthcare or other important urban services. Of course, those who own a Beijing *hukou* don't necessarily want these reforms to take place, since the city's funds will have to be spread across more people.

## Corruption and the environment

There's also the issue of **guanxi** – a well-used term describing personal connections, whether derived from family, business, friendships or out-and-out power. As success is largely dependent on *guanxi*, the potential for **corruption** is enormous; even before being installed as president, Xi Jinping was vowing to crack down on it from the "tigers" at the top to the "flies" at the bottom (though some found this a little funny since Xi himself is the son of one of the Communist Party's founding fathers).

Another descendant of the "Eight Elders" of the Deng era, **Bo Xilai**, found himself implicated in a major scandal in 2012; following the murder of British businessman Neil Heywood, the local chief of police fled to an American consulate to implicate Bo's wife in the killing. Bo is now serving a life sentence, while his wife was given a suspended death sentence – evidence that things are changing, however slowly.

One final issue on the lips of all locals – sometimes in a depressingly literal sense – is **pollution**. Despite the fact that factories were moved far from the city before the Olympics rolled into town, things only seem to be getting worse, even according to the generally untrusted official statistics. In 2009, the US embassy in Beijing began tweeting their own hourly pollution reports; the rest of the world looked on with quizzical amusement on a particularly particle-filled day in 2010, when the hitherto sober reading sailed past "bad" and "hazardous" to a whole new level – "crazy bad". And it really was: the level had passed beyond 500, a full twenty times higher than WHO guidelines, and up until then supposedly the top of the scale. In January 2013, the meter maxed out at 755 – not pleasant at all.

| 2003 | 2007 | 2008 | 2010 |
| --- | --- | --- | --- |
| SARS hits Beijing | Line 5, the first of Beijing's "new" subway lines and only the fourth in the city, opens | Beijing hosts Summer Olympics | Air pollution levels officially hit "crazy bad" level on US Embassy feed |

# Temple life

Beijing's Taoist and Buddhist temples are valuable repositories of heritage: as well as being often the only recognizably Chinese buildings around, they are rich with artefacts and long-preserved traditions. Outside, you'll see a glorious array of tat for sale – from flashing Buddhas to credit card-sized images of gods to be kept in your wallet for luck. Inside, smoke billows from burners – as well as incense, you'll see worshippers burning fake money, ingots or even paper cars to enrich ancestors in heaven. The atmosphere is lively and devout; devotees kowtow before fantastic images and robed monks genuflect.

## Design

In Beijing, as in China as a whole, temples are not as old as they may look; most were trashed during the Cultural Revolution and have been rebuilt from scratch. But the layout and design elements are genuinely ancient, and based on principles set down thousands of years ago. Like private houses, all Chinese temples face **south** (barbarians and evil spirits come from the north), and are surrounded by walls. Gates are sealed by heavy doors and guarded by **statues** – Buddhists use the four Heavenly Kings, while Taoists have a dragon and a lion. Further protection is afforded by a **spirit wall** in the first courtyard – easy enough for the living to walk around but a block to evil, which can supposedly only travel in straight lines.

Following this, there'll be a succession of **halls** and **courtyards**, arranged symmetrically – it's all about maintaining harmony. The courtyards will be enclosed by walls – creating so-called "sky wells" – and will usually feature ornate incense burners full of ash, venerable trees, and perhaps a pond. The buildings are placed according to a strict hierachy, with those facing front and at the rear being the most important. The halls are supported by lacquered **pillars** – Buddhists colour them bright red, Taoists use black. Some of the most elegant details are in the roof, where interlocking beams create a characteristic curved roofline and elegantly made and beautifully painted brackets (*dougongs*) allow the jauntily curving eaves to extend well beyond the main pillars. Look out for the procession of figures, including a dragon and a man riding a phoenix among various mythological beasties, that run along the edges of the roof. They're put there for luck and protection.

## Symbols

The main hall of a **Buddhist temple** is dominated by three large **statues** – the Buddhas of the past, the present and the future – while the walls are lined by rather outlandish **arhats**, or saints. Around the back of the Buddhist trinity will probably be a statue of

---

**TEMPLE FAIRS**

Every Beijing temple holds a fair at **Chinese New Year**, integrating worship, entertainment and commerce. At these boisterous carnivals, the air is thick with incense, and locals queue to kneel to altars and play games that bring good fortune – lobbing coins at the temple bell, for example. Priests are on hand to perform rituals and write prayers.

Beijing's biggest fairs are at the Tibetan **Yonghe Gong** (see p.68) and the Taoist **Baiyun Guan** (see p.88): pick one or the other, as it's considered inauspicious to visit both during the same festival. To help you decide, Taoist festivals concentrate on renewal, Tibetan Lamaist ones on enlightenment.

## A MONK'S LIFE

**Buddhist monks** wear orange robes and keep their heads shaved, while **Taoist monks** wear blue and keep their long hair tied up. Both sets of monks are celibate and vegetarian, and avoid garlic or onion, which are said to enflame the passions. Under the strict rule of an abbot, the monks and nuns live a regimented and quiet life, taken up with study, prayer and observance and celebration of significant dates. There are also plenty of practical tasks concerning the day-to-day running of the institution. Meals are communal and there is at least three hours of prayer and meditation every day

The need to defend the temple, and to balance meditation with activity, led to the development of **martial arts**: Taoist monks generally practice *tai ji quan* (see box, p.80) while Buddhists are famous for having developed kung fu – though you're not likely to see it being practised.

Guanyin, the multi-armed Goddess of Mercy. Believed to help with childbirth, she's very popular, and you'll see the same figure in Taoist temples.

**Taoist** temples are much more diverse in iconography. The Taoist holy trinity is made up of the three **immortals**, who each ride different animals (a crane, tiger and deer) and represent the three levels of the Taoist afterlife. You'll see dragons and phoenixes depicted in all Chinese temples, but **animal carvings** are more popular with the animist Taoists, too: look out for bats and cranes – symbols, respectively, of good luck and longevity. Other figures in Taoist temples include the red-faced God of War, Guan Yu, and the general Zhuge Liang – characters in the ancient story of the *Romance of the Three Kingdoms* (see p.185), and based on real-life figures. Around the edges of the halls you'll see often fantastical depictions of other immortals and saints, usually shown with a magical talisman and evidence of some kind of special power. All are presided over by the stern looking Jade Emperor.

**Confucian temples** are rather formal, with little imagery, though you will see plenty of tombstone-like steles supported by stone tortoises – perhaps a nod towards the Indian story that a tortoise carries the world on its back. Recently, new statues of the great sage have been erected following approval of his official likeness.

# Film

Although Chinese cinema goes back a long way, much of its early produce came from Shanghai, rather than Beijing. The capital finally started to pump out films in quantity during the Great Leap Forward, but output across the nation was choked off with the Cultural Revolution – no film was produced anywhere in the country between 1966 and 1970. Recovery, understandably, took time, but since the early 1980s China in general, and Beijing in particular, have been making larger and larger ripples in world cinema.

## The fifth generation

In 1984 the Chinese film industry was suddenly brought to international attention for the first time by the arrival of the so-called "**fifth generation**" of Chinese film-makers. That year, director **Chen Kaige** and his cameraman Zhang Yimou, both graduates from the first post-Cultural Revolution class (1982) of the Beijing Film School, made the superb art-house film *Yellow Earth*, which told a somewhat sobering tale of peasant life in early Communist times. The film was not particularly well received in China, either by audiences, who expected something more modern, or by the authorities, who expected something more optimistic. Nevertheless, it set the pattern for a series of increasingly overseas-funded films, such as *The Last Emperor* and *Farewell My Concubine*, comprising stunning images of a "traditional" China, irritating the censors at home and delighting audiences abroad.

### Zhang Yimou

Chen Kaige's protégé **Zhang Yimou** was soon stealing a march on his former boss with his first film *Red Sorghum*, based on the Mo Yan novel (see p.185). This film was not only beautiful, and reassuringly patriotic, but it also introduced the world to heartthrob actress **Gong Li**. The fact that Gong Li and Zhang Yimou were soon to be lovers added to the general media interest in their work, both in China and abroad. They worked together on a string of hits, including *Judou*, *The Story of Qiu Ju*, *Raise the Red Lantern*, *Shanghai Triad* and *To Live* (see box, p.180). None of these could be described as art-house in the way that *Yellow Earth* had been, and the potent mix of Gong Li's sexuality with exotic, mysterious locations in 1930s China was clearly targeted at Western rather than Chinese audiences. Chinese like to point out that the figure-hugging *qipao* regularly worn by Gong Li are entirely unlike the period costume they purport to represent. Zhang Yimou has since been warmly embraced by the authorities (as evidenced by his selection as director of the Olympic ceremonies in 2008), though his films have got worse.

## The sixth generation and recent developments

In the 1990s, a new "**sixth generation**" of directors set out to make edgier work. Their films, usually low-budget affairs difficult to catch in China, depict what their makers consider to be the true story of modern urban life: cold apartments, ugly streets, impoverished people. Good examples include *Beijing Bastards* and *In the Heat of the Sun* (see box, p.180). Some commercial films from this period, such as *Beijing Bicycle* and *Spring Subway* (see box, p.180) were influenced by this social realist aesthetic.

The most recent trends in Chinese cinema have seen continuations of the sixth-generation patterns. The **mainstream** directors have become ever more influenced by

## BEIJING ON FILM

**Beijing Bastards** (1993). A story of apathetic, fast-living youths, this was one of China's first independently produced films; it stars rock singer and rebel Cui Jian (see p.183), who is depicted drinking, swearing and playing the guitar.

**Beijing Bicycle** (2001). Given social realist treatment, this is the story of a lad trying to get his stolen bike back – a lot more interesting than it may sound.

**Cell Phone** (2003). Perhaps the most successful work of Feng Xiaogang, one of China's most revered directors, this satirical comedy revolves around two men having affairs. If you like it, try *Be There or Be Square, Sorry Baby, A World Without Thieves* and *Big Shot's Funeral* – all light, clever comedies set in Beijing, made during the 1990s.

★ **Farewell My Concubine** (1994). Chen Kaige's superb take on modern Chinese history. Although the main protagonist – a homosexual Chinese opera singer – is hardly typical of modern China, the tears induced by the film are wept for the country as a whole.

**In the Heat of the Sun** (1995). Directed by Jiang Wen, *In the Heat of the Sun* perfectly captures the post-revolutionary ennui of 1970s Beijing in its tale of a street gang looking for kicks. Written by Wang Shuo, the bad boy of contemporary Chinese literature, it displays his characteristic irreverence and earthy humour.

**The Last Emperor** (1987). This sumptuously shot tale of Puyi, the last of China's long, long line of emperors, remains the most famous Western-made film about China – no surprise, really, since it scooped a full seven Oscars.

**New Socialist Climax** (2009). Jian Yi documentary which explores the way in which revolutionary sites have been turned into tourist attractions.

★ **Out of Phoenix Bridge** (1997). Li Hong's superb documentary, looking at the lives of four young women who move from the countryside to Beijing in search of a new life.

**Spring Subway** (2002). Austere film which employs the capital's gleaming subway stations as a backdrop to the protagonist's soul-searching.

**To Live** (1994). One of Zhang Yimou's most powerful films, this follows the fortunes of a family from "liberation" to the Great Leap Forward and the Cultural Revolution. The essence of the story is that life cannot be lived to prescription, and its power lies in the fact that it is a very real reflection of the experience of millions of Chinese people.

**The World** (2004). Jia Zhangke film set in a world-culture theme park in Beijing, where the workers squabble and fail to communicate against a backdrop of tiny replicas of the world's famous monuments.

---

Western works, and are making big bucks in China's ever-increasing array of multiplex cinemas – in this they've been assisted by a government that still limits the number of Hollywood films shown each year, and pulls them from the screens in order to give home-grown films better sales. Conversely, those at the **art-house** end of the scale have found themselves making low-budget, introspective fare, developed almost exclusively for international consumption and the global film festival circuit.

The mainstream fare is by no means all bad. By way of example, local spaghetti western (does that make it a spaghetti eastern, or a noodle western?) *Let the Bullets Fly* (2010) broke local box-office records, yet also went on to scoop a few international awards. However, the most telling films are those coming from new directors such as **Ying Liang**, whose *The Other Half* (2006) won awards for its depiction of gambling and dysfunctional families in a polluted industrial town, and **Liu Jiayin**, whose *Oxhide* (2004) showed Beijing family life from a documentary-style perspective.

### Documentaries

Beijing does, indeed, have a promising **documentary movement** of its own, one which often skirts, then goes beyond, the line of what's acceptable to the state. Some pertinent (and important) tales of the city have been told in works such as *Out of Phoenix Bridge* (see box above) and *Bumming* (1990), which consists of a series of interviews with disaffected local artists. *Beijing Taxi* (2011), which takes a trip around the city with local cabbies, doesn't perhaps drip with so much meaning, but is illuminating in its own way – expats tend to deplore Beijing's taxi drivers, but here they're painted in a more sympathetic light. *New Socialist Climax* (see box above) is another good example.

# Art

Chinese painting has an ancient history. The earliest brush found in China, made out of animal hairs glued to a hollow bamboo tube, dates from about 400 BC. The Chinese used silk for painting on as early as the third century BC, with paper being used as early as 106 AD. Nowadays, Beijing's modern art scene is up there with the most vibrant in the world, revolving around the superb 798 Art District just to the northeast of the city centre (see p.102). The scene is particularly lively during the Beijing Biennale (ⓦbjbiennale.com.cn), held in late September in even-numbered years.

## Traditional art

The earliest Chinese art dates back to the Neolithic period – **pottery** vessels painted with geometric designs. From the same period come decorated clay heads, and pendants and ornaments of polished stone or jade – a simplified sitting bird in polished jade is a very early example of the Chinese tradition of animal sculpture. The subsequent era, from around 1500 BC, is dominated by **Shang and Zhou bronze vessels** used for preparing and serving food and wine; their design often featured geometric and animal motifs, as well as grinning masks of humans and fabulous beasts. Later, under the **Zhou**, the style of the bronzes became more varied and rich: some animal vessels are fantastically shaped and extravagantly decorated, others seem to be depicting not so much a fierce tiger, for example, as utter ferocity itself.

Although the Shang produced a few small sculpted human figures and animals in marble, **sculptures** and works in stone begin to be found in great quantities in **Han-dynasty** tombs. Indian-style art marked the advent of **Buddhism**; not until the **Tang** do you get the full flowering of a native Chinese style, where the figures are rounder, with movement, and the positions, expressions and clothes are more natural and realistic. The **Song** continued to carve religious figures, but less statuary was produced until the **Ming** with their taste for massive tomb sculptures, as still seen in Beijing.

### Painting

**Traditional Chinese paintings** are light and airy, with empty spaces playing an important element in the design, and rich in symbolism; they're decorated with a few lines of poetry and several names in the form of seals – the marks of past owners. The great flowering of landscape painting came with the **Song dynasty**; an academy was set up under imperial patronage, and different schools of painting emerged which analyzed the natural world with great concentration and intensity. Their style has set a mark on Chinese landscape painting ever since. The **Ming dynasty** saw a willingness by painters to be influenced by tradition: as well as the famous landscapes, look for examples of bamboo and plum blossom, and bird and flower paintings being brought to a high decorative pitch.

The arrival of the Manchu **Qing dynasty** did not disrupt the continuity of Chinese painting, but the art became wide open to many influences. It included the Italian **Castiglione** (Lang Shi-ning in Chinese) who specialized in horses, dogs and flowers under imperial patronage, and individualists such as the Eight Eccentrics of Yangzhou, who objected to derivative art and sought a more distinctive approach to subject and style.

Even today, Chinese art schools emphasize traditional techniques, but many students have been quick to plug themselves into international trends; at its best, this leads to art that is technically proficient and conceptually strong. Recent decades of seismic change in China has, in keeping with the rules of development, seen a recent shift towards more traditional forms of painting, or at least the weaving of the traditional into the contemporary. It has led to works from artists such as **Zhang Daqian** commanding huge prices at auction.

## Contemporary art

**Contemporary art** is flourishing in Beijing, and well worth checking out. The best galleries are owned by expats, and Chinese art is seen as an attractive investment by foreign buyers. Galleries in the city centre are rather more commercial than those in the suburban artsy areas, tending to focus on selling paintings rather than making a splash with a themed show. Still, there are some that display interesting and challenging work.

The scene began in earnest in the 1990s with a group who, with little chance of selling their work – or even exhibiting – banded together to form an arts village in the suburbs of Beijing, near the old Summer Palace. These artists developed a school of painting that expressed their individualism and their sceptical, often ironic and jaundiced view of contemporary China; this was, of course, the generation that had seen its dreams of change shot down at Tian'anmen Square. Nurtured by curator **Li Xianting**, known as "the Godfather of Chinese art", as well as sympathetic foreign collectors, they built the foundations of the art scene as it is today.

The most famous of these so-called **cynical realists** is **Fang Lijun**, whose images of disembodied heads against desolate landscapes are some of the most characteristic images of modern Chinese art. Other art stars who began their career here include **Yue Minjun**, who paints sinister laughing figures, and the satirists **Wang Jinsong** and **Song Yonghong**.

Artists such as **Wang Guangyi** developed a second, distinctly Chinese school of art called **political pop**, where the powerful iconography of the Cultural Revolution was co-opted to celebrate consumerism – workers wave iPods instead of *Little Red Books*. This kind of thing, perennially popular with foreign visitors, is regarded these days as pretty hackneyed in China. Rather more interesting was the deliberately brash "**gaudy art**" movement of the 1990s, whose aesthetic celebrated the tacky and vulgar; look out for **Xu Yihui**'s ceramic confections and the **Luo Brothers**' kitsch extravaganzas.

### Today's trends

It's much harder to pick out trends in today's ferment of activity, but many artists are unsurprisingly preoccupied with documenting the destruction of the Chinese urban landscape and the gut-wrenching changes that have accompanied **modernization**. As spaces for viewing art have increased, artists have diversified into **new media** such as performance and video; two to look out for are **Cao Fei**, who films and photographs fantasy tableaux, and **Yang Fudong**, who makes wistful images of modern life. With all the noise, you need to shout to make yourself heard – and the loudest modern artists are the impresario **Zhang Huang**, who produces witty sculptures on an enormous scale, and art celebrity **Ai Weiwei**, who helped design the concept behind the Bird's Nest Olympic stadium (see p.102).

The contemporary art scene is, however, facing a few major challenges. Artists and photographers have fewer problems with **censorship** than writers or musicians, though the governmental shackles are still in place. Counterfeiting has also become a real issue – unlike Chinese copies of overseas-brand handbags, smartphones or golf clubs, this is having a discernibly negative local impact. There has been a massive surge in **forgeries**, compounded by the fact that only 70 percent of works bought at auction are actually getting paid for. In addition, some of what does actually sell goes for an inflated price – either as status symbols to the nouveau riche, or (allegedly) as tools of high-level bribery. Government regulation may take some time to catch up with these dark inner workings of the local art scene.

# Music

The casual visitor to China could be forgiven for thinking that the only traditional style of music to compete with bland pop is that of the kitsch folk troupes to be heard in hotels and concert halls. Beijing opera, however, is now famous across the globe, while a very different, edgier sound can be heard in certain smoky city bars – the new Chinese rock, with its energetic expressions of urban angst.

## Beijing opera

Chinese musical drama dates back at least two thousand years, and became overwhelmingly popular with both the elite and common people from the Yuan dynasty onwards. Of the several hundred types of regional opera, **Beijing opera**, a rather late hybrid form dating from the eighteenth century, is the most widely known – now heard throughout China, it's the closest thing to a "national" theatre. Many librettos now performed date back to the seventeenth century and describe the intrigues of emperors and gods, as well as love stories and comedy. The rigorous training the form demands – and the heavy hand of ideology that saw it as the most important of "the people's arts" – is graphically displayed in Chen Kaige's film *Farewell My Concubine* (see box, p.180).

While Chinese opera makes a great visual spectacle, musically it is frankly an acquired taste, resembling to the uninitiated the din of cats fighting in a blazing firework factory. The singing style is tense, guttural and high-pitched, while the music is dominated by the bowed string accompaniment of the *jinghu*, a sort of sawn-off *erhu*. It also features plucked lutes, flutes and – for transitional points – a piercing *shawm*. The action is driven by percussion, with drum and clappers leading an ensemble of gongs and cymbals in an assortment of set patterns. Professional opera troupes exist in the major towns but rural opera performances, which are given for temple fairs and even weddings, tend to be livelier. Even in modern Beijing, you may come across groups of old folk meeting in parks to go through their favourite Beijing opera excerpts.

## Indie and electronic music

Controversial local legend **Cui Jian**, a sort of Chinese Bob Dylan, was China's first real rock star, giving up a job as a trumpeter in a Beijing orchestra to perform gravel-voiced guitar rock with lyrics as risqué as he could get away with – look out for his albums *Power to The Powerless* and *Egg Under the Red Flag*. Cui Jian is now seen as the granddaddy of Beijing's thriving **indie music** scene. Nobody makes any money out of it – venues and bands struggle to survive against all-pervasive pop pap, and when an act does take off, piracy eats up any profits the recordings might have made – but fierce dedication keeps the scene alive. Most **bands** of note, many of which perform in English or have a mixed set, are on the Scream, Badhead or Modern Sky labels. Bands to look out for include Rolling Stones-wannnabes Joyside, indie noise merchants Carsick Cars, Mongolian rockers Voodoo Kungfu, indie pros Lonely China Day, and electro popsters Pet Conspiracy. Veteran punks Brain Failure are still going strong, though the mantle of nuttiest punks has passed to younger bands like Demerit.

The best new **electronic music** is on Shanshui Records; look out for iLoop and Sulumi. Not so well represented is **hip-hop** (odd, as it has made plenty of inroads in fashion) though old favourites CMCB carry it off pretty well.

# Books

You won't find much variety in English-language reading materials when buying books in Beijing; your best bet are the many cheap editions of the Chinese classics, published in English translation by two Beijing-based firms, Foreign Languages Press (FLP) and Panda Books (some of whose titles are published outside China, too). In the reviews below, books that are especially recommended are marked ★; o/p signifies that a book is out of print.

## HISTORY

**Peter Fleming** *The Siege at Peking*. A lively account of the events that led up to June 20, 1900, when the foreign legations in Beijing were attacked by the Boxers and Chinese imperial troops.

**Paul French** *Midnight in Peking*. A real-life murder mystery, revolving around the search for the killer of Pamela Warner, an English girl whose body was found in Beijing, minus heart and blood, in 1937.

**Jan Wong** *Red China Blues*. Jan Wong, a Canadian of Chinese descent, went to China as an idealistic Maoist in 1972 at the height of the Cultural Revolution, and was one of only two Westerners permitted to enrol at Beijing University. She describes the six years she spent in China and her growing disillusionment, which led eventually to her repatriation. A touching, sometimes bizarre, inside account of the bad old days.

## CULTURE AND SOCIETY

★**Jasper Becker** *The Chinese*; *City of Heavenly Tranquility: Beijing in the History of China*. *The Chinese* is a classic, weighty, erudite but very comprehensible introduction to Chinese society and culture; lighter and breezier, *City of Heavenly Tranquility* is a great collection of stories about Beijing's history, including a hard-hitting condemnation of how most physical remains of that history have recently been destroyed.

**Ian Buruma** *Bad Elements: Chinese Rebels from Los Angeles to Beijing*. Interviews with Chinese dissidents, both at home and in exile, make for a compelling, if inevitably rather jaundiced, view of the country.

**Martin Jacques** *When China Rules the World*. Comprehensive overview, both troubling and enlightening, of the ascendancy of the Chinese state and the impact that

it is having on the rest of the world.

**James Kynge** *China Shakes the World*. Another critical but acute overview of Chinese society and government and the challenges ahead.

★**Michael Meyer** *The Last Days of Old Beijing*. Combines a history of Beijing's *hutongs* with a memoir of what it was like to live in them, immersed in the local community.

**Morris Rossabi** (ed.) *The Travels of Marco Polo*. Said to have inspired Columbus, *The Travels* is a fantastic read, full of amazing insights picked up during Marco Polo's 26 years of wandering in Asia between Venice and the Peking court of Kublai Khan. It's not, however, a coherent history, having been ghost-written by a romantic novelist from Marco Polo's notes.

## GUIDES AND REFERENCE BOOKS

**Giles Beguin and Dominique Morel** *The Forbidden City: Heart of Imperial China*. A good introduction to the complex, and to the history of the emperors who lived there, though the best thing about this pocket book (as with most books about the Forbidden City) is the illustrations.

**Lin Xiang Zhu and Lin Cuifeng** *Chinese Gastronomy* (o/p). A classic work, relatively short on recipes but strong on

cooking methods and the underlying philosophy. It wavers in and out of print, sometimes under different titles – look for "Lin" as the author name. Essential reading for anyone serious about learning the finer details of Chinese cooking.

**Mary Tregear** *Chinese Art*. Authoritative summary of the main strands in Chinese art from Neolithic times, through the Bronze Age and up to the twentieth century. Clearly written and well illustrated.

## RELIGION AND PHILOSOPHY

**Asiapac Comics Series**. Available at Beijing's Foreign Language Bookstore, this entertaining series of books presents ancient Chinese philosophy in cartoon format,

making the subject accessible without losing too much complexity. They're all well written and well drawn; particularly good is the *Sayings of Confucius*.

**Confucius** *The Analects*. There are various good translations of this classic text, a collection of Confucius's teachings focusing on morality and the state. *I Ching*, also known as *The Book of Changes*, is another classic volume from Confucius that teaches a form of divination. It includes coverage of some of the fundamental concepts of Chinese thought, such as the duality of *yin* and *yang*.

**Lao Zi** *Tao Te Ching*. The *Daodejing* in pinyin, this is a collection of mystical thoughts and philosophical speculation that form the basis of Taoist philosophy.
**Arthur Waley** (trans.) *Three Ways of Thought in Ancient China*. Translated extracts from the writings of three of the early philosophers – Zhuang Zi, Mencius and Han Feizi. A useful introduction.

## BIOGRAPHY AND AUTOBIOGRAPHY

**Pallavi Aiyar** *Smoke and Mirrors: An Experience of China*. There are plenty of memoirs about the expat experience in Beijing; this one stands out as it was written from an Indian perspective. Amusing, anecdotal and full of acute observations.
**E. Backhouse and J.O. Bland** *China Under the Empress Dowager* (o/p). Classic work on imperial life in late nineteenth-century China. It's based around the diary of a court eunuch, which is now generally accepted to have been forged (Backhouse was the prime suspect; see the review of *Hermit of Peking* by Hugh Trevor-Roper).
**Rachel Dewoskin** *Foreign Babes in Beijing*. Breezy account of an American girl's adventures among the city's artsy set in the 1990s. The most interesting parts concern the author's experiences working as an actress on a Chinese soap opera.
**Jia Yinghua** *The Last Eunuch of China: the Life of Sun Yaoting*. The title of this book basically says it all: it's a fantastic peek at the colourful life of Sun Yaoting, who died in 1996 after rising from humble farmyard origins to the imperial court.
★ **Jung Chang** *Wild Swans*; *Mao: The Untold Story* and *Empress Dowager Cixi: The Concubine Who Launched Modern China*. Enormously popular in the West, *Wild Swans* is a family saga covering three generations that chronicles the horrors of life in turbulent twentieth-century China. A massive and well-researched character assassination, *Mao* serves as an excellent introduction to modern Chinese history, as well as being a good read. Lastly, *Cixi* is one of several recent books to paint the dowager in a more forgiving light, arguing that she was more savvy, and less evil, than the world gives her credit for.
**Pu Yi** *From Emperor to Citizen*. The autobiography of the last Qing emperor, Pu Yi, who lost his throne as a boy and was later briefly installed as a puppet emperor during the Japanese occupation. He ended his life employed as a gardener.
**Hugh Trevor-Roper** *Hermit of Peking: The Hidden Life of Sir Edmund Backhouse*. Sparked by its subject's thoroughly obscene memoirs, *Hermit of Peking* uses external sources in an attempt to uncover the facts behind the extraordinary and convoluted life of Edmund Backhouse – Chinese scholar, eccentric recluse and phenomenal liar – who lived in Beijing from the late nineteenth century until his death in 1944.

## CHINESE LITERATURE

**Cao Xueqing** *Dream of Red Mansions*. Sometimes published under the English title *Dream of the Red Chamber*, this intricate eighteenth-century comedy of manners follows the fortunes of the Jia clan through the emotionally charged adolescent lives of Jia Baoyu and his two female cousins, Lin Daiyu and Xue Baochai. *The Story of the Stone*, a version published in the West by Penguin, fills five paperbacks; the FLP edition, available in Beijing, is much simplified and abridged.
**Chun Sue** *Beijing Doll*. This rambling confessional details the teenage writer's adventures in the indie music scene. With plenty of sex and drugs, it caused quite a stir when it came out and was, predictably, banned.
**Lao She** *Rickshaw Boy*. One of China's great modern writers, Lao She was driven to suicide during the Cultural Revolution. This story is a haunting account of a young rickshaw puller in pre-1949 Beijing.
★ **Lu Xun** *The Real Story of Ah Q and Other Tales of China*. Widely read in China today, Lu Xun is regarded as the father of modern Chinese writing. *Ah Q* is one of his best tales:

short, allegorical and cynical, about a simpleton who is swept up in the 1911 revolution.
**Luo Guanzhong** *Romance of the Three Kingdoms*. One of the world's greatest historical novels. Though written 1200 years after the events it depicts, this vibrant tale vividly evokes the battles, political schemings and myths surrounding China's turbulent Three Kingdoms period.
★ **Ma Jian** *Red Dust*; *The Noodle Maker*; *Beijing Coma*. Satirist Ma Jian is one of China's most insightful living writers, though most of his work is banned in China. *Red Dust* is a travelogue about an epic, beatnik-style jaunt around China in the 1980s, documenting a set of chaotic lives, not least the narrator's own. *The Noodle Maker* is a dark novel concerning the friendship between a writer of propaganda and a professional blood donor; and *Beijing Coma*, his weightiest tome, concerns the events of 1989.
★ **Mo Yan** *The Red Sorghum Clan*; *The Garlic Ballads*. China's only winner of the Nobel Prize for Literature, Mo Yan (whose name, meaning "don't speak", speaks volumes about how popular he is with the regime) is most famed for

*The Garlic Ballads*, a hard-hitting novel of rural life; and *The Red Sorghum Clan*, parts of which were turned into *Red Sorghum*, a Zhang Yimou film (see p.180). Both books were banned in China; though neither were set in Beijing, their thinly veiled social commentary is still appropriate reading.

**Wang Shuo** *Playing For Thrills*; *Please Don't Call Me Human*. The bad boy of contemporary Chinese literature, Wang Shuo writes in colourful Beijing dialect about the city's seamy underbelly. These are his only novels translated into English: the first is a mystery story whose boorish narrator spends most of his time drinking, gambling and chasing girls; the second, banned in China, a bitter satire portraying modern China as a place where pride is nothing and greed is everything, and a dignified martial artist is emasculated in order to win an Olympic gold medal.

★ **Wu Cheng'en** *Journey to the West*. Absurd, lively rendering of the Buddhist monk Xuanzang's pilgrimage to India to collect sacred scriptures, aided by – according to popular myth – Sandy, Pigsy, and the irrepressible Sun Wu Kong, the monkey king. Arthur Waley's version, published in the West under the title *Monkey*, retains the tale's spirit while shortening the hundred-chapter opus to paperback length.

**Yiyun Li** *A Thousand Years of Good Prayers*; *Gold Boy, Emerald Girl*. Two short stories looking at how China's rapid changes have affected the lives of ordinary folk, from a Beijinger now living in the States.

# Mandarin Chinese

As the most widely spoken language on earth, Chinese is hard to overlook. Mandarin Chinese, derived from the language of Han officialdom in the Beijing area, has been systematically promoted over the past hundred years to be the official, unifying language of the Chinese people, much as modern French, for example, is based on the original Parisian dialect. It is known in mainland China as *putonghua*, "common language". All Beijingers will speak and understand it, but note that working-class Beijingers have a distinctive accent, adding an "r" sound to the end of many words – pronounced in a manner similar to the "r" of Americans or Irish (or pirates), it's most noticeable with older folk, particularly men who've been at the beer or *bai jiu*.

Chinese **grammar** is delightfully simple. There is no need to conjugate verbs, decline nouns or make adjectives agree – Chinese characters are immutable, so words simply cannot have different "endings". Instead, context and fairly rigid rules about word order are relied on to make those distinctions of time, number and gender that Indo-European languages are so concerned with. Instead of cumbersome tenses, the Chinese make use of words such as "yesterday" or "tomorrow" to indicate when things happen; instead of plural endings they simply state how many things there are. For English speakers, Chinese word order is very familiar, and you'll find that by simply stringing words together you may well be producing perfectly grammatical Chinese. Basic sentences follow the subject–verb–object format; adjectives, as well as all qualifying and describing phrases, precede nouns.

From the point of view of foreigners, the main thing that distinguishes Mandarin from familiar languages is that it's a **tonal** language. In order to pronounce a word correctly, it is necessary to know not only the sounds of its consonants and vowels but also its correct tone – though with the help of context, intelligent listeners should be able to work out what you are trying to say even if you don't get the tones quite right.

## Pinyin

Back in the 1950s, the Communist government hoped to eventually replace Chinese characters with an alphabet of Roman letters; though near-certain mass riots brought an end to this plan, the **pinyin system**, a precise and exact means of representing all the sounds of Mandarin Chinese, had already been devised. It comprises all the Roman letters of the English alphabet, with the four tones represented by diacritical marks, or accents, which appear above each syllable. The old aim of replacing Chinese characters with *pinyin* was abandoned long ago, but in the meantime *pinyin* has one very

---

### THERE'S AN APP FOR THAT

Travellers are increasingly using their mobile phones to counter linguistic difficulties faced during their time in China. One of the most useful apps is the **Waygo Visual Translator** (⑩ waygoapp.com), which allows the steady-handed to scan Chinese characters, then translates them for you – particularly handy in restaurants with no English-language menu. Better for word-to-word translation is the excellent **Pleco** app (⑩ pleco.com), which also has scanning facilities if you're prepared to pay extra fees; the **Dian Hua** app (⑩ dianhuadictionary .com) is similar, and nearly as good.

important function, that of helping foreigners pronounce Chinese words. However, there is the added complication that in *pinyin* the letters don't all have the sounds you would expect, and you'll need to spend an hour or two learning the correct sounds.

You'll often see *pinyin* in Beijing, on street signs and shop displays, but only well-educated locals know the system very well. The establishments in this book have been given both in characters and in *pinyin*; the pronunciation guide below is your first step to making yourself comprehensible. For more information, see the *Rough Guide Mandarin Chinese Phrasebook*.

## PRONUNCIATION

There are four possible **tones** in Mandarin Chinese, and every syllable of every word is characterized by one of them, except for a few syllables, which are considered toneless. In English, to change the tone is to change the mood or the emphasis; in Chinese, to change the tone is to change the word itself. The tones are:

**First** or "high" *ā ē ī ō ū* A high, flat pitch often used in English when mimicking robotic or very boring, flat voices.
**Second** or "rising" *á é í ó ú* Used in English when asking a question showing surprise, for example "eh?" Try raising your eyebrows when attempting to make a sound with this tone – it never fails.
**Third** or "falling-rising" *ǎ ě ǐ ǒ ǔ*. Used in English when echoing someone's words with a measure of incredulity. For example, "John's dead.""De-ad?!"
**Fourth** or "falling" *à è ì ò ù*. Often used in English when counting in a brusque manner – "One! Two! Three! Four!" Try stamping your foot lightly when attempting to make a sound with this tone.
**Toneless** A few syllables do not have a tone accent. These are pronounced without emphasis, much like that lovely word "meh".

Note that when two words with the third tone occur consecutively, the first word is pronounced as though it carries the second tone. Thus *nĕ* (meaning "you") and *hăo* ("well, good"), when combined, are pronounced *ní ăǎo*, meaning "how are you?"

## CONSONANTS

Most consonants, as written in *pinyin*, are pronounced in a similar way to their English equivalents, with the following exceptions:
**c** as in ha**ts**
**g** is hard as in **g**od (except when preceded by "n", when it sounds like sa**ng**)
**q** as in **ch**eese
**x** has no direct equivalent in English, but you can make

the sound by sliding from an "s" to an "sh" sound and stopping midway between the two
**z** as in su**ds**
**zh** as in fu**dge**

## VOWELS AND DIPHTHONGS

As in most languages, the vowel sounds are rather harder to quantify than the consonants. The examples below give a rough description of the sound of each vowel as written in *pinyin*.
**a** usually somewhere between f**a**r and m**a**n
**ai** as in **eye**
**ao** as in c**ow**
**e** usually as in f**ur**
**ei** as in g**ay**
**en** as in hyph**en**
**eng** as in s**ung**
**er** as in b**ar** with a pronounced "r"
**i** usually as in b**ee**, except in zi, ci, si, ri, zhi, chi and shi, when i is a short, clipped sound, like the American military "s**ir**".
**ia** as in y**ak**
**ian** as in y**en**
**ie** as in y**eah**
**o** as in s**aw**
**ou** as in sh**ow**
**ü** as in the German **ü** (make an "ee" sound and glide slowly into an "oo"; at the mid-point between the two sounds you should hit the ü-sound); in pinyin, it's sometimes written as a V
**u** usually as in f**ool**, though whenever u follows j, q, x or y, it is always pronounced **ü**
**ua** as in s**ua**ve
**uai** as in **why**
**ue** as though contracting "you" and "air" together, **you'air**
**ui** as in **way**
**uo** as in w**ore**

## USEFUL WORDS AND PHRASES

When writing or saying the name of a Chinese person, the surname is given first; thus Mao Zedong's family name is Mao. Also note that Chinese famously has no precise words for "yes" and "no"; the terms for "is" (是, shì) or "correct"

(对, duì) are usually used as a positive response, while for negatives the term 不 (bù) goes behind the verb in question.

## BASICS

| | | |
|---|---|---|
| I | 我 | wǒ |
| You (singular) | 你 | nǐ |
| He | 他 | tā |
| She | 她 | tā |
| We | 我们 | wǒmen |
| You (plural) | 你们 | nǐmen |
| They | 他们 | tāmen |
| I want... | 我要 | wǒ yào... |
| No, I don't want... | 我不要 | wǒ bú yào... |
| Is it possible...? | 可不可以 | kě bù kěyǐ...? |
| It is (not) possible | (不)可以... | (bù) kěyǐ |
| Is there any.../Have you got any...? | 你有没有 | nǐ yǒu méiyǒu...? |
| There is/I have | 有... | yǒu... |
| There isn't/I haven't | 没有... | méiyǒu |
| Please help me | 请帮我忙.. | qǐng bāng wǒ máng |
| Mr... | ...先生 | xiānshēng |
| Mrs... | ...太太 | tàitai |
| Miss... | ...小姐 | xiǎojiě |

## COMMUNICATING

| | | |
|---|---|---|
| I don't speak Chinese | 我不会说中文 | wǒ búhuì shuō zhōngwén |
| Can you speak English? | 你会说英语吗 | nǐ huì shuō yīngyǔ ma? |
| Can you get someone who speaks English? | 请给我找一个会说英文的人 | qǐng gěiwǒ zhǎo yīgè huìshuō yīngwén de rén? |
| Please speak slowly | 请说得慢一点 | qǐng shuōde màn yīdiǎn |
| Please say that again | 请再说一遍 | qǐng zài shuō yī biàn |
| I understand | 我听得懂 | wǒ tīngdedǒng |
| I don't understand | 我听不懂 | wǒ tīngbùdǒng |
| I can't read Chinese characters | 我看不懂汉字 | wǒ kànbùdǒng hànzì |
| What does this mean? | 这是什么意思 | zhèshì shénme yìsi? |
| How do you pronounce this character? | 这个字怎么念 | zhègè zì zěnme niàn? |

## GREETINGS AND BASIC COURTESIES

| | | |
|---|---|---|
| Hello/How do you do?/How are you? | 你好 | nǐhǎo |
| I'm fine | 我很好 | wǒ hěnhǎo |
| Thank you | 谢谢 | xièxie |
| Don't mention it/You're welcome | 不客气 | búkèqi |
| Sorry to bother you... | 麻烦你 | máfán nǐ... |
| Sorry/I apologize | 对不起 | duìbùqǐ |
| It's not important/No problem | 没关系 | méiguānxì |
| Goodbye | 再见 | zàijiàn |
| Excuse me (when getting attention) | 不好意思 | bùhǎoyìsi |

## CHIT-CHAT

| | | |
|---|---|---|
| What country are you from? | 你哪个国家来的？ | nǐ nǎgè guójiā lái de mǎ? |
| Britain | 英国 | yīngguó |
| England | 英国/英格兰 | yīngguó/yīnggélán |
| Scotland | 苏格兰 | sūgélán |
| Wales | 威尔士 | wēi'ěrshì |
| Ireland | 爱尔兰 | ài'érlán |
| America | 美国 | měiguó |
| Canada | 加拿大 | jiānádà |

| | | |
|---|---|---|
| Australia | 澳大利亚 | àodàlìyà |
| New Zealand | 新西兰 | xīnxīlán |
| South Africa | 南非 | nánfēi |
| China | 中国 | zhōngguó |
| Outside China | 外国 | wàiguó |
| What's your name? | 你叫什么名字 | nǐ jiào shénme míngzi? |
| My name is... | 我叫.... | wǒ jiào... |
| Are you married? | 你结婚了吗? | nǐ jiéhūn le ma? |
| I am (not) married | 我(没有)结婚了 | wǒ (méiyǒu) jiéhūn le |
| Have you got children? | 你有没有孩子? | nǐ yǒu méiyǒu háizi? |
| Do you like...? | 你喜不喜欢.....? | nǐ xǐ bù xǐhuān....? |
| I (don't) like... | 我不喜欢.... | wǒ (bù) xǐhuān... |
| What's your job? | 你干什么工作? | nǐ gàn shénme gōngzuò? |
| I'm a foreign student | 我是留学生 | wǒ shì liúxuéshēng |
| I'm a teacher | 我是老师 | wǒ shì lǎoshī |
| I work in a company | 我在一个公司工作 | wǒ zài yígè gōngsī gōngzuò |
| I don't work | 我不工作 | wǒ bù gōngzuò |
| I'm retired | 我退休了 | wǒ tuìxīu le |
| Clean/dirty | 干净/脏 | gānjìng/zāng |
| Hot/cold | 热/冷 | rè/lěng |
| Fast/slow | 快/慢 | kuài/màn |
| Good/bad | 好/坏 | hǎo/huài |
| Big/small | 大/小 | dà/xiǎo |
| Pretty | 漂亮 | piàoliang |
| Interesting | 有意思 | yǒuyìsi |

**NUMBERS**

| | | |
|---|---|---|
| Zero | 零 | líng |
| One | 一 | yī |
| Two | 二/两 | èr/liǎng* |
| Three | 三 | sān |
| Four | 四 | sì |
| Five | 五 | wǔ |
| Six | 六 | liù |
| Seven | 七 | qī |
| Eight | 八 | bā |
| Nine | 九 | jiǔ |
| Ten | 十 | shí |
| Eleven | 十一 | shíyī |
| Twelve | 十二 | shíèr |
| Twenty | 二十 | èrshí |
| Twenty-one | 二十一 | èrshíyi |
| One hundred | 一百 | yībǎi |
| Two hundred | 二百 | èrbǎi |
| One thousand | 一千 | yīqiān |
| Ten thousand | 一万 | yīwàn |
| One hundred thousand | 十万 | shíwàn |
| One million | 一百万 | yībǎiwàn |
| One hundred million | 一亿 | yīyì |
| One billion | 十亿 | shíyì |

* 两/liǎng is used when enumerating, for example "two people" is liǎnggè rén.
二/èr is used when counting.

## TIME

| | | |
|---|---|---|
| Now | 现在 | xiànzài |
| Today | 今天 | jīntiān |
| (In the) morning | 早上 | zǎoshàng |
| (In the) afternoon | 下午 | xiàwǔ |
| (In the) evening | 晚上 | wǎnshàng |
| Tomorrow | 明天 | míngtiān |
| The day after tomorrow | 后天 | hòutiān |
| Yesterday | 昨天 | zuótiān |
| Week/month/year | 星期/月/年 | xīngqī/yuè/nián |
| Next/last week/month/year | 下/上星期/月/年 | xià/shàng xīngqī/yuè/nián |
| Monday | 星期一 | xīngqī yī |
| Tuesday | 星期二 | xīngqī èr |
| Wednesday | 星期三 | xīngqī sān |
| Thursday | 星期四 | xīngqī sì |
| Friday | 星期五 | xīngqī wǔ |
| Saturday | 星期六 | xīngqī liù |
| Sunday | 星期天 | xīngqī tiān |
| What's the time? | 几点了？ | jǐdiǎn le? |
| Morning | 早上 | zǎoshàng |
| Afternoon | 中午 | zhōngwǔ |
| Evening | 晚 | wǎn |
| 10 o'clock | 十点钟 | shídiǎn zhōng |
| 10.20 | 十点二十 | shídiǎn èrshí |
| 10.30 | 十点半 | shídiǎn bàn |

## TRAVELLING AND GETTING AROUND TOWN

| | | |
|---|---|---|
| North | 北 | běi |
| South | 南 | nán |
| East | 东 | dōng |
| West | 西 | xī |
| Airport | 机场 | jīchǎng |
| Ferry dock | 船码头 | chuánmǎtóu |
| Left-luggage office | 寄存处 | jìcún chù |
| Ticket office | 售票处 | shòupiào chù |
| Ticket | 票 | piào |
| Can I have a ticket to…? | 可不可以卖给我到…的票 | kěbùkěyǐ màigěi wǒ dào…de piào? |
| I want to go to… | 我想到…去 | wǒ xiǎng dàoqù |
| I want to leave at (8 o'clock) | 我想(八点钟)离开 | wǒ xiǎng (bādiǎnzhōng) líkāi |
| When does it leave? | 什么时候出发？ | shénme shíhòu chūfā? |
| When does it arrive? | 什么时候到？ | shénme shíhòu dào? |
| How long does it take? | 路上得多长时间？ | lùshàng děi duōcháng shíjiān? |
| CITS | 中国国际旅行社 | zhōngguó guójì lǚxíngshè |
| Train | 火车 | huǒchē |
| (Main) train station | (主要)火车站 | (zhǔyào) huǒchēzhàn |
| Bus | 公共汽车 | gōnggòng qìchēzhàn |
| Bus station | 汽车站 | qìchēzhàn |
| Long-distance bus station | 长途汽车站 | chángtú qìchēzhàn |
| Express train/bus | 特快车 | tèkuài chē |
| Fast train/bus | 快车 | kuɨi chē |
| Ordinary train/bus | 普通车 | pǔtōng chē |
| Timetable | 时间表 | shíjiān biǎo |
| Map | 地图 | dìtú |

| Where is…? | …在哪里？ | …zài nǎlǐ? |
| Go straight on | 往前走 | wǎng qián zǒu |
| Turn right | 往右走 | wǎng yòu zǒu |
| Turn left | 往左拐 | wǎng zuǒ guǎi |
| Taxi | 出租车 | chūzū chē |
| Please use the meter | 请打开记价器 | qǐng dǎkāi jìjiàqì |
| Underground/subway station | 地铁站 | dìtiě zhàn |
| Bicycle | 自行车 | zìxíng chē |
| Can I borrow your bicycle? | 能不能借你的自行车 | néngbùnéng jiè nǐdē zìxíngchē? |
| Bus | 公共汽车 | gōnggòng qìchē |
| Which bus goes to…? | 几路车到…去？ | jǐlùchē dào … qù? |
| Number (10) bus | (十)路车 | (shí) lù chē |
| Does this bus go to…? | 这车到…去吗？ | zhè chē dào … qù ma? |
| When is the next bus? | 下一班车几点开？ | xiàyìbānchē jǐdiǎn kāi? |
| The first bus | 头班车 | tóubān chē |
| The last bus | 末班车 | mòbān chē |
| Please tell me where to get off | 请告诉我在哪里下车？ | qǐng gàosù wǒ zài nǎlǐ xiàchē? |
| Museum | 博物馆 | bówùguǎn |
| Temple | 寺庙 | sìmiào |
| Church | 教堂 | jiàotáng |

**ACCOMMODATION**

| Accommodation | 住宿 | zhùsù |
| Hotel (upmarket) | 宾馆 | bīnguǎn |
| Hotel (cheap) | 招待所, 旅馆 | zhāodàisuǒ, lǚguǎn |
| Hostel | 旅舍 | lǚshè |
| Do you have a room available? | 你们有房间吗？ | nǐmen yǒu fángjiān ma? |
| Can I have a look at the room? | 能不能看一下方向？ | néngbùnéng kàn yíxià fángjiān? |
| I want the cheapest bed you've got | 我要你这里最便宜的床位 | wǒ yào nǐ zhèlǐ zuìpiányi de chuángwèi |
| Single room | 单人房 | dānrén fáng |
| Twin room | 双人房 | shuāngrén fáng |
| Double room with a big bed | 双人房间带大床 | shuāngrénfángjiān dài dàchuáng |
| Three-bed room | 三人房 | sānrén fáng |
| Dormitory | 多人房 | duōrén fáng |
| Suite | 套房 | tàofáng |
| (Large) bed | (大)床 | (dà) chuáng |
| Passport | 护照 | hùzhào |
| Deposit | 押金 | yājīn |
| Key | 钥匙 | yàoshi |
| I want to change my room | 我想换房 | wǒ xiǎng huànfáng |

**SHOPPING, MONEY AND THE POLICE**

| How much is it? | 这是多少钱？ | zhèshì duōshǎo qián? |
| That's too expensive | 太贵了 | tài guì le |
| I haven't got any cash | 我没有现金 | wǒ méiyǒu xiànjīn |
| Have you got anything cheaper? | 有没有便宜一点的？ | yǒu méiyǒu piányì yìdiǎn de? |
| Do you accept credit cards? | 可不可以用信用卡？ | kě bù kěyǐ yòng xìnyòngkǎ? |
| Department store | 百货商店 | bǎihuò shāngdiàn |
| Market | 市场 | shìchǎng |
| ¥1 (RMB) | 一块（人民币） | yí kuài (rénmínbì) |
| US$1 | 一块美金 | yí kuài měijīn |
| £1 | 一个英镑 | yí gè yīngbàng |
| €1 | 一欧元 | yí ōuyuán |

| Change money | 换钱 | huàn qián |
| Bank | 银行 | yínháng |
| Travellers' cheques | 旅行支票 | lǚxíngzhīpiào |
| ATM | 提款机 | tíkuǎnjī |
| PSB | 公安局 | gōng'ānjú |

## COMMUNICATIONS

| Post office | 邮电局 | yóudiànjú |
| Envelope | 信封 | xìnfēng |
| Stamp | 邮票 | yóupiào |
| Airmail | 航空信 | hángkōngxìn |
| Surface mail | 平信 | píngxìn |
| Telephone | 电话 | diànhuà |
| Mobile/cell phone | 手机 | shǒujī |
| SMS message | 短信 | duǎnxìn |
| International telephone call | 国际电话 | guójì diànhuà |
| Reverse charges/collect call | 对方付钱电话 | duìfāngfùqián diànhuà |
| Phone card | 电话卡 | diànhuàkǎ |
| I want to make a telephone call to (Britain) | 我想给（英国）打电话 | wǒ xiǎng gěi (yīngguó) dǎ diànhuà |
| Internet | 网路 | wǎngluò |
| Internet café/bar | 网吧 | wǎngbā |
| Email | 电子邮件 | diànzǐyóujiàn |

## HEALTH

| Hospital | 医院 | yīyuàn |
| Pharmacy | 药店 | yàodiàn |
| Medicine | 药 | yào |
| Doctor | 医生 | yīshēng |
| Chinese medicine | 中药 | zhōngyào |
| Diarrhoea | 腹泻 | fùxiè |
| Vomit | 呕吐 | ǒutù |
| Fever | 发烧 | fāshāo |
| I'm ill | 我生病了 | wǒ shēngbìng le |
| I've got flu | 我感冒了 | wǒ gǎnmào le |
| I'm (not) allergic to… | 我对…(不)过敏 | wǒ duì … (bù) guòmǐn |
| Antibiotics | 抗生素 | kàngshēngsù |
| Condom | 避孕套 | bìyùntào |
| Tampons | 卫生棉条 | wèishēng miántiáo |

## A MENU READER

### GENERAL

| Restaurant | 餐厅 | cāntīng |
| House speciality | 招牌菜 | zhāopái cài |
| How much is that? | 多少钱 | duōshǎo qián? |
| I don't eat (meat) | 我不吃(肉) | wǒ bùchī (ròu) |
| I would like… | 我想要… | wǒ xiǎng yào... |
| Local dishes | 地方菜 | dìfāng cài |
| Snacks | 小吃 | xiǎochī |
| Menu/set menu/English menu | 菜单/套菜/英文菜单 | càidān/tàocài/yīngwéncàidān |
| Small portion | 少量 | shǎoliàng |
| Chopsticks | 筷子 | kuàizi |
| Knife and fork | 刀叉 | dāochā |
| Spoon | 勺子 | sháozi |

| Waiter/waitress | 服务员 | fúwùyuán |
| Bill/cheque | 买单 | mǎidān |
| Cook these ingredients together | 原料混合一块儿做 | yuánliào hùnhé yíkuàir zuò |
| Not spicy/no chilli please | 请不要辣椒 | qǐng búyào làjiāo |
| Only a little spice/chilli | 一点辣椒 | yìdiǎn làjiāo |
| 50 grams | 两 | liǎng |
| 250 grams | 半斤 | bànjīn |
| 500 grams | 斤 | jīn |
| 1 kilo | 1公斤 | yī gōngjīn |

## DRINKS

| Beer | 啤酒 | píjiǔ |
| Coffee | 咖啡 | kāfēi |
| Milk | 牛奶 | niúnǎi |
| (Mineral) water | (矿泉)水 | (kuàngquán) shuǐ |
| Wine | 葡萄酒 | pútáojiǔ |
| Yoghurt | 酸奶 | suānnǎi |
| Tea | 茶 | chá |
| Black tea | 红茶 | hóngchá |
| Green tea | 绿茶 | lǜchá |
| Jasmine tea | 茉莉花茶 | mòlìhuā chá |
| Juice | 果汁 | guǒzhī |

## STAPLE FOODS

| Aubergine | 茄子 | qiézi |
| Bamboo shoots | 笋尖 | sǔnjiān |
| Bean sprouts | 豆芽 | dòuyá |
| Beans | 豆子 | dòuzi |
| Beef | 牛肉 | niúròu |
| Bitter gourd | 苦瓜 | kǔguā |
| Black bean sauce | 黑豆豉 | hēidòuchǐ |
| Bread | 面包 | miànbāo |
| Buns (filled) | 包子 | bāozi |
| Buns (plain) | 馒头 | mántou |
| Carrot | 胡萝卜 | húluóbo |
| Cashew nuts | 腰果 | yāoguǒ |
| Cauliflower | 菜花 | càihuā |
| Chicken | 鸡 | jī |
| Chilli | 辣椒 | làjiāo |
| Chocolate | 巧克力 | qiǎokèlì |
| Coriander (leaves) | 香菜 | xiāngcài |
| Crab | 蟹 | xiè |
| Cucumber | 黄瓜 | huángguā |
| Dough stick (fried) | 油条 | yóutiáo |
| Duck | 鸭 | yā |
| Dumplings | 饺子 | jiǎozi |
| Eel | 鳝鱼 | shànyú |
| Eggs (fried/ordinary) | 煎鸡蛋/鸡蛋 | jiānjīdàn/jīdàn |
| Fish | 鱼 | yú |
| Garlic | 大蒜 | dàsuàn |
| Ginger | 姜 | jiāng |
| Lamb | 羊肉 | yángròu |
| Lotus root | 莲藕 | liánǒu |
| MSG | 味精 | wèijīng |

| Mushrooms | 磨菇 | mógū |
| Noodles | 面条 | miàntiáo |
| Omelette | 摊鸡蛋 | tānjīdàn |
| Onions | 洋葱 | yángcōng |
| Oyster sauce | 蚝油 | háoyóu |
| Pancake | 摊饼 | tānbǐng |
| Peanut | 花生 | huāshēng |
| Pepper (green)/capsicum | 青椒 | qīngjiāo |
| Pork | 猪肉 | zhūròu |
| Potato (stir-fried) | (炒)土豆 | (chǎo) tǔdòu |
| Prawns | 虾 | xiā |
| Preserved egg | 皮蛋 | pídàn |
| Rice noodles | 河粉 | héfěn |
| Rice porridge (aka "congee") | 粥 | zhōu |
| Rice, boiled | 白饭 | báifàn |
| Rice, fried | 炒饭 | chǎofàn |
| Salt | 盐 | yán |
| Sesame oil | 芝麻油 | zhīma yóu |
| Shuijiao (dumplings in soup) | 水铰 | shuǐjiǎo |
| Sichuan pepper | 四川辣椒 | sìchuān làjiāo |
| Snake | 蛇肉 | shéròu |
| Soup | 汤 | tāng |
| Soy sauce | 酱油 | jiàngyóu |
| Squid | 鱿鱼 | yóuyú |
| Straw mushrooms | 草菇 | cǎogū |
| Sugar | 糖 | táng |
| Tofu | 豆腐 | dòufu |
| Tomato | 蕃茄 | fānqié |
| Vegetables (green) | 绿叶蔬菜 | lǜyè shūcài |
| Vinegar | 醋 | cù |
| Water chestnuts | 马蹄 | mǎtí |
| White radish | 白萝卜 | báiluóbo |
| Wood-ear fungus | 木耳 | mùěr |
| Yam | 红薯 | hóngshǔ |

## COOKING METHODS

| Boiled | 煮 | zhǔ |
| Casseroled (see also "Claypot") | 焙 | bèi |
| Deep-fried | 油煎 | yóujiān |
| Fried | 炒 | chǎo |
| Poached | 白煮 | báizhǔ |
| Red-cooked (stewed in soy sauce) | 红烧 | hóngshāo |
| Roast | 烤 | kǎo |
| Steamed | 蒸 | zhēng |
| Stir-fried | 清炒 | qīngchǎo |

## EVERYDAY DISHES

| Braised duck with vegetables | 蔬菜炖鸭 | shūcài dùnyā |
| Cabbage rolls (stuffed with meat or vegetables) | 菜卷 | càijuǎn |
| Chicken and sweetcorn soup | 玉米鸡丝汤 | yùmǐ jīsī tāng |
| Chicken with bamboo shoots and baby corn | 笋尖嫩玉米炒鸡片 | sǔnjiān nènyùmǐ chǎojīpiàn |

| Chicken with cashew nuts | 腰果鸡片 | yāoguǒ jīpiàn |
|---|---|---|
| Claypot/sandpot (casserole) | 砂锅 | shāguō |
| Crispy aromatic duck | 香酥鸭 | xiāngsū yā |
| Egg flower soup with tomato | 蕃茄蛋汤 | fānqié dàntāng |
| Egg fried rice | 蛋炒饭 | dànchǎofàn |
| Fish ball soup with white radish | 白萝卜鱼蛋汤 | báiluóbo yúdàn tāng |
| Fish casserole | 砂锅鱼 | shāguōyú |
| Fried shredded pork with garlic and chilli | 大蒜辣椒炒肉片 | dàsuàn làjiāo chǎo ròupiàn |
| Hotpot | 火锅 | huǒguō |
| Kebab | 串肉 | chuànròu |
| Noodle soup | 汤面 | tāngmiàn |
| Pork and mustard greens | 芥菜叶炒猪肉 | jiècàiyè chǎo zhūròu |
| Pork and water chestnut | 马蹄猪肉 | mǎtízhūròu |
| Prawn with garlic sauce | 蒜汁虾 | suànzhīxiā |
| "Pulled" noodles | 拉面 | lā miàn |
| Roast duck | 烤鸭 | kǎyā |
| Scrambled egg with pork on rice | 滑蛋猪肉饭 | huádàn zhūròufàn |
| Sliced pork with yellow bean sauce | 黄豆肉片 | huángdòu ròupiàn |
| Squid with green pepper and black beans | 豆豉青椒炒鱿鱼 | dòuchǐ qīngjiāo chǎo yóuyú |
| Steamed eel with black beans | 豆豉蒸鳝 | dòuchǐ zhēng shàn |
| Steamed rice packets wrapped in lotus leaves | 荷叶蒸饭 | héyè zhēngfàn |
| Stewed pork belly with vegetables | 回锅肉 | huíguōròu |
| Stir-fried chicken and bamboo shoots | 笋尖炒鸡片 | sǔnjiān chǎo jīpiàn |
| Stuffed bean-curd soup | 豆腐汤 | dòufu tāng |
| Sweet and sour spare ribs | 糖醋排骨 | tángcù páigǔ |
| Sweet bean paste pancakes | 赤豆摊饼 | chìdòu tānbǐng |
| White radish soup | 白萝卜汤 | báiluóbo tāng |
| Wonton soup | 馄饨汤 | húntun tāng |

## VEGETABLES AND EGGS

| Aubergine with chilli and garlic sauce | 大蒜辣椒炒茄子 | dàsuàn làjiāo chǎoqiézi |
|---|---|---|
| Aubergine with sesame sauce | 芝麻酱拌茄子 | zhīmájiàng bànqiézi |
| Egg fried with tomatoes | 蕃茄炒蛋 | fānqié chǎodàn |
| Fried tofu with vegetables | 豆腐炒蔬菜 | dòufu chǎoshūcài |
| Fried bean sprouts | 炒豆芽 | chǎodòuyá |
| Pressed tofu with cabbage | 白菜豆腐 | báicài dòufu |
| Spicy braised aubergine | 炖香辣茄子条 | dùn xiānglà qiézitiáo |
| Stir-fried bamboo shoots | 炒冬笋 | chǎodōngsǔn |
| Stir-fried mushrooms | 炒鲜菇 | chǎo xiāngū |
| Tofu and spinach soup | 菠菜豆腐汤 | bōcài dòufu tāng |
| Tofu slivers | 豆腐花 | dòufuhuā |
| Tofu with chestnuts | 栗子豆腐 | lìzi dòufu |
| Vegetable soup | 蔬菜汤 | shūcài tāng |

## REGIONAL DISHES
### NORTHERN

| Aromatic fried lamb | 炒羊肉 | chǎoyángròu |
|---|---|---|
| Fish with ham and vegetables | 火腿蔬菜鱼片 | huǒtuǐ shūcài yúpiàn |
| Fried prawn balls | 炒虾球 | chǎoxiāqiú |

| Mongolian hotpot | 蒙古火锅 | ménggǔ huǒguō |
| Beijing (Peking) duck | 北京烤鸭 | běijīng kǎoyā |
| Red-cooked lamb | 红烧羊肉 | hóngshāo yángròu |
| Lion's head (pork rissoles casseroled with greens) | 狮子头 | shīzitóu |

## SICHUAN AND WESTERN CHINA

| Boiled beef slices (spicy) | 水煮牛肉 | shuǐzhǔ niúròu |
| Crackling-rice with pork | 爆米肉片 | bàomǐ ròupiàn |
| Crossing-the-bridge (spicy) noodles | 过桥米线 | guòqiáo mǐxiàn |
| Carry-pole noodles (with a chilli-vinegar-sesame sauce) | 担担面 | dàndànmiàn |
| Deep-fried green beans with garlic | 大蒜煸四季豆 | dàsuàn biānsìjìdòu |
| Dong'an chicken (poached in spicy sauce) | 东安鸡子 | dōng'ān jīzi |
| Doubled-cooked pork | 回锅肉 | huíguōròu |
| Dry-fried pork shreds | 油炸肉丝 | yóuzhà ròusi |
| Fish-flavoured aubergine | 鱼香茄子 | yúxiāng qiézi |
| Gongbao chicken (with chillies and peanuts) | 公保鸡丁 | gōngbǎo jīdīng |
| Green pepper with spring onion and black bean sauce | 豆豉洋葱炒青椒 | dòuchǐ yángcōng chǎo qīngjiāo |
| Hot and sour soup (flavoured with vinegar and white pepper) | 酸辣汤 | suānlà tāng |
| Hot-spiced bean curd | 麻婆豆腐 | mápódòufu |
| Rice-flour balls, stuffed with sweet paste | 汤圆 | tāngyuán |
| Smoked duck | 熏鸭 | xūnyā |
| Strange-flavoured chicken (with sesame-garlic-chilli) | 怪味鸡 | guàiwèijī |
| Stuffed aubergine slices | 馅茄子 | xiànqiézi |
| Tangerine chicken | 桔子鸡 | júzijī |
| "Tiger-skin" peppers (pan-fried with salt) | 虎皮炒椒 | hǔpí qīngjiāo |
| Wind-cured ham | 扎肉 | zhāròu |

## SOUTHERN CHINESE/CANTONESE

| Baked crab with chilli and black beans | 辣椒豆豉焙蟹 | làjiāo dòuchǐ bèi xiè |
| Barbecued pork ("char siew") | 叉烧 | chāshāo |
| Casseroled bean curd stuffed with pork mince | 豆腐碎肉煲 | dòfu suìròu bǎo |
| Claypot rice with sweet sausage | 香肠饭 | xiāngchángfàn |
| Crisp-skinned pork on rice | 脆皮肉饭 | cuìpíròufàn |
| Fish-head casserole | 焙鱼头 | bèiyútóu |
| Fish steamed with ginger and spring onion | 清蒸鱼 | qīngzhēngyú |
| Fried chicken with yam | 芋头炒鸡片 | yùtóu chǎo jīpiàn |
| Honey-roast pork | 叉烧 | chāshāo |
| Lemon chicken | 柠檬鸡 | níngméngjī |
| Litchi (lychee) pork | 荔枝肉片 | lìzhīròupiàn |
| Salt-baked chicken | 盐鸡 | yánshuǐjī |

## DIM SUM

| | | |
|---|---|---|
| Dim sum | 点心 | diǎnxīn |
| Barbecued pork bun | 叉烧包 | chāshāobāo |
| Crab and prawn dumpling | 蟹肉虾饺 | xièròu xiājiǎo |
| Custard tart | 蛋挞 | dàntà |
| Doughnut | 油炸圈饼 | yóuzhà quānbǐng |
| Pork and prawn dumpling | 烧麦 | shāomài |
| Fried taro and mince dumpling | 蕃薯糊饺 | fānshǔ hújiǎo |
| Lotus paste bun | 莲蓉糕 | liánrónggāo |
| Moon cake (sweet bean paste in flaky pastry) | 月饼 | yuèbǐng |
| Paper-wrapped prawns | 纸包虾 | zhǐbāoxiā |
| Prawn crackers | 虾片 | xiā piàn |
| Prawn dumpling | 虾饺 | xiā jiǎo |
| Spring roll | 春卷 | chūnjuǎn |
| Steamed spare ribs and chilli | 辣椒蒸排骨 | làjiāo zhēngpáigǔ |
| Stuffed rice-flour roll | 肠粉 | chángfěn |
| Stuffed green peppers with black bean sauce | 豆豉馅青椒 | dòuchǐ xiànqīngjiāo |
| Sweet sesame balls | 芝麻球 | zhīmá qiú |

## FRUIT

| | | |
|---|---|---|
| Fruit | 水果 | shuǐguǒ |
| Apple | 苹果 | píngguǒ |
| Banana | 香蕉 | xiāngjiāo |
| Grape | 葡萄 | pútáo |
| Honeydew melon | 哈密瓜 | hāmìguā |
| Longan | 龙眼 | lóngyǎn |
| Lychee | 荔枝 | lìzhī |
| Mandarin orange | 橘子 | júzi |
| Mango | 芒果 | mángguǒ |
| Orange | 橙子 | chéngzi |
| Peach | 桃子 | táozi |
| Pear | 梨 | lí |
| Persimmon | 柿子 | shìzi |
| Plum | 李子 | lǐzi |
| Pomegranate | 石榴 | shíliú |
| Pomelo | 柚子 | yòuzi |
| Watermelon | 西瓜 | xīguā |

## GLOSSARY

**Arhat** Buddhist saint.

**Bei** North.

**Binguan** Hotel; generally a large one, for tourists.

**Bodhisattva** A follower of Buddhism who has attained enlightenment, but has chosen to stay on earth to teach rather than enter nirvana; Buddhist god or goddess.

**Boxers** The name given to an anti-foreign organization that originated in Shandong in 1898. Encouraged by the Qing Empress Dowager Cixi, they roamed China attacking westernized Chinese and foreigners in what became known as the Boxer movement.

**Canting** Restaurant.

**Cheongsam** Another word for a *qipao*.

**CITS** China International Travel Service. Tourist organization primarily interested in selling tours, though they can help with obtaining train tickets (see p.26).

**Cultural Revolution** Ten-year period beginning in 1966 and characterized by destruction, persecution and fanatical devotion to Mao.

**Dagoba** Another name for a stupa.

**Dong** East.

**Fandian** Restaurant or hotel.

**Fen** Smallest denomination of Chinese currency – there are one hundred fen to the yuan.

**Feng** Peak.

**Feng shui** A system of geomancy used to determine the positioning of buildings.

**Gong** Palace.

**Guanxi** Literally "connections": the reciprocal favours inherent in the process of official appointments and transactions.

**Guanyin** The ubiquitous Buddhist Goddess of Mercy, who postponed her entry into paradise in order to help ease human misery. Derived from the Indian deity Avalokiteshvara, she is often depicted with up to a thousand arms.

**Gulou** Drum tower; traditionally marking the centre of a town, this was where a drum was beaten at nightfall and in times of need.

**Guomindang (GMD)** The Nationalist Peoples' Party. Under Chiang Kaishek, the GMD fought Communist forces for 25 years before being defeated and moving to Taiwan in 1949, where it remains a major political party.

**Han Chinese** The main body of the Chinese people, as distinct from other ethnic groups such as Uigur, Miao, Hui or Tibetan.

**Hui** Muslims; officially a minority, China's Hui are, in fact, ethnically indistinguishable from Han Chinese.

**Hutong** A narrow alleyway.

**Immortal** Taoist saint.

**Jiao (or mao)** Ten fen.

**Jie** Street.

**Jiuba** Bar or pub.

**Lamaism** The esoteric Tibetan and Mongolian branch of Buddhism, influenced by local shamanist and animist beliefs.

**Laowai** A slang term for foreigner.

**Ling** Tomb.

**Little Red Book** A selection of "Quotations from Chairman Mao Zedong", produced in 1966 as a philosophical treatise for Red Guards during the Cultural Revolution.

**Lu** Street.

**Luohan** Buddhist disciple.

**Maitreya Buddha** The Buddha of the future, at present awaiting rebirth.

**Mandala** Mystic diagram which forms an important part of Buddhist iconography, especially in Tibet; they usually depict deities and are stared at as an aid to meditation.

**Men** Gate/door.

**Miao** Temple.

**Middle Kingdom** A literal translation of the Chinese words for China.

**Nan** South.

**Pagoda** Tower with distinctively tapering structure.

**Palanquin** A covered sedan chair, used by the emperor.

**Peking** The old English term for Beijing.

**Pinyin** The official system of transliterating Chinese script into Roman characters.

**PLA** The People's Liberation Army, the official name of the Communist military forces since 1949.

**PSB** Public Security Bureau, the branch of China's police force which deals directly with foreigners.

**Putonghua** Mandarin Chinese; literally "Common Language".

**Qiao** Bridge.

**Qipao** Long, narrow dress slit up the thigh.

**Red Guards** The unruly factional forces unleashed by Mao during the Cultural Revolution to find and destroy brutally any "reactionaries" among the populace.

**Renmin** The people.

**Renminbi** The official term for the Chinese currency, literally, "people's money".

**RMB** Renminbi. Another name for Chinese currency literally meaning "the people's money".

**Si** Temple, usually Buddhist.

**Siheyuan** Traditional courtyard house.

**Spirit wall** Wall behind the main gateway to a house, designed to thwart evil spirits, which, it was believed, could move only in straight lines.

**Spirit Way** The straight road leading to a tomb, lined with guardian figures.

**Stele** Freestanding stone tablet carved with text.

**Stupa** Multitiered tower associated with Buddhist temples; usually contains sacred objects.

**Ta** Tower or pagoda.

**Tai ji** A discipline of physical exercise, characterized by slow, deliberate, balletic movements.

**Tian** Heaven or the sky.

**Uigur** Substantial minority of Turkic people, living mainly in Xinjiang.

**Waiguoren** Foreigner.

**Xi** West.

**Yuan** China's unit of currency. Also a courtyard or garden (and the name of the Mongol dynasty).

**Zhan** Station.

**Zhong** Middle.

**Zhongnanhai** The compound, next to the Forbidden City, that serves as Communist Party headquarters.

**Zhonglou** Bell tower, usually twinned with a drum tower. The bell it contained was rung at dawn and in emergencies.

**Zhuang** Villa or manor.

# Small print and index

## A ROUGH GUIDE TO ROUGH GUIDES

Published in 1982, the first Rough Guide – to Greece – was a student scheme that became a publishing phenomenon. Mark Ellingham, a recent graduate in English from Bristol University, had been travelling in Greece the previous summer and couldn't find the right guidebook. With a small group of friends he wrote his own guide, combining a highly contemporary, journalistic style with a thoroughly practical approach to travellers' needs.

The immediate success of the book spawned a series that rapidly covered dozens of destinations. And, in addition to impecunious backpackers, Rough Guides soon acquired a much broader readership that relished the guides' wit and inquisitiveness as much as their enthusiastic, critical approach and value-for-money ethos.

These days, Rough Guides include recommendations from budget to luxury and cover more than 120 destinations around the globe, as well as producing an ever-growing range of eBooks.

Visit **roughguides.com** to find all our latest books, read articles, get inspired and share travel tips with the Rough Guides community.

## Rough Guide credits

**Editor**: Edward Aves
**Layout**: Ankur Guha
**Cartography**: Katie Bennett
**Picture editor**: Mark Thomas
**Proofreaders**: Diane Margolis, Xiaosong Que
**Managing editor**: Keith Drew
**Assistant editor**: Prema Dutta
**Photographer**: Tim Draper

**Production**: Charlotte Cade
**Cover design**: Sarah Stewart-Richardson, Mark Thomas, Ankur Guha
**Editorial assistant**: Rebecca Hallett
**Senior pre-press designer**: Dan May
**Programme manager**: Helen Blount
**Publisher**: Joanna Kirby

## Publishing information

This fifth edition published June 2014 by
**Rough Guides Ltd**,
80 Strand, London WC2R 0RL
11, Community Centre, Panchsheel Park,
New Delhi 110017, India
**Distributed by Penguin Random House**
Penguin Books Ltd,
80 Strand, London WC2R 0RL
Penguin Group (USA)
345 Hudson Street, NY 10014, USA
Penguin Group (Australia)
250 Camberwell Road, Camberwell,
Victoria 3124, Australia
Penguin Group (NZ)
67 Apollo Drive, Mairangi Bay, Auckland 1310,
New Zealand
Penguin Group (South Africa)
Block D, Rosebank Office Park, 181 Jan Smuts Avenue,
Parktown North, Gauteng, South Africa 2193
Rough Guides is represented in Canada by Tourmaline
Editions Inc. 662 King Street West, Suite 304, Toronto,
Ontario M5V 1M7
Printed in Malaysia by Vivar Printing Sdn.Bhd.

216pp includes index
A catalogue record for this book is available from the
British Library
ISBN: 978-1-40934-198-7

MIX
Paper from
responsible sources
FSC™ C018179

## Help us update

We've gone to a lot of effort to ensure that the fifth edition of **The Rough Guide to Beijing** is accurate and up-to-date. However, things change – places get "discovered", opening hours are notoriously fickle, restaurants and rooms raise prices or lower standards. If you feel we've got it wrong or left something out, we'd like to know, and if you can remember the address, the price, the hours, the phone number, so much the better.

Please send your comments with the subject line "**Rough Guide Beijing Update**" to @mail @uk.roughguides.com. We'll credit all contributions and send a copy of the next edition (or any other Rough Guide if you prefer) for the very best emails.

Find more travel information, connect with fellow travellers and plan your trip on @roughguides.com

## ABOUT THE AUTHOR

**Martin Zatko** has been visiting Beijing regularly since his first trip there in 2003, and likes to think of the place as some sort of endlessly changing home. Still on the way towards fulfilling his childhood dream of visiting every country in the known universe, he has also worked on the Rough Guides to China, Japan, Tokyo, Korea, Seoul, Vietnam, Turkey and Europe on a Budget.

## Acknowledgements

**Martin Zatko** would like to thank two people in particular: Jee Young Lee for being a great travel partner in Beijing and beyond, and Eivind Hestetun Thomassen for almost everything else (the gorgeous place to stay, the beer, the snus, the inside knowledge, the rides around town, and the more dubious sight of him doing work in his underpants every morning). Other big-ups to the ever-bubbly Caroline Tan, Irmun Demberel for a few memorable nights out, Nick and Simon from Koryo Tours, Ali for the bicycle, and the incredibly long list of locals who made my time in Beijing such a pleasure.

## Readers' updates

Thanks to all the readers who have taken the time to write in with comments and suggestions (and apologies if we've inadvertently omitted or misspelt anyone's name):

Allan Dreyer Andersen; Mark & Lynn Davis; Erin Henshaw; Jendra Jarnagin; Joanne Opthof; Joan Redemer; Steinar Saethre.

## Photo credits

# Index

Maps are marked in **grey**

# Map index

## Listings key

■ Accommodation

● Eating

■ Drinking and nightlife

● Shopping

# City plan

The **city plan** on the pages that follow is divided as shown:

N

0                                   500
metres

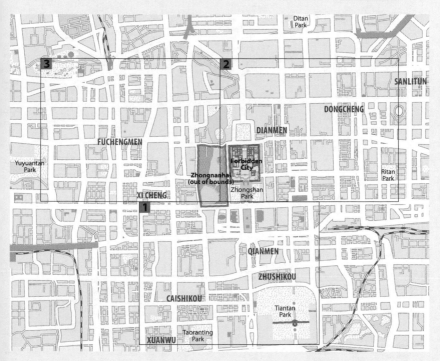

## Map symbols

| | | | | | | | |
|---|---|---|---|---|---|---|---|
| ✈ | Airport | ⊠ | Post office | ⛳ | Golf course | ▪ | Building |
| ★ | Bus stop | ⊠ | Gate | ⚊ | Swimming/pool | ⬭ | Stadium |
| Ⓜ | Subway | ♦ | Place of interest | ▲ | Hill | ⬚ | Park |
| Ⓐ | Bus station/depot | 🕌 | Mosque | ♠ | Museum | | |
| ⓘ | Information office | 🏛 | Chinese temple | ▬ | Wall | | |
| ⊞ | Hospital | ▲ | Dagoba | ●--● | Cable car | | |

**2**

Bell Tower

Drum Tower

JIUGULOU DAJIE

HOUHAI BEYAN

HOUHAI NAN YAN

Yinding Bridge

Qianhai

QIANHAI DONGYAN

QIANHAI NANYAN

BAIMI CANG JIE

Guo Moruo's Former Residence

GULOU DONG DAJIE

JIAODAOKOU DONGDAJIE

JIAODAOKOU

BEITOU TIAO

Beixinqiao

QIANGULOUYUAN HUTONG

JU'ER HUTONG

XIANG'ER HUTONG

Mao Dun's Former Residence

HOEYUANENSI HUTONG

FANGZHUANCHANG HUTONG

SHAJING HUTONG

QIANYUANENSI HUTONG

QINLAO HUTONG

XIGUAN HUTONG

JINGYANG HUTONG

MAO'ER HUTONG

BEIBINGMASI HUTONG

BAIMICANG HUTONG

Central Academy of Drama

DONGMIANHUA HUTONG

FU XUE HUTONG

YU'ER HUTONG

Penghao Theatre

BANCHANG HUTONG

Zhangzizhong

FUXIANG HUTONG

CHAODOU HUTONG

DI'ANMEN WAI DAJIE

DI'ANMEN XI DAJIE

DI'ANMEN DONG DAJIE

ZHANGZI ZHONG LU

Entrance

Nanluoguxiao

BEIHE HUTONG

Beijing Hospital of Traditional Chinese Medicine

XIEZUO HUTONG

WANGZHIMA HUTO

Five Dragons Pavilion

DI'ANMEN NAN DAJIE

LANZHI HUTONG

SHANLAO HUTONG

WEIJIA HUTONG

HUANGHUAMEN XIE

DONGQIANGJIE

BEI HEYAN DAJIE

DONGHUANGCHENGEN BEILIE

MEISHUGUAN HOUJIE

SHIJINHUAYUAN HUTONG

Beihai Park

BEIHEYANZA TIAO

JINGSHAN HOU JIE

NAFU HUTONG

YUQUN HUTONG

ZIZAIYUAN HUTONG

JIANGSOUTOU XIANG

SANYANJING HUTONG

QIANLIANG HUTONG

JINGSHAN XI JIE

JINGSHAN DONG JIE

National Art Museum of China

Jingshan Park

SHATAN HOUJIE

DIANMEN

SHATAN BEIJIE

North Gate (exit only)

JINGSHANQIAN JIE

WUSI DAJIE

DONGSI XIDAJIE

Dong

BEICHIZI DAJIE

DONGCHANG HUTONG

DUOFU XIANG

Capital Theatre

BAOFANG HUTONG

YINCHA HUTONG

DONGHUANGCHENGEN NAN JIE

FUQIANG HUTONG

WANGFUJING DAJIE

QIHELOU JIE

ZHIDE BEI XIANG

DENGSHIKOU XI JIE

DENGSHIKOU DONG JIE

Dengshiko

St Joseph's Church

BAISHU HUTONG

SHAOJIU HUTONG

GANYU HUTONG

Intime Lotte

XILA HUTONG

XITANGZI HUTONG

Courtyard Gallery

DONGHUANMEN DAJIE

DONG'ANMEN DAJIE

JINYU HUTONG

Beijing Mil Kung Fu Sch

**Forbidden City**

East Gate (exit only)

Dong'anmen Night Market

APM

JINYU HUTONG

West Gate (exit only)

Wumen

NANCHIZI DAJIE

Beijing Department Store

Sun Dong'an Plaza

MEIZHA HUTONG

Peki Unic Hosp

West entrance

Forbidden City ticket office

DATIANSHUIJING HUTONG

Wangfujing Arts & Crafts Store

DONGDAN SAN TIAO

Forbidden City Concert Hall

Ancestral Temple

Wangfung Gallery

Oriental Plaza

Zhongshan Park

Working People's Cultural Palace

CHENGUANG JIE

NAN HEYAN DAJIE

Star City

Grand Hyatt

Tian'anmen

XIAGONGFU JIE

Beijing Hotel

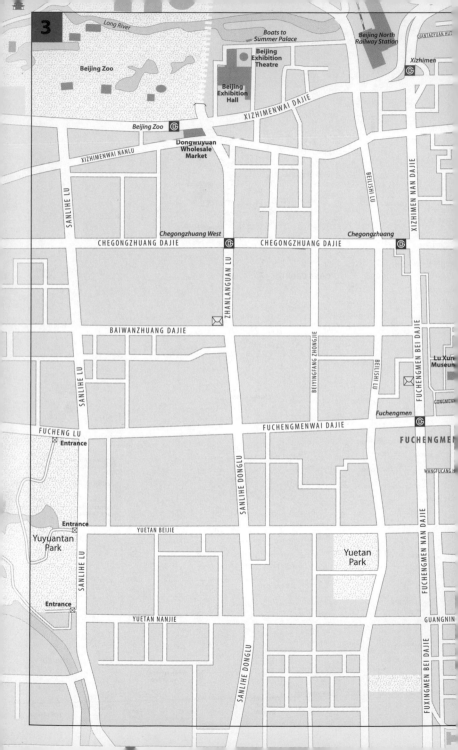

## 3

Long River

Boats to
Summer Palace

Beijing North
Railway Station

QIANTAOYUAN HUT

Beijing
Exhibition
Theatre

Xizhimen

Beijing Zoo

Beijing
Exhibition
Hall

XIZHIMENWAI DAJIE

Beijing Zoo

Dongwuyuan
Wholesale
Market

XIZHIMENWAI NANLU

BEILISHI LU

XIZHIMEN NAN DAJIE

SANLIHE LU

Chegongzhuang West

Chegongzhuang

CHEGONGZHUANG DAJIE

CHEGONGZHUANG DAJIE

ZHANLANGUAN LU

BAIWANZHUANG DAJIE

BEIYINGFANG ZHONGJIE

FUCHENGMEN BEI DAJIE

Lu Xun
Museum

SANLIHE LU

BEILISHI LU

GONGMEN

Fuchengmen

FUCHENG LU

FUCHENGMENWAI DAJIE

FUCHENGMEN

Entrance

WANGFUCANG H

SANLIHE DONGLU

Entrance

Yuyuantan
Park

YUETAN BEIJIE

FUCHENGMEN NAN DAJIE

Yuetan
Park

SANLIHE LU

Entrance

YUETAN NANJIE

GUANGNIN

SANLIHE DONGLU

FUXINGMEN BEI DAJIE

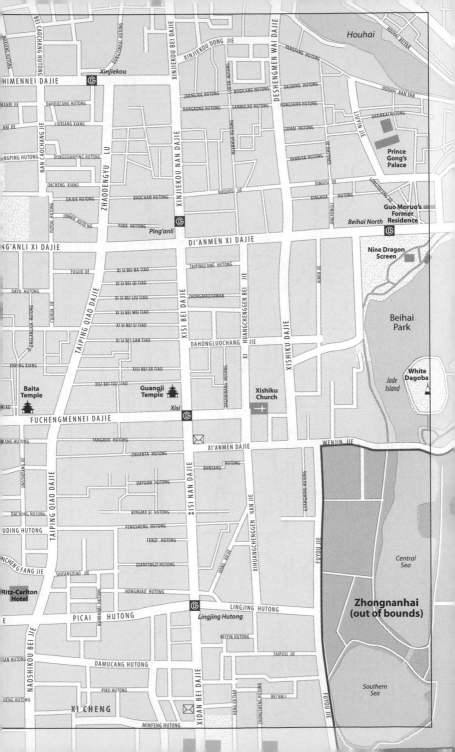

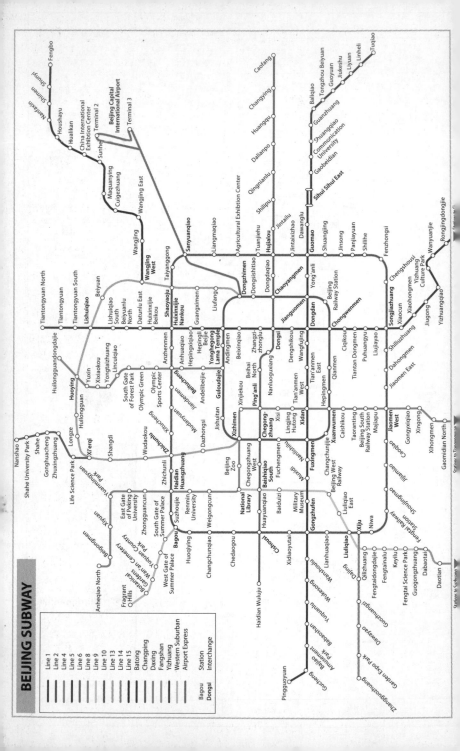